ARAB
CONTEMPORARIES

ARAB
CONTEMPORARIES
THE ROLE OF
PERSONALITIES
IN POLITICS

 MAJID KHADDURI

THE JOHNS HOPKINS UNIVERSITY PRESS

BALTIMORE AND LONDON

Manufactured in the United States of America

The Johns Hopkins University Press, Baltimore, Maryland 21218
The Johns Hopkins University Press Ltd., London

Library of Congress Catalog Card Number 72-12576
ISBN 0-8018-1453-7

Library of Congress Cataloging in Publication data
will be found on the last printed page of this book.

DEDICATED

TO THE MEMORY OF

MY WIFE

Contents

Preface

This work is a sequel to *Political Trends in the Arab World.* In that volume, I discussed the role of ideas and ideals in politics, and I pointed out that Arab politics in the modern age has become essentially a "great debate" about reform among thinkers and leaders. In the present volume, I intend to explore the role of representative leaders—how they were drawn into the political scene, their endeavors to formulate goals, and the methods they pursued to achieve their goals by participation in politics.

Needless to say, *Arab Contemporaries* lays no claim to studying the role of all Arab leaders; it is devoted to a study of only a dozen of them—all of whom I have known, though some more intimately than others. I have followed the activities of all with almost equal interest, and I have consciously chosen them to illustrate three types of leadership—military, professional, and intellectual. Each represents a school of thought in political participation, as I shall explain more fully in the introductory chapter. In each case, I do not, strictly speaking, present a biographical, but a political, study of each leader (although some biographical material has been deemed necessary), stressing his personal qualities and qualifications, his behavior patterns, and the pathway pursued to acquire power. I have also tried to give a general assessment of the character, achievements, and capacity for leadership of each personality, illustrated by events and situations which I have known directly or indirectly. I am aware that personal contacts with these men might have induced me to accept *post hoc, ergo propter hoc* personal views which are likely to influence judgment; I have, however, tried to verify opinions and to give as detached an assessment as I sought in *Political Trends*. It is hoped that these essays, taken as a whole, will form not separate but correlated studies and will throw some light on our understanding of contemporary Arab politics.

Though it is impossible to cite by name all those who have readily given me assistance or counsel during the preparation of this work, it is a pleasure to acknowledge their kindnesses. Some, who have either given me oral or written comments on various parts, have preferred to remain anonymous; the names of others are cited in the text or in footnotes. Above all, I am grateful to all the men who form the subject matter of this work, many of whom graciously agreed to provide material about their political roles and discussed some of the problems and situations in which they were involved. Some have already passed away, but of those still alive, several have read the essays relating to them either in the original or in translation.

I should like to thank Dr. Ashraf Ghurbal and Ambassadors Raymond Hare and John Badeau for their comments on the essay on Nasir; C. J. Edmonds, for the essay on Nuri al-Sa'id; Ambassador Akram Zu'aytar and Dr. Yusuf Haykal, for the essay on the Mufti; Ambassadors Ibrahim al-Suwayyil and Hermann F. Eilts, for the essay on King Faysal; Habib Bourguiba, Jr., for the essay on his father; Ambassador George Tu'ma (Tomeh), for the essays on Bakdash and 'Aflaq; Jibran Majdalani, Hani Hindi, and Elie Salim, for the essays on Junblat and 'Aflaq; and Ahmad Haykal, for the essay on his father, Muhammad Husayn Haykal. I also want to thank William Sands, R. K. Ramazani, and John D. Anthony, who read the work in whole or in part. Finally, I want to thank Eileen Donlin, who rendered invaluable secretarial assistance while the work was in preparation, and Alexandra Grochol who prepared the index. Needless to say, none is responsible for any error of fact or judgment which the work may contain.

MAJID KHADDURI

School of Advanced International Studies
The Johns Hopkins University

CHAPTER I

Introduction

My companions are like stars in Heaven;
whomever you follow would provide the right guidance.

The Prophet Muhammad

An inquiry into the role of personalities in politics necessarily raises questions of scope and method. For instance,
are we to consider political leaders as "authors" of political
movements or merely as "instruments" who somehow appear on
the political scene to achieve social demands? Considerable disagreement surrounds this question among writers: at one end of the
spectrum are those who endorse the "great man" theory (Carlyle's
hero), and at the other end are those who consider leaders as mere
"puppets" (Herbert Spencer) who derive their power from a public
desirous of changing social conditions. If either of these views is
regarded as valid, the outstanding interest would be the motivations
of the leader: whether he was motivated by sheer political ambition
or by a set of ideas and ideals (ultimate goals). Even if it is assumed,
for the sake of analysis, that political ambition dominates the minds
of most leaders, for such ambition to be pursued, it would appear
necessary for the leader to be identified with some overriding goals
in order to justify publicly his political involvement. In *Political
Trends in the Arab World,* I explained how ideas and ideals (goals)
evolved and were debated among Arab political thinkers and leaders.
In the present volume, I intend to indicate how different Arab
leaders have tried to implement some of these ideas.

Apart from goals and methods, the role of personalities may be

1

examined from another perspective. For example, we should examine who the leaders are. Do they come from a privileged small group within society, or are they the acknowledged leaders of a much larger circle of men, among whom there may be others who fill important political roles? Here, again, there is considerable disagreement among writers. Some contend, for example, that in the less advanced societies, it is the paramount leader who is most likely to play a decisive role in politics; others maintain that it is not so much the qualities of the individual leader as it is the political system which determines who the leader will be and the nature of his political role. For example, in a democracy, a political leader may be a spokesman either for the group in power, or for any one of a number of groups contesting for power; in authoritarian systems, political power and political leadership are the monopoly of the few at the top.

If we assume that the most decisive political roles are performed by the few at the top, the question arises whether it is better to study them collectively or separately, assuming in the latter case that each leader has his own goals and methods. The former approach, which is popular among experts in the behavioral sciences, seems to presuppose that leaders ordinarily react similarly to stimuli and in accordance with a recognizable pattern of political behavior. If this were to be the approach, the function of the investigator would be to study the outward conduct of the political leaders of a given society and to formulate from their conduct a generalized behavior pattern of leadership in that society. While this method might well prove illuminating, it tends to ignore other variables, such as social morality and cultural values, which in certain societies, govern the minds and actions of leaders to a larger extent than in others.

In this volume, which seeks to deepen our understanding of the role of personalities in politics, our approach will be to describe and analyze the individual skills and the general level of sophistication of a number of contemporary leaders who have played significant roles in the Arab world and to determine the relevance of their values and goals to the conditions existing in their respective countries. While particular attention will be given to these variables, the general patterns of political behavior will not be ignored, since they are likely to sharpen our insight into the leadership role that each of these men has performed. This method may strike the reader as idealistic, since it seeks to explore the relationship of such intangible variables as values, skills, and sophistication to the role of leadership in politics. However, these variables will not be studied in the abstract but rather in relation to the particular events and movements in which these men have been involved. Consequently, our method might well be called "empirical idealism," since it views ideas and ideals not as abstract principles but as guidelines for political action, and because it endeavors to investigate the extent to which such guidelines have relevance to reality.

I have categorized the leaders under study into three basic types. The first category consists of leaders whose goals had little relevance to existing conditions and realities and, in some instances, ran counter to the requirements of the country. These extremists, realizing that their goals were ahead of the times, have either withdrawn from politics altogether or have tried to prepare the way for a new generation of leaders to achieve their goals. In the present study, such leaders are classified as idealists, owing to their tendency to place ideals above realities.

The second type consists of men who, like the idealists, regard goals as overriding. They differ in that they are also prepared to use revolutionary means to achieve their goals. The fact that the regimes established by revolutions often fail to pursue their declared goals is often overlooked, though such leaders frequently continue to assert that their goals will be achieved ultimately. Such leaders are usually the spokesmen for a particular ideology.

A third group of leaders occupies an intermediate position in that they realize that the goals they pursue, while embodying their countrymen's hopes and expectations, must be modified by reality if they are ever to be realized. Men in this group, whom we shall call "realists," are usually prepared to limit themselves to goals that they believe can be achieved, and to disregard or to modify others. In short, they are leaders who are prepared to subordinate ideals to realities. These leaders often seem to possess greater flexibility and, therefore, a greater capacity for political survival than those who are less inclined to compromise with reality.

It goes without saying that each of these three groups—the idealistic, the ideological, and the realistic—may, and often do, include within their ranks one or more variants, but in the main these variations are differences in degree only and not in kind. The pathway to leadership positions varies considerably from one group to another; indeed they vary from one leader to another in accordance with the methods acceptable to each country.

In addition to the horizontal categorization of political figures according to goals and methods along idealistic, realistic, and ideological lines, vertical divisions can be established on the basis of the methods by which they assumed leadership. For example, those who entered the political scene on horseback, leading by the sword in a manner reminiscent of the legionnaire, might well be called military politicians (Part I); others, who came on foot and tended to be distinguished by a high level of skill and sophistication, might be referred to as the professional politicians (Part II); still others, who also came on foot and were armed only with their pens, might be called the intellectual politicians (Part III). These categories of leaders, differentiated by goals and methods, are not mutually exclusive. A military or intellectual politician might be just as inspired by idealistic or ideological goals as the more experienced politician, and he might prove just as capable of achieving a realistic and effective leadership.

The contemporary Arab world has been chosen for the examination of the role of personalities in politics—their requisite qualifications, their goals and methods, the political ladders they climbed, their fundamental achievements, and their relative impact. In the final chapter, an attempt will be made to answer some of the basic questions raised here in the light of the experience of different Arab leaders in their respective countries.

PART ONE

THE MAN OF THE SWORD
THE MILITARY
POLITICIAN

 The sword is truer in tidings
    than any writings:
In its edge is the boundary
    between earnestness and sport.

Abu Tammam (d. 854)

'Aziz 'Ali al-Misri

CHAPTER II

The Idealistic School
'Aziz 'Ali al-Misri

I founded the 'Ahd [Covenant] Society in 1912 with the
avowed purpose of protecting the rights and privileges
of all the nationalities of the Ottoman Empire, provided
that the Empire would become a grand federal union
within which all people regardless of race or religion
would live in peace and harmony.

'Aziz 'Ali al-Misri

The basic issues that faced the military politicians were essentially the same as those that confronted other Arab
leaders—issues arising from the changes within contemporary Arab society that were brought about by the impact of foreign
ideas and pressures.[1] Some leaders adopted goals that had been
formulated by others and were primarily concerned with achieving
them, either through practical reform measures to be carried out
peacefully or through revolutionary processes. Others tried to
formulate their own reform proposals and goals and then attempted
to institute them by participation in politics. The military politicians,
taking the goals with which they were identified for granted, entered
the political scene with a sword—by seizure of power, notwithstand-

---

[1] For the basic issues with which Arab leaders were involved and the setting in which they
operated, see my *Political Trends in the Arab World* (Baltimore, 1970).

7

ing the fact that they were renowned as guardians of public order: *Nam si violandum est ius, regnandi gratia violandum est; aliis rebus pietatem colas* (Julius Caesar). They also stayed in power by the weapons of their profession, although they denied these procedures to their opponents and sought to achieve goals by peaceful albeit authoritarian methods.

Three types of military politicians, each representing a different school of thought, have been distinguished for the purpose of this study. 'Aziz 'Ali al-Misri represents the first type: the military politician who identified himself with goals aimed at creating basic social changes regardless of their relevance to actual conditions. He was the first to pursue political goals with military methods in contemporary Arab society. The second type, seeking sweeping changes by revolution, military or otherwise, in accordance with ideological formulations, comprises almost all those who styled themselves "Free Officers" and who have taken an active part in politics ever since their armies seized power by military *coups d'etat.* Jamal 'Abd al-Nasir, possessing more impressive potentials of leadership than other officers, represents this school as the example *par excellence.* The third type, the military politician who possesses the skills and methods of professional politicians, is eminently represented by Nuri al-Sa'id.

'Aziz 'Ali is regarded as the "father" of contemporary Arab officers who have taken part in politics. His participation in the founding of secret Arab societies before World War I and his trial and expulsion from Turkey in 1914 created a sensation in Arab lands and made him, in T. E. Lawrence's words, "an idol of the Arab officers."[2] And yet, during World War I, when an opportunity to achieve national objectives offered itself, he failed to seize it because he refused to compromise ideals, even though they no longer were relevant to new conditions. Nevertheless, he continued to inspire disciples to the end of his life.

Perhaps 'Aziz 'Ali's ethnic background was partly responsible for his inability to identify himself with the political activities into which he was drawn. His ancestors were neither Arabian by origin nor, strictly speaking, native Egyptian. It was well known that both his father and grandfather were Circassian, although his father,

---

[2] T. E. Lawrence, *Seven Pillars of Wisdom* (London, 1935), p. 59.

Zakariya, was born in Egypt.[3] The family's Circassian name,
Chahlpe, was also well known in Egypt before 'Aziz, after settling
in Istanbul, adopted the name of al-Misri in order to distinguish
himself from the Arabic-speaking officers who came from other
Arab countries. Thus 'Aziz 'Ali was quite aware that he was not an
Arab by origin, although, having been born in Egypt, his native
tongue was Arabic. It is true that not all 'Aziz 'Ali's Arab associates
in Istanbul were Arab by origin either; but perhaps they were not as
conscious of their ancestry as was 'Aziz, for all claimed to have been
the descendants of Arab ancestors, real or imaginary.[4]

In Istanbul, 'Aziz 'Ali found himself in a congenial atmosphere,
where he could speak his mind freely against the British occupation
and about Egypt's attachment to the Ottoman sultanate. He distinguished himself as an able cadet at the Military Academy and later
at the Staff College, graduating with distinction four years before
the Turkish revolution of 1908. Upon graduation, he was commis-
sioned to serve in Macedonia and was remarkably successful in
pursuing Bulgarian bands and in the fighting along Greek, Bulgarian,
and Albanian frontiers. It was during his service in the Balkans that
'Aziz joined the secret Committee of Union and Progress (C.U.P.),
some of whose members were his schoolmates, and contributed to
its final success. "When the Army of Operations," says Jamal
(Cemal) Pasha, "marched on Constantinople after the reactionary
movement of 31 March (13 April) 1909, he ['Aziz 'Ali] was commanding one of its detachments, and after Galata Bridge had been
seized, he attacked Tophana Barracks and displayed great skill in
clearing the rebels out of there."[5]

Following the restoration of constitutional life, a short period of

---

[3] See *al-Ahram* (Cairo), July 21, 1959. See also Ronald Storrs, *Orientations* (London,
1944), p. 179: "His ['Aziz 'Ali's] ancestor was one Salim 'Arafat, a merchant of Basra,
who used to trade annually in the Caucasus by the Black Sea. His 'correspondent' in
those parts was a Circassian, Hassan Bey, who finally bestowed upon 'Arafat the hand of
his sister, at the same time formally adopting him in the tribe. All this is in the reign of
Sultan Mahmud. The third generation of this alliance migrated to Constantinople and
thence, realizing by the sale of their slaves, settled down in Egypt, having by this time become more Circassian than Arab, though still aware of, and maintaining their Basra connection: besides enjoying, on account of it, the friendship of Arabs, especially those west
of Egypt."

[4] 'Aziz 'Ali was born either in 1879 or in 1880.

[5] Djemal Pasha, *Memories of a Turkish Statesman* (London, 1922), pp. 60-61. See also
Francis McCullough, *The Fall of Abdul-Hamid* (London, 1910), pp. 218-19.

fraternization was enjoyed by the various national communities who hoped that an era of liberty and equality might emerge. But the situation was much more complex than the C.U.P. leaders realized, since they were utterly unprepared to deal with the nationality problem. Their extremists, who advocated a policy of Turkification, frightened other nationalities. Even the three principal leaders—Tal'at, Enver, and Jamal—failed to agree on a common symbol of unity, for Tal'at seems to have preferred Ottomanism, Enver was reputed to be in sympathy with Pan-Islamism, and Jamal encouraged nationalism, although all agreed on the need to maintain Ottoman unity. Lack of agreement on a common national policy led to an anarchy of ideas that ultimately prompted the various national communities to seek their salvation in separation from Ottoman unity.

'Aziz 'Ali, who had been an influential member of the C.U.P. and a staunch supporter of Ottoman unity, saw a grave danger in the policy of Turkification and counseled moderation. He had come to the conclusion that in so composite a society as the Ottoman Empire the best way to maintain its integrity was not by attempting to suppress nationalities but by recognizing them, each as an autonomous unit within the Ottoman superstructure. He held that in order to maintain Ottoman unity the identity of the various national communities should be maintained. He was therefore on good terms with a few leaders of the national communities and tried to bring about an understanding between them and the C.U.P.

Such ideas, espoused by a man who was not a Turk by origin, aroused the suspicion of his rivals in the C.U.P. and gave the false impression that he was supporting the dissatisfied nationalities. His visits to the Muntada al-Adabi, an Arab cultural club frequented by both Arab and Ottoman leaders, led to the belief that he was sympathetic to the cause of the Arab community, whose language he spoke. At this time he had also joined the secret Arab society of al-Qahtaniya, organized in 1909 by his friend Salim al-Jaza'iri, and the names of its members seem to have become known to the government.[6] His outspoken views on the nationality problem and his tactless dealings with C.U.P. leaders must have contributed to the

[6] George Antonius, *The Arab Awakening* (London, 1938), p. 111.

government's failure to recognize his services to the state.[7]

Most damaging of all was his quarrel with Enver Pasha. Its origin seems to have been purely personal, for 'Aziz 'Ali, even when he was still active in C.U.P. circles, was critical of Enver. When the two were in Cyrenaica, 'Aziz, resenting the fact that Enver was his superior officer, made derogatory remarks about him in the company of Turks and Arabs. When Enver returned to Istanbul to become Minister of War, 'Aziz continued to attack him, even though Enver had become the head of his department. The Arabs, who claimed 'Aziz 'Ali as a member of their community, joined in denouncing Enver and his colleagues, which prompted a few members of the C.U.P. to accuse 'Aziz of stirring up Arab nationalism and espousing the idea of Arab independence. Thus, although the personal element seems to have been the underlying factor in the antagonism between these two army officers, the quarrel was fully exploited by rival nationalists.[8]

The final rupture of 'Aziz 'Ali's relations with C.U.P. leaders was marked by his arrest and departure from Istanbul in April 1914. The incident gave Enver Pasha a pretext to denounce 'Aziz 'Ali as an Arab revolutionary leader who sought an Arab rebellion, and much to 'Aziz 'Ali's dismay, it put him in a somewhat different light in the eyes of those working for Turko-Arab collaboration. Arab leaders, already provoked by real grievances against the Turks, exploited the incident as grounds to denounce the C.U.P. leaders and to proclaim 'Aziz 'Ali as the champion of Arab liberation from Turkish oppression. The Arab leaders claimed that their appeal to foreign diplomatic missions saved 'Aziz from death. In fact, moderate Turkish elements were by no means pleased with Enver's move to crush 'Aziz 'Ali, and it was Jamal Pasha, alarmed by the impact

---

[7]Jamal Pasha hinted this by saying: "Up to this time [1909] I did not know that this man ['Aziz 'Ali] had Arabian connections" (Djemal Pasha, *Memories,* p. 61).

[8]In his *Memories,* Jamal Pasha expressed the real feeling of the Turkish leaders when he said:

"When Enver Pasha ultimately became Minister of War, 'Aziz 'Ali Bey was literally beside himself. He could not bear the thought that he, who had been Enver's contemporary at the military school and had done such good work and displayed such a high degree of patriotism, should have been left a simple major on the General Staff while his rival became Minister of War and he came to the conclusion that cooperation with the Turks brought him neither profit nor glory. 'Long live the Arab Revolution'" (pp. 62-63).

of Enver's vindictive action, who intervened to put an end to it. Recalling these events in his memoirs, Jamal Pasha states that he realized that "public opinion condemn[ed] Enver Pasha more severely than 'Aziz 'Ali." He therefore moved to save him; he wrote Enver Pasha:

> Notwithstanding all the evidence which the court martial has accumulated against 'Aziz 'Ali Bey, and the fact that sentence has been passed upon him, it is you whom public opinion condemns. Your condemnation in this way will do you a thousand times more harm than anything 'Aziz 'Ali will suffer from a few years in prison. Please try and get him the Imperial pardon and I will take good care that he leave Constantinople, and never returns to Constantinople.[9]

"The next day," added Jamal Pasha, "Enver Pasha rang me up to say that His Majesty had pardoned 'Aziz 'Ali Bey."[10] When 'Aziz 'Ali's brother called on Jamal Pasha to thank him, he was advised that 'Aziz 'Ali must leave for Egypt at once and that he should leave Turkish politics. "I heard subsequently," Jamal Pasha wrote, "that although 'Aziz 'Ali Bey had given me his word of honour at the time, he placed himself at the service of Sherif Hussein during the World War when the latter rose against the Caliphate. . . . Today it is I who cannot forgive him."

A narrative of 'Aziz 'Ali's career after he left Istanbul may be found elsewhere,[11] but it is important to remember here that his ideas and goals changed very little after World War I, even though new conditions had been created that offered him the opportunity, through participation in the Revolt of 1916, to achieve Arab independence. He continued to hold that Ottoman unity must be preserved, perhaps in the form of a broad federal union, modeled after the Austro-Hungarian *Ausgleich,* in which Turks and Arabs as well as other nationalities would be given autonomous status. He advocated collaboration with Germany, because he was confident that

---

[9]*Ibid.,* p. 64.

[10]Cf. T. E. Lawrence, who says that 'Aziz 'Ali was "saved by *The Times* and Lord Kitchener" (*Seven Pillars,* p. 75). See also Storrs, *Orientations,* p. 179.

[11]See n. 17, below.

she would support the Ottoman federal scheme and because he saw dangers for the future of Ottoman unity from Allied victory. He candidly stated these ideas to the Sharif of Makka, who led the Arab Revolt of 1916, and said that he was not in favor of complete separation from Ottoman unity. 'Aziz 'Ali, in an interview in 1958, told me that he advised the Sharif that the immediate objective of the Arab revolt should be merely to prevent the spread of hostility between Great Britain and Turkey into the Hijaz and to achieve Arab autonomy within the Ottoman unity.[12] Sharif Husayn, finding this young officer highly opinionated, was not very anxious to entrust him with high military command; but the British authorities, realizing the Sharif's urgent need for trained army officers, advised him to employ 'Aziz 'Ali, as well as other army officers, because of their prior training in the Ottoman army. Reluctant to entrust the command of the tribal forces to regular army officers, Sharif Husayn employed 'Aziz 'Ali and other Arab officers, provided they agreed to serve under the command of his sons.

No sooner had 'Aziz 'Ali begun to carry on his work as chief of staff in the Sharif's army than conflict between the two men over the conduct of the war led to his dismissal from the post and his departure from the Hijaz. After his return to Cairo toward the end of 1916, he was deported to Spain, where he spent the last two years of the war, because of his uncompromising position toward British policy. He spent the next twenty years in relative obscurity until World War II broke out in 1939. He was appointed Chief of Staff of the Egyptian army in 1940, when pro-Axis feeling was growing in the country, but he was dropped under British pressure and put under police surveillance for the rest of the war years. From 1940 until the Egyptian Revolution of 1952, he was secretly in touch with the Free Officers who laid down the plan of the Revolution, giving them moral support and encouraging them to pursue revolutionary activities. He almost agreed to lead the military uprising, but declined, pleading ill health. After the revolution, he was appointed Egyptian Ambassador to the Soviet Union in 1954 but retired very soon because of old age. He died in 1965.

---

[12] See also a statement to this effect in Fa'iz al-Ghusayn, *Mudhakkirati 'An al-Thawra al-'Arabiya* [My Memoirs about the Arab Revolt] (Damascus, 1956), p. 238.

III

What were his methods?

'Aziz 'Ali was a revolutionary officer who believed that violence was the only effective method to translate ideas into realities. He did not believe in half-measures or compromises: the only way to achieve goals was to defeat enemies by war or revolution. He was hot-tempered and incapable of persuading others to accept his views and therefore saw in violence the only means to achieve ends. When he and Enver Pasha disagreed, he failed to reason with Enver— the latter was no less hot-tempered than 'Aziz—and the conflict degenerated into a personal quarrel and ended in 'Aziz 'Ali's expulsion from Istanbul. In like manner, 'Aziz 'Ali's disagreement with Sharif Husayn on the objectives of the Arab Revolt prompted 'Aziz 'Ali first to negotiate secretly with the Ottoman authorities in Madina and then to use the Arab army to capture Makka. When the news of the plot reached Husayn, 'Aziz 'Ali was relieved of duty and sent back to Cairo.

Nor was 'Aziz 'Ali patient enough to lay down well-thought-out plans. His opponents often succeeded in frustrating his plans because they used subtle methods while he relied almost exclusively on force and revolutionary tactics. In 1941, when the German army was advancing toward Egypt, he claimed to have contacted the Germans and that an aircraft was sent to pick him up.[13] It is improbable that a German aircraft was sent to pick him up, but it is highly probable that the Free Officers provided a plane that would enable him to escape to German lines. The aircraft, it is said, hit a post on take-off and crashed. 'Aziz 'Ali was imprisoned on a charge of conspiring against the security of the state. He was released in 1944.[14]

Because he failed to calculate the possible dangerous consequences of his adventures, 'Aziz 'Ali often discouraged others from cooperating with him in politics.[15] Above all, 'Aziz 'Ali's lack of

---

[13] Anwar al-Sadat, *Revolt on the Nile* (London, 1957), pp. 36-37.

[14] *Ibid.*, p. 38. See also Muhammad Husayn Haykal, *Mudhakkirat Fi al-Siyasa al-Misriya* [Memoirs on Egyptian Politics] (Cairo, 1953), Vol. II, pp. 214-15.

[15] 'Abd al-Razzaq al-Sanhuri, a Cabinet Minister and President of the Council of State, told me that when he once suggested to Nuqrashi, leader of the Sa'dist Party, that he seek the cooperation of 'Aziz 'Ali in the establishment of a nationalist society, Nuqrashi discouraged him by the remark: "Be careful; that man is an adventurer!"

flexibility and his refusal to change his views even when events proved their falsity made it impossible for him to play the role of leader in any prospective political movement. His inability to bend, which was highly commended in military circles, was not sheer obstinancy: he honestly believed that sound principles in politics, as in morality, should be fully observed if a leader were to enjoy the confidence of the people; and thus he was not prepared to compromise.

It is abundantly clear that 'Aziz 'Ali, though he inspired many fellow officers to participate in politics, was not fit himself to become a leader. Perhaps only later in his career did he come to realize these shortcomings and tend to evade responsibility, even when circumstances appeared fairly favorable for success.[16]

IV

Why did 'Aziz 'Ali fail to become a political leader?

From early life, 'Aziz 'Ali possessed certain qualities—moral courage, physical strength, and sharp intelligence—which would enable any young man to work his way up in society and to participate in politics. But the conditioning of early life produced certain attitudes that adversely affected his political career and inhibited his leadership.

Growing up in the Egypt of the late Cromer regime, when anti-British feeling reached a high pitch, 'Aziz 'Ali was molded in an atmosphere of aversion to European political domination. Opposed to the British occupation, Egyptian leaders consciously aroused in the nation a nostalgic attachment to the Ottoman caliphate, and Egyptian nationalism was mixed with traditional Islamic zeal. It was in this emotional atmosphere that 'Aziz 'Ali received his early education, and these emotional factors determined his decision, after graduation from high school, to pursue his studies in Istanbul rather than in Paris or London. Had he not been imbued with these prejudices against European influence, he might have received a more solid education in Europe and his views on Anglo-Arab relations would probably have been more balanced. Ottoman school-

---

[16] See Chapter IV, p. 54.

ing could hardly have broadened his educational experience, except, perhaps, by providing him with professional military training. Even in this field, 'Aziz 'Ali accepted uncritically Ottoman admiration for German military discipline and German methods of warfare.

The Istanbul of the late Hamidian period had another impact on 'Aziz's future. While still a cadet, he was associated with a group of army officers who keenly felt a patriotic duty to take an active part in politics in order to end the Hamidian despotism and reestablish constitutional government. The political activities of the army officers resulted in the overthrow of the Hamidian regime, and they eventually led to the transfer of power from civilian to military hands and the elevation of some of 'Aziz's friends and associates to high political office. Though the main impetus behind these events was military rather than political, appreciation of the role of political forces was crucial to personal success in the new power structure. Men like 'Aziz 'Ali, who could not subordinate military discipline to political forces, were bound to remain in less influential positions, while their more politically minded compatriots naturally rose in the hierarchy.

Idealism proved another obstacle for the would-be politician within the military man, for politics requires certain qualities which the military man, in his career as a good soldier, cannot tolerate if high standards of discipline are to be maintained. 'Aziz 'Ali expected to achieve political success by the sheer fact that he had achieved high military discipline. He looked with envy on Enver Pasha, whose military achievements may not have been as high but who had attained high political office because he had the ability to manipulate political forces to his advantage, as 'Aziz 'Ali was incapable of doing. 'Aziz 'Ali's conflict with Enver Pasha was exploited by opposition groups, especially Arab leaders, who used it as a pretext to denounce the government's policy toward non-Turkish elements of the Ottoman Empire. The opposition factions were thus able to put 'Aziz in the false position of being the champion of the nationalities against Ottoman unity. Consequently, though at heart a firm believer in Ottoman unity, he almost inevitably found himself involved in antigovernmental activities detrimental to Ottoman unity. This aroused the suspicion of his friends in high government positions, but he could not extricate himself from this situation.

The acid test which proved 'Aziz 'Ali's commitment to ideal
goals and his firm personal convictions was the opportunity given
him to join the Arab Revolt in 1916. If he had been a political op-
portunist, seeking power and prestige, he would have been able to
attain an office higher than those given to his subordinates, Ja'far
al-'Askari and Nuri al-Sa'id, who later rose to Cabinet rank. 'Aziz
'Ali went to the Hijaz with no intention of breaking Ottoman unity,
although he honestly believed that the Arabs should be given an
autonomous status within it. When, to his surprise, he discovered
that Sharif Husayn aimed at a complete separation from the Ottoman dominion, which was not clear in official proclamations, he
turned to the Germans, hoping that German victory over Britain
might produce an understanding between Turks and Arabs and thus
further the cause of Ottoman unity.

'Aziz 'Ali proved to be an idealist who was prepared to step
aside from power in favor of a dream the practicability of which
was questionable but which had dominated his mind since his
Istanbul days. He was not a realist who could appreciate the play
of political forces. There were, it is true, certain emotional factors
which may have influenced his fateful decision to seek German
rather than British collaboration, such as his admiration for German military discipline and a latent dislike for Britain, owing to
her occupation of Egypt; but his decision seems to have been remote from a desire for immediate returns. It has been maintained
that Sharif Husayn's dissatisfaction with 'Aziz 'Ali was due, at least
in part, to personal rather than political reasons, to 'Aziz's insub-
ordination of superiors. If this personal element had any significant
bearing on 'Aziz's decision, it must indeed reflect on the strength
of his character and personality.

'Aziz was a social reformer who sympathized with the oppressed
and downtrodden. He passionately desired to achieve a just society
in which liberty, equality, and other liberal principles could be
realized, and violence was the only means he knew to achieve this
goal. However, he devoted much more time to the problem of how
to establish his utopia than to its nature and type. The ways and
means by which he could achieve his goal seemed to him much more
important than the goal itself, because he was not essentially a social
thinker, but an amateur, attracted by certain fanciful ideas which
he sought to realize by revolutionary means. His utopia through

revolution remained a mirage, for none of the schemes he laid down had the slightest chance of success, although the Egyptian Revolution of 1952, whose leaders derived inspiration from his revolutionary ideas, may well be regarded as a partial vindication of his long-cherished ideal.[17]

[17]The writer has drawn freely from his article "'Aziz 'Ali al-Misri and the Arab Nationalist Movement," *St. Antony's Papers,* ed. Albert Hourani (London, 1964), pp. 140-63.

CHAPTER III

The Realistic School
Nuri al-Sa'id

I derived my political doctrine from the study of military command. Once a German colonel told us in class that the right spirit for a commander is to do the job with the resources he has available. It is his duty to use his brain and energy with what he has at hand. That gave me the idea I have followed all my life—to be practical, not idealistic. My critics always want the ideal. If everything comes as you like, what is the use of ability? This is my doctrine: Never be an idealist. Use what is available and don't wait till everything is perfect and miss your chance.

Nuri al-Sa'id

Nuri al-Sa'id was a disciple of 'Aziz 'Ali al-Misri, but no master and disciple could be farther apart in outlook and methods. True, the two were agreed on ultimate goals, and both were influenced by the same nationalist stirrings that dominated the Arab community in Istanbul after the Revolution of 1908. But when they went to the Hijaz in 1916 to take part in the Arab Revolt they differed radically on how to relate goals to conditions. Nuri saw that the future of Arab countries lay in their complete separation from Ottoman rule and the achievement of independence; to him, this was the logical outcome of the war. 'Aziz 'Ali, on the other hand, was not prepared to depart from commitments to Ottoman unity; he refused to adjust his goals in accordance with new conditions, even though he was entrusted with mili-

19

Nuri al-Saʿid

tary command which might have elevated him to the highest position of responsibility. Nuri, though less sophisticated than 'Aziz 'Ali, possessed a far more judicious eye which enabled him to peer more deeply below the surface of things and to play a more constructive role in the service of his country; 'Aziz 'Ali, unyielding to realities, lived for the rest of his life in almost complete obscurity. Needless to say, Nuri belonged to a different school of military politicians—the realistic school—from that which placed ideals and military discipline above political realities. Nuri possessed the flexible mind of a practical politician while 'Aziz 'Ali's mind was conditioned by idealistic principles.

II

Long before Baghdad came under Ottoman rule, reduced circumstances had become the way of life for the residents in that once-opulent city of the caliphs. Many men who played an important role in 'Iraq after World War I came from poor families, and Nuri was no exception. His father, Sa'id Taha, though a respected official in the Awqaf department,[1] was a poor man when Nuri was born in 1888.[2]

Nuri's homeland, part of the Ottoman dominion, was governed directly by Turkish officials, and natives were permitted to serve either in religious institutions or in the army. Because his father was in the service of a religious department, Nuri, after a brief course in an elementary school, went to a cadet academy, which would give him an opportunity for an army career and a chance to climb the social ladder. In 1903, Nuri was transferred to the Military Academy of Istanbul at the age of fourteen, and he was graduated three years later.

Returning to 'Iraq, Nuri joined a mounted infantry unit whose principal task was to collect taxes, mostly on sheep, from unwilling

---

[1] The department of "Pious Foundation" was designed to supervise estates for charitable purposes.

[2] Little is known about Nuri's ancestors. The family claims descent from an Arab tribe and more specifically from Mulla Lowlow, a legendary figure who lived in Baghdad some three centuries ago, but there is no evidence to confirm either connection. Cf. Lord Birdwood, *Nuri as-Sa'id* (London, 1959), pp. 8-9.

tribesmen all over the country. This unattractive duty helped the future politician to get acquainted with the countryside and to establish friendships with tribal chiefs. In 1908, when the Young Turks achieved power, Nuri began to pay attention to politics and to talk about freedom, constitutional government, and reform. He aspired to be in the center of activities, and his ambition to rise under the new regime was awakened. His services in Baghdad and his unquestionable loyalty to the Ottoman Porte were rewarded by his superior's approval for further military training.

In 1910 he returned to Istanbul to enter the Staff College. By this time he had married. His wife's brother was Ja'far al-'Askari, a schoolmate, who married Nuri's sister. These two officers, bound together by friendship and family loyalty, cooperated in the pursuit of common political objectives while in the military service and later in politics. Nuri's only son, Sabah, was born in Istanbul in 1911.[3] While in the Staff College, Nuri learned French and attended lectures by German instructors on European history and strategy. After graduation, he gained some experience in the operations against the Bulgarians during the Balkan wars.

While in Istanbul, Nuri's mind was preoccupied with political problems. Like 'Aziz 'Ali, with whom he was in close touch, he supported the reform program of the Young Turks, some of whom had been his classmates at the Staff College; but he also shared the misgivings of the Arab community in Istanbul about Ottoman misrule in Arab lands and the discrimination in military and civil services between Arab and Turk. As we have noted before, Arab leaders in Istanbul organized secret societies to defend Arab rights, but Nuri took no part in these activities.

In 1912 'Aziz 'Ali, in pursuit of a compromise plan to preserve Ottoman unity, organized the 'Ahd Society. Nuri joined in the hope that Arab countries might obtain self-government within the Ottoman superstructure. As a nationalist, he joined in agitations with other Arab leaders, some of whom were members of Parliament, such as Sulayman Faydi, a lawyer from Basra, and Jamil Sidqi al-Zahawi, the liberal poet.[4] He became particularly active at the time

---

[3] He was killed in Baghdad during the Revolution of 1958.

[4] For a brief account of Zahawi's life and ideas, see my *Political Trends*, pp. 235-37; and for Faydi's own account of this period see his memoirs, *Fi Ghamrat al-Nidal* [In the Midst of the Struggle] (Baghdad, 1952), pp. 140-67.

of the arrest and trial of 'Aziz 'Ali and endeavored with other Arab leaders to seek British intervention to secure his release. In foreign affairs he seems to have become suspicious of German objectives in their support of the Young Turks and to have begun to think that the future of the Arabs would depend on British support. 'Aziz 'Ali's expulsion from Istanbul in 1914 left Nuri with a sense of loneliness. He was discouraged by the loss of the leader under whom he was to defend his country's rights, and he decided that returning to his country was the only way to engage in a struggle against Ottoman domination.[5]

Nuri's departure from Istanbul was a turning point in his life. Had he remained there, when the war broke out, he would have been compelled to fight against Britain since he was an officer in the Ottoman army. He and one of his countrymen, 'Abd-Allah al-Damluchi, decided to escape from Istanbul and seek refuge in Arab lands. Nuri was debating in his mind whether he should proceed to Cairo, where 'Aziz 'Ali had gone, or whether he should return to his own country and then perhaps go to Arabia—provinces relatively free from Ottoman control—where he could engage in Arab nationalist activities without being threatened by Ottoman authorities. According to Sulayman Faydi, then a member of Parliament, it was he who suggested to Nuri that he visit Sayyid Talib al-Naqib, a man of considerable influence in the Basra province and also a member of Parliament, and work under his guidance for the Arab cause. Sayyid Talib headed an Arab society in Basra which advocated reforms in Arab lands. He had long been consolidating his position in Basra and stood as a defender of Arab rights. The Young Turks, unable to influence him, recognized his authority and compromised with him. Because he suspected that the Young Turks might trap him in Istanbul, Sayyid Talib remained in Basra during the two years preceding the outbreak of war.

Nuri and Damluchi left Istanbul secretly for Basra, armed with a letter of introduction to Sayyid Talib from Sulayman Faydi.[6] They arrived on June 12, 1914, and went first to Sayyid Talib to seek protection from possible Ottoman arrest. With the help of

---

[5] For Nuri's own account of this period, see *al-Zaman* (Baghdad), January 31 and February 1, 1947; reprinted in Nuri's *Ahadith* (Baghdad, 1947), pp. 90-91. (Hereafter referred to as Nuri's *Ahadith*.)

[6] Faydi, *Fi Ghamrat al-Nidal*, p. 174.

Sayyid Talib, they then tried to escape to Ibn Saud and the Sultan of Masqat (Muscat) where they could work without fear. But Nuri fell ill before they were ready to leave for Arabia, and Damluchi left alone. Damluchi stayed in Arabia in the service of Ibn Saud for the next decade and a half until he returned in 1930 to 'Iraq as Nuri's Minister of Foreign Affairs, when Nuri himself had become Prime Minister.

When Nuri recovered in November 1914, an Indian Expeditionary Force had already occupied Basra. He began to give thought to the course he should follow. At this time 'Aziz 'Ali seems to have sent a message to Arab leaders in 'Iraq advising against cooperation with Britain because of the danger to Ottoman unity. But Nuri saw that Arab interests would be best served if he sided with the British, and he wrote Sir Percy Cox, British Resident in the Persian Gulf, offering his services.[7] According to Nuri, he asked Cox to give him permission to go to Egypt. Because Nuri was an officer in the Ottoman army, Cox sent him to India to be interned; from there he was sent to Cairo, where he became engaged with other Arab leaders in the preparations for the military operations in the Hijaz against the Turks.[8]

Nuri's participation in the Arab Revolt was the beginning of a life-long association with the Hashimi house. He entered military service under Husayn, Sharif of Makka, who led the revolt; later he served under Husayn's son, Faysal, in the Hijaz, in Syria, and in 'Iraq. He was still with the Hashimi house serving Faysal's son and grandson when he was killed, with the King and Crown Prince, in the Revolution of 1958.

The story of Nuri's participation in the Arab Revolt belongs to military history, the details of which have been recorded by Nuri himself as well as by others.[9] It was during this period that Nuri became Faysal's loyal servant and followed him first to Damascus and then to 'Iraq.

While still in Damascus, Nuri's eyes were fixed on 'Iraq—his homeland—whose future had not yet been decided. Nuri and some

[7] Sir Percy Cox also became Chief Political Officer after the British Expeditionary Force landed in Basra in 1914.

[8] See Nuri's Ahadith, pp. 91-92.

[9] Nuri al-Sa'id, Mudaharat 'An al-Harakat al-'Askariya Li al-Jaysh al-'Arabi fi al-Hijaz wa Suriya [Lectures on the Military Operations of the Arab Army in the Hijaz and Syria] (Baghdad, 1947); T. E. Lawrence, Seven Pillars of Wisdom (London, 1935).

of his compatriots who had been watching events in 'Iraq were alarmed by the actions of Sir Arnold Wilson, Acting Civil Commissioner, who seemed to be perpetuating direct British administration of the country. Wilson represented a view supported by the Colonial Office, which saw 'Iraq from an Indian perspective and tried to keep it within the orbit of Anglo-Indian administration. Others among Nuri's British associates followed the Foreign Office school of thought, which sought to exercise British influence through an Arab (Hashimi) administration. Nuri indicated to the British that he and his fellow 'Iraqi officers would cooperate with Britain if the administration was placed in 'Iraqi hands.[10] Some of Nuri's compatriots, on the other hand, began to arouse feelings against Britain, which culminated in an uprising in 1920; Nuri took no part in these events, although he did hope that Britain might change her policy and appoint a commissioner sympathetic with Arab aspirations.

Before returning to 'Iraq, Nuri went to London with Faysal at the time when Britain was reviewing the 'Iraqi situation. Faysal had already been considered as a possible candidate for the throne, and when it was offered to him by the British, Faysal replied that he would accept the throne if formally offered to him by the 'Iraqi people. Sir Percy Cox, well known for his sympathies with the Arabs, was appointed High Commissioner and returned to 'Iraq to carry out the new arrangement. Upon his arrival in October 1920, Cox invited a few 'Iraqi officers who had served under Faysal in Damascus, including Ja'far al-'Askari and Nuri al-Sa'id, to return to 'Iraq. Ja'far went to serve as Minister of Defence in the newly established Provisional Government of 'Iraq; Nuri remained with Faysal in London.

Nuri arrived in 'Iraq in February 1921 and began to associate with old friends and acquaintances who were fully immersed in local politics. One group included politicians who desired the head of the regime to be an Arab from 'Iraq. In this group was the Naqib of Baghdad, head of the Provisional Government, and Sayyid Talib al-Naqib, Minister of Interior, whose friendship, it will be remembered, Nuri had cultivated in Basra in 1914. Another group

---

[10] For Nuri's views in conversations with Hubert Young, see Sir Hubert Young, *The Independent Arab* (London, 1933); and Birdwood, *Nuri as-Sa'id*, p. 115.

was comprised of nationalists who had worked under Faysal in the Hijaz and Syria and supported Faysal's candidacy for the throne. Nuri had no hesitation as to whom his loyalty belonged, and he thus had to part company with his friend, Sayyid Talib, who had presented himself as a candidate for president of a republican regime.

In March 1921, Faysal was formally nominated for the throne of 'Iraq in a conference held in Cairo. The nomination was confirmed by a plebiscite held in the same year,[11] and Faysal was proclaimed King in August 1921.

From 1921 to 1930 Nuri preferred to remain in the background of the ensuing struggle for independence. All political leaders were agreed in principle on independence, but they disagreed on the way to achieve it. Some wanted independence at once as a matter of right; others were prepared to wait until the country was ready for it. Nuri saw the need for British advice and urged rapid development before full independence. He endeavored to organize a national army, and served for almost a decade either as Chief of Staff or as Minister of Defence. He was rarely out of office in the constant reshuffling of cabinets—which caused one friendly critic to describe him as the perennial minister.

In 1930, when Britain finally decided to recognize 'Iraq's independence and replace the Mandate by a treaty of alliance, Nuri appeared the man ideally fitted to deal with Britain as head of a government. He stood up to the task for which he was selected—to conclude a treaty of alliance and achieve independence. For two years he worked assiduously to reconcile differences among rival groups, on the one hand, and to negotiate a treaty of alliance with Britain, on the other.

The treaty, signed on June 30, 1930, provided for the termination of British control and recognition of 'Iraqi independence. 'Iraq would consult Britain on foreign policy, and Britain would come to the defense of 'Iraq if she were attacked. As *quid pro quo,* 'Iraq granted Britain two air bases and the use of all means of communi-

---

[11] The Cairo Conference, held in 1921, was presided over by Winston Churchill and attended by high British civil and military authorities. It dealt with formulating a new policy not only for 'Iraq but also for other countries. See A. S. Klieman, *Foundations of British Policy in the Arab World: The Cairo Conference of 1921* (Baltimore, 1970), Chap. 7.

cations in the event Britain became involved in war. These obligations were to become binding after 'Iraq became independent. The
entry of 'Iraq into the League of Nations on October 3, 1932, as a
sovereign state demonstrated Nuri's skills as a leader and his ability
to achieve national goals. After independence, he continued to serve
as Premier or Foreign Minister, becoming his country's leading ex-
pert in foreign affairs. It is not the purpose of this essay to give a
narrative of 'Iraq's political development and Nuri's active participation in it, since these have been dealt with elsewhere,[12] but to
study Nuri's role as a political leader.

III

After he became Prime Minister in 1930, Nuri is considered to
be the principal architect of his country's domestic and foreign
policy. From 1930 to his death in 1958 he was Prime Minister fourteen times (thirteen as Premier for 'Iraq and once for the Arab
Federation), and many more times, he was a minister (usually for
foreign affairs) in cabinets in which he was the principal figure.
Even when he did not serve as minister, he was not really out of
power, for he either influenced policy through a protégé or through
the head of state as a privy counselor. While out of power, he usually preferred to reside outside the country—either in an Arab or a
European capital. Even then he participated in formal and informal
negotiations, sometimes returning to form a new government to
carry out a particular agreement if the existing government failed
to honor his commitments. What were Nuri's objectives?
   Ever since 1916 when he went to the Hijaz to participate in the
Arab Revolt, he had been firmly convinced that Arab national
aspirations—independence, unity, etc.—would be more effectively
achieved under the leadership of the Hashimi house. More specifically, he found in Faysal leadership qualities—prudence, moderation,
and the ability to handle men—which he admired and cherished. He
remained loyal to the Hashimi house after Faysal's death, although
he questioned the ability of Faysal's son, King Ghazi (especially

[12] See my *Independent 'Iraq* (2nd. ed.; London, 1960); and *Republican 'Iraq* (London,
1969).

after the *coup d'état* of 1936), to rule and had some difficulties with Faysal's nephew, Amir 'Abd al-Ilah, who served as Regent until Faysal's grandson (Faysal II) came of age in 1953. Nuri believed that his country's interests would be better served by supporting the royal dynasty, and he tried to build the stature of young King Faysal in the public eye. For this reason he went so far as to kiss the king's hands in public in order to give an example of loyalty and respect.

No less significant than loyalty to king and country was Nuri's concern about Arab independence and unity. Like Faysal I, he served outside his country before he returned to 'Iraq. He seems to have come to the conclusion that Arab national interests would be best served if 'Iraq—as well as every Arab country—were first to achieve independence. He found in Faysal I the kind of leader whom he believed could achieve ultimate Arab national interests. After Faysal's death and the achievement of his country's independence, Nuri's enthusiasm for Arab unity may have cooled off, since Faysal's descendants proved unequal to the task—indeed, they were unacceptable to other Arab countries. But he never really gave up the desire for Arab unity whenever the circumstances to achieve it were favorable. During World War II, when French influence began to recede from Syria and Lebanon and Britain declared herself in favor of a union acceptable to the Arabs,[13] Nuri lost no time in negotiating for unity with other Arab countries. This negotiation led eventually to the establishment of the Arab League, although his preference was for a more intimate union of the Levant countries and 'Iraq (the Fertile Crescent) as a prelude to an overall Arab union.[14] When the so-called Fertile Crescent unity scheme did not materialize, he supported the Arab League as an instrument for cooperation in inter-Arab relations. Nevertheless, he did not completely give up the possibility of Arab unity, as shown by his initial support for King 'Abd-Allah's Greater Syria plan and in the subsequent federal union between 'Iraq and Jordan over whose government he presided in 1958.

[13] Statements in favor of Arab unity were made by Anthony Eden, Secretary of State for Foreign Affairs, in 1941 and 1943.

[14] See Nuri al-Sa'id, *Arab Independence and Unity* (Baghdad, 1943); and also exchange of telegrams with King Ibn Sa'ud about Syria and Lebanon dated July 24, 1943 (text in Khayr al-Din al-Zirkli, *Shubh al-Jazira fi 'Ahd al-Malik 'Abd al-'Aziz* [The Peninsula during the Time of King 'Abd al-'Aziz] [Bayrut, 1970], Vol. III, pp. 1148-50).

Arab inability to unite or coordinate activities revealed a weakness which may have indicated to Nuri the need for a Great Power's support, not only to aid them against possible foreign aggression but also to provide economic and technical assistance for internal development. From his early Istanbul days, no less than from his experiences during and after World War I, he had seen in Great Britain the power most likely to support Arab nationalism; he believed that the British and the Arabs had many common interests and that their subsequent conflicts were not necessarily irreconcilable. Britain's willingness to terminate the Mandate and her support in strengthening 'Iraq confirmed his belief in Britain's friendship. He hoped that after other Arab countries had achieved independence a grand Anglo-Arab alliance, based on mutual respect for independence and national unity, would be established on a permanent basis to work for progress and stability in the Arab world.

After World War II, when the Cold War developed, Nuri came into conflict with other Arab leaders over cooperation with the West. Nuri urged an alliance with the West in the West-East conflict, while these leaders advocated neutrality (a stance later put forth by Nasir as "positive neutrality"). Nuri held that Soviet penetration into Arab lands would endanger their newly acquired independence but that an alliance with the Western powers would protect it. He did not think neutrality was feasible because of the important strategic position of Arab lands between Western and Eastern blocs and because of the weakness of the Arabs, which would necessarily invite Great Power intervention. Nuri conceded that there were certain conflicts between the West and the Arabs— the question of Palestine, Western support of some Arab regimes against others, unduly prolonged British control of some Arab countries—but in his view these problems eventually would be favorably resolved if the Arabs would seek cooperation with the West and strengthen their position in the world.

Nuri maintained that Britain was prepared to withdraw her control gradually from the entire Arab world, if the Arabs would cooperate in Western defense plans. Under the treaty of 1930, Britain retained possession of two 'Iraqi air bases; in 1955, when Britain agreed to relinquish them, 'Iraq joined the Baghdad Pact. 'Iraq had already begun to receive Western military and economic assistance a year before (under a separate agreement with the

United States in 1954). Nuri hoped that other Arab countries would join the Pact and through Western economic and military assistance become united and strong. Only then, he thought, could they try to influence the Western powers to resolve the Arab-Israeli conflict in the Arabs' favor. He realized that the Palestine problem was the greatest stumbling block in Anglo-Arab (and later Western-Arab) rapprochement, but he always held that this issue was secondary to other defense questions and that it would be eventually resolved in favor of the Arabs if they cooperated with the West.[15]

Nuri's views on foreign policy were not shared by most Arab leaders, particularly the military leaders of Egypt, because there was a widespread suspicion that European powers were not prepared to withdraw their influence from Arab lands, nor were they ready to supply arms in considerable quantities to strengthen them. Consequently, the Arab leaders desired to remain neutral in the Cold War. They did not think that the Soviet threat was imminent. Their immediate enemy, they argued, was Israel and not the Soviet Union. If the Western powers were prepared to provide them with arms for defense against any attack—Soviet or Israeli—they were prepared to accept the assistance without commitment to either side. Nuri's failure to persuade his Western friends to accept the Arab point of view and the refusal of Arab leaders to cooperate with the Western powers weakened his position in the Arab world and led to his final demise.[16] He was compelled to concentrate on building up 'Iraq's strength by pursuing a policy of internal reconstruction in order to demonstrate the soundness of his policy in general; but before his countrymen were able to obtain the benefit of his reconstruction plans, the Revolution of 1958 swept away both his regime and some of his plans.

---

[15] It is deemed outside the scope of this essay to discuss the origins and purposes of the Baghdad Pact. For Nuri's role in the Pact, see W. J. Gallman, *Iraq under General Nuri* (Baltimore, 1964). See Fadil Jamali's criticism of this book in *Forum,* Vol. XL (Autumn 1964), pp. 13-24; and Khaldun al-Husri's reply, *ibid.,* Vol. XLI (Autumn 1965), pp. 25-28, and Vol. XLII (Winter, 1965), pp. 24-29.

[16] For Nuri's warnings to the West, see his article "Last Testament of Iraqi Premier," *Life International,* Vol. XXV (August 18, 1958), pp. 26-28. Shortly before the Revolution of 1958, Nuri tried to counteract Pan-Arab opposition by forming a tripartite bloc of three Arab countries—'Iraq, Jordan and Kuwayt—but Britain was reluctant to allow Kuwayt to slip from her control and join the Arab Federation. See Harold Macmillan, *Riding the Storm, 1956-1959* (London, 1970), p. 504.

IV

'Iraq has been described in Arab chronicles as a very difficult country to govern. The methods suggested to control its people have varied from one extreme to another. On his deathbed Mu'awiya, founder of the Umayyad dynasty (d. 680), is reported to have advised his son Yazid to change the governor every day if the 'Iraqis asked him to. Another extreme view was advocated by al-Hajjaj,[17] governor of 'Iraq under the Caliph 'Abd al-Malik, who urged that only a harsh and repressive policy could succeed, and he ruled the country with an iron hand. Neither policy succeeded: disorder prevailed under Caliph Yazid's rule, and serious uprisings followed Hajjaj's tenure of office. The two extreme policies reflected simplistic methods applied to a highly complex society. The social structure of 'Iraq was divided into three principal parts. The first was the tribal and semi-tribal communities of the south, essentially a mixture of emigrés who entered the country in increasing numbers after the Arab conquests of the seventh century and intermarried with the natives. The second was composed of the urban centers in the middle of the Tigris-Euphrates valley. These centers had formed the backbone of the once highly civilized society of Islam's golden age and of earlier civilizations that flourished in the country. Peace and order were crucial for the urban population, for without them they could not have maintained their relatively advanced civilization. Aware of the dangers of periodic tribal raids, the caliphs (and later, the Ottoman sultans) were often forced to recruit mercenary armies to protect the constructive work of these centers. The third part of 'Iraqi society—the Kurdish community— had only become part of the country after World War I; it had never before been regarded as part of 'Iraq, since it formed a portion of the region known as Jazirat Ibn 'Umar. This non-Arab section, to say nothing of other religious and ethnic groups, added to the complexity of 'Iraq's social structure. It is a very difficult task to govern a people that has not yet developed cohesion and social solidarity and has even been reluctant to accept in principle a common 'Iraqi nationality.

Against this background it is clear why Faysal I, who had ex-

[17] Al-Hajjaj Ibn Yusuf al-Thaqafi (d. 714).

perienced life in desert and town, urged his ministers upon his assumption of authority to follow a policy of moderation and to dampen hopes for radical reform until 'Iraq could form a nation-state in the modern sense. So long as Faysal was alive, his prestige and balanced leadership held the country together. All political leaders, though they often quarreled among themselves, acknowledged his supreme authority and served the country to the best of their abilities.

After Faysal's death (1933), it devolved upon Nuri to assert leadership over rival groups and political figures in order to keep the country from falling apart. There was a short period of tribal uprisings and military intervention in politics, during which Nuri was ousted from power on more than one occasion. He was finally able to purge the army of political opponents after the military uprising of 1941. However, it was not until World War II that the problem of overhauling the political system was seriously tackled, notwithstanding a constitutional amendment in favor of strengthening the head of state that had been adopted during the war.[18]

In principle, Nuri was in favor of a parliamentary democracy which would operate within the monarchical system. For almost a decade after the war, he toyed with the idea of developing a two-party system which would prevent the army and palace entourage from interfering in the political process. In 1946, when political parties were allowed to be formed, Nuri, then out of power, tried to enlist the support of a few elder politicians and moderate elements to form a right-wing party and to encourage liberals to form a "loyal opposition"; he was opposed to allowing communists to form a party. Nuri's efforts failed because most of the elder politicians preferred to operate without a party system; those who were prepared to work under his leadership refused to cooperate with each other for personal reasons.[19] Thus, the political parties that were formed in 1946 were left-wing and center parties.

In 1950, Nuri made another attempt and formally organized the Constitutionalist Party, hoping to attract both older and

[18] See my *Independent 'Iraq*, pp. 289-99, 302-6.

[19] Nuri succeeded in enlisting the cooperation of Sawaydi and Sa'd Salih to join a political party, but they later refused when they discovered that Salih Jabr, one of Nuri's chief supporters, was to be included. Jabr later formed his own party, in opposition to Nuri, when the two leaders parted company on the question of the Portsmouth Treaty in 1948.

younger men to counteract the left-wing parties. While this party attracted a few able young men like Diya' Ja'far and Khalil Kanna, (the latter defected from the liberal-nationalist groups), he failed again to persuade the leading politicians to join. Since Nuri himself was an elder politician who moved only in higher circles, he left the actual operation of the party on the popular level to younger men— to Khalil Kanna, in particular—and failed to utilize his popularity as a leader to carry the country in support of a parliamentary democracy.

There were renewed efforts to strengthen the parliamentary system in 1953, when Faysal II came of age. 'Abd al-Ilah, the King's uncle and Crown Prince, was to cease to exercise power as Regent, and the King, in assuming his constitutional prerogatives, was to consult the leaders of political parties and other groups without necessarily abandoning his uncle's palace entourage. Liberal opposition leaders admonished the elder politicians to let the King exercise his right to consult all the country's leaders without discrimination in the interest of the monarchy itself.[20] At the outset the King's uncle agreed to withdraw from active politics, retaining only his position as Crown Prince; and a cabinet composed essentially of moderate elements was formed to hold "free elections" as a step toward strengthening the parliamentary system. The political parties that participated in the elections of 1954 won only a few seats in Parliament; the majority were held either by elder politicians or by members of Nuri's Constitutionalist Party.[21] Nuri might have been satisfied with the returns, had he not discovered the Crown Prince's hidden manipulation of the elections and his attempt to create a new palace entourage under the patronage of a "liberal cabinet." Nuri, who was out of the country during the elections, is reported to have said that he would never again take responsibility as long as the Crown Prince continued to interfere in politics. Since it became clear that the position of elder politicians would be completely undermined by a small but active opposition in the new Parlia-

---

[20] Fa'iq al-Samarra'i, an influential leader of the Istiqlal Party, welcomed the King's assumption of his prerogatives and called in an article for cooperation with the monarchy if the elder politicians would cease to use the palace as a base of operation.

[21] See Frank Stoakes and S. H. Longrigg, *'Iraq* (London, 1958), pp. 105-6; and George Grassmuck, "The Electoral Process in 'Iraq, 1952-1958," *The Middle East Journal,* Vol. XIV (1960), pp. 397-415.

ment, the Crown Prince was urged to reconcile his differences with Nuri in the interest of the monarchy itself. In July 1954, the Crown Prince made the journey to Paris to make peace. Nuri agreed to return to Baghdad only on condition that he would have a free hand in governing the country.

After he formed a government on August 2, 1954, Nuri followed a policy which contradicted all previous efforts to strengthen the parliamentary system. He dissolved Parliament after it had only one sitting—the shortest in its history—and he disbanded all political parties including his own. He also censored and arrested opposition leaders, ostensibly to rid the country of communist agitation. These actions rendered the political system anything but parliamentary: Nuri ruled with almost dictatorial powers. True, he did succeed temporarily in reducing the influence of the Crown Prince and his entourage, a necessary step toward strengthening the parliamentary system, but he utterly failed to create a popular base for it. While in power—from 1954 to 1957 and again for some three months in 1958—he was able to keep the country under firm control even when there were signs of revolt, as the abortive coup of 1956 demonstrated, but when he relinquished power, leaving the country to lesser hands, disorder and chaos reigned. It became evident that the country was moving quickly to an almost inevitable calamity—he and the monarchy were overthrown and liquidated in 1958.

V

Nuri is reported to have said shortly before the downfall of the monarchy that if his countrymen would only realize how prosperous and contented they would be in a decade when his reconstruction schemes were carried out they would no longer listen to a handful of troublemakers. In his old age, he seems to have given up the hope of developing a truly parliamentary system and to have begun to rely on the prospect of prosperity and development as a means to win loyalty for the regime. He was unaware that his opponents were not merely a handful of lawyers and schoolteachers, as he often said, but a growing number of formidable leaders and well-organized groups, especially the communists, who were determined to overthrow him as the bulwark of the ruling oligarchy.

After he returned to power in 1954, Nuri had decided to crush
the opposition before embarking on his ambitious reform schemes.
He maintained that the opponents to the regime who were agitating
for reform and democracy were inspired by motives very different
from their declared intentions. The communists, he held, were determined to destroy the existing regime by revolutionary means in
order to establish a communist dictatorship, even though they
talked about democracy and social reform.[22] But Nuri's methods
of dealing with the communists were wholly negative and too
simplistic—he moved only to bring their leaders to trial for seditious activities and to give them various sentences of imprisonment
in accordance with their respective crimes. If necessary, he was
prepared to put to death their principal leaders and to exile others
from the country—as he had done in 1946 and 1949. Those who
pledged to abandon the communist creed and never again to engage in communist activities were pardoned—or their prison terms
shortened—and put under police surveillance.[23] In 1958, shortly
before the July Revolution, Sa'id Qazzaz, Minister of the Interior,
told me with apparent complacency that the communist movement
had been completely liquidated and that there were no longer any
communists in the country. True, the principal leaders seemed to
have virtually disappeared from the scene, but there is no doubt
that the movement went deeper under the surface. The people may
have had certain mental reservations about radical ideas, but the
tenacity and endurance with which communists defied authority
aroused public sympathy and their activities appeared in the public
eye as a form of national struggle against tyranny. The communists
maintained that their struggle was as patriotic as any other group's
and that their objective, like that of other nationalists, was to
achieve democracy and national unity combined with socialism.
Small wonder, therefore, that the communist movement spread
widely and rapidly immediately after the July Revolution.[24] Nuri's
methods, though temporarily restricting subversive activities, by no
means nipped the communist movement in the bud. Popular
grievances continued, and the communists and other opponents of
the regime fully exploited them.

[22] See Nuri's *Ahadith*, pp. 19-20.

[23] *Ibid.*, pp. 83-88; and my *Independent 'Iraq*, pp. 361 ff.

[24] See my *Republican 'Iraq*, pp. 117 ff.

As to other opponents—including nationalists—Nuri maintained that they were self-seeking, notwithstanding the fact that he was in agreement with them about the need for reform. Consequently, he always tried to reason with them and perhaps to win them over by offering them high political posts. From among those who agreed to cooperate, however, he often chose opportunists whose self-seeking motives he could expose; he did not really take into his confidence young men of integrity who enjoyed good reputation. Actually, Nuri failed to enlist the cooperation of men who genuinely disagreed with him; when he denied them the right of free expression, they often resorted to violence on the ground of redeeming freedom.[25]

Nuri's concern about reform was indeed genuine, and he earnestly sought to meet his countrymen's urgent need for development. Perhaps he instinctively realized that before he could grapple with the problems of the political system and institute an enduring parliamentary democracy, sweeping social and economic reforms must be carried out. In 1950 he created the Development Board for reconstruction as an autonomous body under the chairmanship of the Prime Minister in order to insure efficiency and limit bureaucratic influences. Seventy percent of the oil royalties were earmarked for development, and other sources, such as loans from the International Bank, were also considered and used.[26] In 1951 the oil agreement with the 'Iraq Petroleum Company was revised on the basis of fifty-fifty profit sharing, which increased the amount of funds available for development. The Board launched ambitious schemes for irrigation and drainage, designed to save the country from the perennial threat of floods and to store river waters for increasing agricultural production. At the outset the Board supported no short-term projects but concentrated its resources on irrigation and flood control plans. But once these grandiose projects were completed, other short-term plans were considered, and shortly before the July Revolution the Board did initiate some such projects, including the construction of roads and bridges and the building of hospitals and schools. Had some of the plans to improve the condi-

[25] For the attitude of 'Iraqi liberals toward authority, see Chapter VIII, below.

[26] For a study of the achievements of the Development Board, see F. Qubain, *The Reconstruction of 'Iraq* (New York, 1958).

tions of the poor been carried out before 1958, Nuri's critics might
not have been able to arouse the masses against him. The big projects, though regarded by experts as necessary for an essentially
agricultural country,[27] failed to impress the public because most of
them were built outside towns and cities and because they were
thought to serve only the landowning class. Nuri hoped that his
development schemes would eventually bring about general prosperity and, as a result, raise the standard of living of the common man,
who at last would reap the fruits of his lifelong public service. It
was, indeed, a race between development and revolution; but time
ran short for development. Two days after his opponents rose in
revolt on July 14, 1958, the very crowd whose interests Nuri had
had at heart precipitated his death and dragged his naked corpse
down the streets.[28]

VI

Nuri was not unaware of the possibility of a military uprising,
but, like his handling of civilian opponents, his techniques for ward-
ing it off were too simplistic: he either tried to ignore the young
officers or to fraternize with senior ones in the belief they would
be able to keep the armed forces under control.

From the time he became Cabinet minister, Nuri operated as a
civilian politician and never thought that the army should be used
as a political instrument. He was confident that political conflicts
could be resolved by peaceful methods, and he hoped that 'Iraq's
political system would eventually evolve into a true parliamentary
democracy. He was horrified when the 'Iraqi army became involved
in politics in 1936 and admonished both civil and military leaders
against military interference in political issues. But Nuri's warning
went unheeded; and as has happened in other countries, once the
military has intervened in politics such intervention is likely to continue. Nuri himself used the army when power slipped from his hands

---

[27] For conflicting views on the Development Board as well as an evaluation of its projects,
see Lord Salter, *The Development of 'Iraq* (London, 1955); 'Abd al-Rahman al-Jalili,
al-I'mar Fi al-'Iraq [Reconstruction of 'Iraq] (Bayrut, 1968); Michael Ionides, *Divide and
Lose* (London, 1960), pp. 197 ff.

[28] For an account of Nuri's assassination, see my *Republican 'Iraq*, pp. 52-56.

in the first military coup in 1936, but he vainly thought that after his return to power he would be able to isolate the army from politics. He tried at first to retire some officers and appoint others to diplomatic posts; by 1941, when these measures had not discouraged young officers from political ventures, he went so far as to throw some in prison and execute others.

After World War II, Nuri began to pay special attention to the army and large sums were earmarked in annual budgets to equip it with modern weapons. It is true that Nuri's main purpose was perhaps primarily political—to divert the attention of officers from domestic to foreign affairs and to use the army as a means to achieve foreign policy objectives (for example, Western defense plans)—but he also intended to win the good will of some leading officers by entrusting them with real responsibility. In particular, he cultivated the company of senior officers in order to inspire them with confidence in their position and enhance their loyalty to king and country. His foreign policy, however, though appealing to and supported by almost all senior officers, was very unpopular among the younger officers, who had fallen under the ideological influences of civilian leaders. He was aware of the widespread dissatisfaction with Western policy among the younger officers, but he did nothing really constructive to win them over, perhaps believing that his influence over the senior officers would automatically carry the entire army behind him.

Nuri, it is true, had received his training in military sciences and spent his early career in the service, but he never really distinguished himself as an army officer, and after he left the army to become a politician, he was no longer counted as military. Unlike 'Aziz 'Ali, who kept an interest in military affairs, Nuri lost touch with the army. When he got an echo of the spread of revolutionary ideas in the army, he fully appreciated the gravity of the matter, but he did nothing constructive to check it. He warned some officers alleged to have been involved, but he left the matter to army intelligence.

Nuri's warning to one of the officers, Midhat al-Hajj Sirri, was almost prophetic. He said to Sirri shortly before the July Revolution:

> I hear you are engaged in a plot against the regime. Is this true? Look [added Nuri], if your plot ever succeeds, you and the other officers will be engaged in a struggle

among yourselves which will not end until each of you hangs the other.[29]

No sooner did the military seize power than conflict ensued among them, and the first to be executed by a rival military faction were Sirri himself and his fellow officers.

Though he was aware of the dangers of military uprisings, he was never really able to isolate the army from politics. It is the irony of fate that Ja'far al-'Askari, the first Minister of Defense, and Nuri, first Chief of Staff, who were primarily responsible for organizing the army when the 'Iraqi government was established in 1921, were put to death during army rebellions: the first during the 1936 coup and the second during the 1958 revolution.

VII

Had he died before 1958, Nuri might have been hailed as one of the great leaders in the Arab world—perhaps the greatest among his contemporaries. At that time, he was the Prime Minister of the Arab Federation, not of 'Iraq. But when events in 'Iraq got out of hand, and the July Revolution swept away the monarchy, some of Nuri's friends were reported to have said: "Nuri was a grand old man, but he had been out of touch."[30] Others dispassionately remarked, "Nuri had had enough glory," implying that his opponents— the younger leaders in particular—must now be given their chance. Nuri was not opposed in principle to younger leaders sharing responsibility either in high political posts or in "loyal opposition" groups, but he warned against violent methods and disorder. "One must not destroy anything," he warned once in a press conference, "before he finds a better substitute."[31] His opponents, however, seeing no signs that the existing regime was likely to change, became too impatient with Nuri's methods to continue to support the ruling oligarchy.

---

[29] It is reported that he also added: "If the rebellion does not succeed you will be seen hanging on scaffolds set-up between the northern and southern gates of Baghdad" (see my *Republican 'Iraq*, p. 86).

[30] He was seventy years old when he was assassinated.

[31] Nuri's *Ahadith*, p. 15. For his remarks against violence and disorder, see *ibid.*, p. 98.

Nuri, like many other contemporary leaders, had indeed made a number of mistakes. In his early career, it is alleged that he was involved in the assassination of Tawfiq al-Khalidi, an opposition member of Parliament who often criticized Cabinet ministers for irregularities.[32] He was also charged with the killing of young King Ghazi, with whom he had differences of opinion; in fact, the King's death was accidental.[33] He seriously tried to avenge the assassination of his brother-in-law Ja'far al-'Askari, killed in 1936 by an order of Bakr Sidqi, by implicating Hikmat Sulayman (who had inspired Sidqi to rebel in 1936) in an alleged plot against the state in 1939.[34] Though public opinion was manifestly against the hanging or exile of political leaders, Nuri executed the leading officers who took part in the 1941 coup, and he dealt harshly with communists for alleged subversive activities. Believing that conspiracy against the state is a very serious crime, Nuri sought by public punishment to discourage adventurers from resorting to violence. In retrospect, Nuri's methods did not prevent recurrence of *coups.* Pardon or life imprisonment for political criminals might have saved his own life by avoiding an eventual vendetta. Soft-hearted though he may have been toward the downtrodden, Nuri did not hesitate to inflict harsh punishments. He was not afraid for his own safety, and in defiance of those who threatened his life he once said: "The man has not been born who can assassinate me."[35] In his old age, he grew careless and overconfident and was thus destroyed by opponents he had underestimated.

Nuri was also reproached for his lack of respect for democratic

[32] I have often heard this accusation from some of Nuri's opponents based essentially on hearsay, but no positive evidence has ever been given for complicity in the matter.

[33] See the memoirs of Colonel Salah al-Din al-Sabbagh, one of the "four colonels" responsible for the military uprising of 1941, who was subsequently hanged in 1945 for his action (Salah al-Din al-Sabbagh, *Fursan al-'Uruba Fi al-Mizan* [Arab Heroes on the Scale] [n.d.], pp. 80-84).

[34] For an account of the incident and the trial of Sulayman by a Military Court, see my *Independent 'Iraq,* pp. 137-40.

[35] It is said that Nuri either shot himself or was killed by passers-by two days after the Revolution of July 14, 1958, when he was walking in disguise down a street in southern Baghdad. There is reason to believe that his death was suicide rather than assassination. He always carried a revolver and often said that he would never hesitate to shoot himself if he ever found himself unable to escape death. Since no one claimed the credit for having killed Nuri at a time when such an act would have been regarded as heroic and a reward of £10,000 was put for his head, I am of the opinion that Nuri shot himself when he was identified by passers-by and was not assassinated by an unknown person.

procedures. He often acted without regard to the views and sensitivities of his supporters and not infrequently he made decisions
without Cabinet discussions. It is said, not without justification,
that he treated most of his Cabinet colleagues as youngsters, who
often stood speechless before him. He appeared to many observers,
as indeed to the present writer, to act thoughtlessly to subordinates.
But in reality he never meant to slight colleagues, old or young, unless they turned against him or tried to hurt him. He was indeed a
kind person at heart, always warm to friends and considerate to
visitors. True, he was often impatient with democratic processes—
if one could regard the 'Iraqi parliamentary system as democratic—
because he demanded efficiency, and his opponents, more effective
speakers in parliamentary debates than himself, often tried to oppose measures urgently needed.

In his dealings with foreign statesmen, Nuri made a greater impression as a dignified and effective statesman than on his countrymen; he was the diplomat who knew exactly what he wanted and
sought by compromise and flexible methods to achieve primary
objectives. In his negotiations, he was not lacking in resourcefulness;
indeed, he was always ready with fresh ideas and proposals—one
foreign observer is reported to have described him "as full of tricks
as a monkey."[36] He was able to acquire the confidence of many,
especially that of British statesmen, with whom he established
cordial relations. He believed that trust and mutual respect in the
conduct of foreign affairs are likely to enhance the national interest
much more than unwarranted suspicion and lack of credibility. Even
if he disagreed, he never lost his temper. He would even try to en-
liven the negotiations. Matin Daftari, a former Persian Prime Minister,
once told me that when he was in Baghdad in 1951 (while on his
way to the United Nations to take part in the discussion on the
Persian oil conflict), Nuri sent him a message consisting of a verse
by the Persian poet Sa'di (d. 1291) in which he hinted that his
country was headed in the wrong "direction." Sa'di's verse, in translation is as follows:

> I fear, oh (noble) Arab
>   You might ne'er reach the (holy) Ka'ba;

[36] See Gallman, *Iraq Under General Nuri*, p. 104.

> The path thou has chosen
> Will take thee to Turkistan![37]

Nuri's leadership qualities were noticed very early in his career. T. E. Lawrence, who associated with the Arab officers during the Hijaz operations in 1916-18, remarked about Nuri: "Most men talked faster under fire, and acted with betraying ease and joviality. Nuri grew calmer . . . . His courage, authority and coolness marked him as the ideal leader."[38] Few Arab leaders have possessed such fine qualities. All who have known him, including his critics, were agreed that he possessed two salient characteristics: courage and integrity. However, Nuri was not a popular leader—he lacked the ability to appeal directly to the people. At a time when the masses were excited by fiery speakers—Nasir, Bourguiba, and others— Nuri tried to appeal to reason rather than emotions. No politician is likely to succeed if he is unable to appeal to emotions, notwithstanding the fact that reason is necessary for the development of public policies. Nuri excelled in laying down plans and policies but proved utterly incapable of explaining them to the people.

[37]Tarsam narasi be-Ka'ba ay A'rabi
In rah keh tow miravi be-Torkistan ast.
                              Sa'di
[38]Lawrence, *Seven Pillars*, pp. 519-42.

CHAPTER IV

The Ideological School
Jamal ʿAbd al-Nasir

The pages of history are full of heroes who created their own roles
and also of roles which found no heroes to perform them. It seems
to me that there is one such role waiting for its heroic performer
within the Arab world. Now, I cannot say why, but I feel that at
last, exhausted by its wanderings, this role has halted near the borders
of our country and is beckoning to us to bestir ourselves, study
the lines and don the costume, since we alone are qualified to
play the part.

Nasir

Of all the contemporary Arab leaders dealt with in this work,
no one proved more controversial than Nasir, notwithstanding his being the youngest of them and the most recent to
enter the political scene. No less significant is the fact that his political career was cut short by premature death at a crucial moment
when he was grappling with the consequences of the Six-Day War
and pursuing a domestic policy of sweeping social reforms. For these
reasons, Nasir's role in politics is the most difficult to assess, even
though there exists a greater amount of published material on his
life and political activities than on others. More difficult, indeed, is
the task of presenting the real image of a man about whom there
have been conflicting accounts and opinions. A final judgment on
him will therefore have to await future writers who will view him
from a perspective different from ours.

Jamal 'Abd al-Nasir

II

Nasir appeared to Western writers as the Arab leader whose
ambition conflicted with essential Western interests; therefore his
policies and methods were looked upon by the West with suspicion
and disfavor. He was not unaware of misrepresentations, but he
took no serious steps to correct them. Some of his actions and
angry public statements—the Czech (Russian) arms deal, recognition of the People's Republic of China, nationalization of the Suez
Canal Company, support of revolutionary movements in Algeria, the
Congo, and other countries, intervention in the Yaman, the closure
of the Straits of Tiran—weighed against him and led many Westerners
to confuse his goals with his rhetorical statements. It is therefore
in order first to outline his goals before we discuss his leadership
and actions.

Nasir possessed a practical turn of mind and tried to solve problems by tackling them one after the other in the order of their
urgency. Yet he was committed to certain national goals which
were considered almost sacrosanct and therefore not subject to
compromises. As a native Egyptian who grew up in a social environment sensitive to deprivation, Nasir was bound to voice his
countrymen's grievances against social fetters, on the one hand, and
to seek national freedom from foreign rule, on the other. Influenced
by emotional as well as by socioeconomic forces, Nasir may well be
regarded as essentially belonging to an ideological rather than to a
realistic school of leaders. Yet it would be wrong to depict him as
merely a doctrinaire unwilling to modify his actions in the light of
experience. After he seized power by force, he tried to achieve his
objectives by peaceful and practical methods, or as he said, by trial
and error. What were those objectives or ultimate goals?

First and foremost was the achievement of Egypt's full independence, which meant in practice the elimination of all encroachments on the country's sovereignty, whether resulting from military
occupation, treaty stipulations, or political pressures. To achieve
these goals, Nasir decided to bring about the fall of the old regime
and the establishment of a new one which would first bring pressure on Britain to evacuate all her forces from the Canal Zone and
then abrogate treaties and other international instruments considered
likely to compromise his country's independence. The next step

would be to prepare the way for internal reforms. Nasir also sought to insure Egypt's national security from foreign dangers. The insistence that Egyptians should be free to manage their own affairs was the product of a strong and compelling emotional force and not merely the cherished desire of intellectuals.

As an ideological objective, Nasir was demanding recognition not only of Egypt's own sovereign rights but also of the sovereign rights of other dependent countries that desired full independence, especially the Arab countries that had not yet achieved any form of independence—Algeria, the Sudan, and the South Arabian and Persian Gulf principalities—but also the countries and peoples of Africa and Asia who were still struggling to achieve freedom from colonial rule. In some independent countries of the Third World, his appeal to assert sovereign rights was even stronger. He, along with Nehru and Tito, consciously developed this ideological commitment, and it was not a reaction to a popular appeal, as was his commitment to Arab nationalism. In the pursuit of ideological goals, Nasir went so far as to antagonize Western powers—France and Britain in particular—by extending help to some countries struggling for independence; but he was not prepared to go to war with them unless they deliberately sought to encroach on his own country.

Second, and as a corollary to independence and national security, Nasir was committed to the principle of nonalignment in the East-West conflict on the ground that the Cold War, generated by rivalry among the Great Powers, was a conflict in which Egypt (as well as other Afro-Asian countries) was not directly concerned. He maintained that it was not in Egypt's interests to heighten tensions but rather to reduce them by refusing to take sides in the struggle among the Great Powers. Consequently, any attempt by a foreign power to draw Egypt into this struggle was considered incompatible with her freedom of action. For the same reason Nasir objected to having his Arab neighbors become unwilling participants in Western defense alliances—that is, because this, too, could possibly draw Egypt into war.

As a third goal, Nasir was no less committed in principle to serving the interests of "the common man"—and the majority of the Egyptian people were common men. He grew up in a society of glaring social and economic inequality and felt bitterness toward the small ruling oligarchy which exploited and oppressed the people and showed utter disregard for their welfare. This bitter feeling compelled him to commit himself ideologically to social reform—a commitment which was quite genuine on his part.[1] It is true that he had no clear idea at the outset as to how he would achieve this goal, but after he seized power he began to experiment with social reform in accordance with his pragmatic method of trial and error. This was the objective of a "social revolution," to use his words, which he intended to carry out, after a "political revolution"—the overthrow of the old regime—had been achieved. A new political structure was first necessary because that of the old regime had failed to carry out basic social changes.[2]

Fourth, Nasir consciously tried to instill a sense of pride and dignity among people who for centuries had been dominated by foreigners. Before Nasir, 'Urabi and Zaghlul had tried to inspire pride and self-confidence among the Egyptian people, but they had failed to create the necessary conditions. Nasir's achievement of full independence and his defiance of the West by obtaining arms from the East created a deep emotional appeal which went beyond Egypt's boundaries. After the tripartite attack on his country in 1956, Nasir's appeal in the Arab world rose still higher. His drive to achieve national freedom aroused high excitement in the Arab world and his call was associated with unity. In his pursuit of Arab unity, Nasir thought in imperial terms and sought by the association of Egypt with Arab national identity to give the Egyptian people a new meaning to life—something higher and more vast than their own parochial feelings. True, Arab nationalism, and Pan-Arabism in particular, had been asserted by a few leaders in Arab lands to the east of Egypt, but no Egyptian leader before Nasir had ever identified Egyptian with Arab nationalism

[1] Once when he was asked by a visitor what was his most pressing problem of the moment, Nasir replied: "The fact that another 175,000 people will be born in this country this month and have to be fed" (Robert Stephens, *Nasser* [London, 1971], p. 8).

[2] See Nasir's *Philosophy of the Revolution* (Cairo, n.d.), p. 26. It is deemed outside the scope of this essay to discuss the content of Nasir's "social" and "political" revolutions, as these have been dealt with in my *Political Trends in the Arab World* (Baltimore, 1970), Chaps. 6-7. Nasir's plans, in which he stressed Egypt's needs for technological development to catch up with modern progress, have been fully explained in his speech at the National Conference of Popular Forces in 1962. See *Mahadir Jalsat al-Mu'tamar al-Watani li al-Quwa al-Sha'biya* [Proceedings of the National Conference of Popular Forces] (Cairo, 1962), pp. 124-35.

or sought to inspire confidence, self-assurance, and dignity among the Arab people as a whole.[3]

Which of these goals was the center of Nasir's interests? Was it Arab unity, as some have suggested, or his concern for the common man? These two goals—to become the "head" of an Arab empire or the "servant" of the common man—are not necessarily contradictory, although in the achievement of one the other might be hurt or permanently sacrificed. In his public utterances, Nasir always insisted that the improvement of social conditions and the welfare of the people were his ultimate goals, but in practice his constant preoccupation with the country's national security and foreign ventures proved overriding in his mind.

It may seem strange indeed to outside observers that domestic demands should be subordinated to foreign ventures, especially in a country where the majority of the people live at the subsistence level. In theory, revolutionary reformers pay more attention to social than to political problems, but the Egyptian order of priorities must be fully understood in the light of Egypt's long history of servitude to foreign rule, which rendered Egyptians more self-conscious about freeing their minds than about feeding their bodies.[4] Nasir's readiness to subordinate the promise of improving "social conditions" to the requirements of "security" was demonstrated when he mortgaged Egypt's principal crop to obtain defense weapons; he did this because Egypt's security had appeared in his eyes to be jeopardized by his neighbor's encroachments.

Nasir's preoccupation with national security prompted him to seek ways and means for enhancing Egypt's power. Her position at the crossroads of continents and international waterways, though often inviting Great Power interventions, was an asset which might enable her to secure the support of neighbors and to play an influential role in regional and international affairs. Egyptian writers

---

[3] On the contrary, Zaghlul spoke disparagingly of the importance of the Arab countries; he is reported to have remarked that the strength of each Arab country was equal to zero, and that there was no advantage to adding one zero to another. For Arab reaction to Zaghlul's assessment, see Sati' al-Husri, al-'Uruba Awwalan [Arabism First] (Bayrut, 1955), pp. 60-67.

[4] Ahmad Lutfi al-Sayyid had for long lectured Egyptians that there was something more important than the "necessary food for life"—national freedom. See a quotation from Lutfi al-Sayyid on p. 175 below. Nasir had read Lutfi al-Sayyid's writings and was influenced by him.

had long been urging an active foreign policy reminiscent of Egypt's role under the pharaohs, Mamluks, and Muhammad 'Ali; but in recent years King Faruq and other leaders who had tried to play this role had failed utterly. After 1952, when the Free Officers seized power, they tried at the outset to avoid involvement in their neighbor's affairs; but Nasir, more conscious of Egypt's historical role than his fellow officers, thought about other things. Since he had been acclaimed as leader of Arab nationalism, he maintained that Egyptian participation in an Arab union would enable her, with the moral and material support of her Arab neighbors, to play a more important role in international councils. Although he did not seek a special position for Egypt in the Arab union, the Egyptian people were not satisfied with an equal partnership with other countries, and the Egyptian functionaries who served in other Arab lands betrayed a feeling of cultural superiority which worked against Egypt's own interests. Nasir seems to have given up the idea of Arab unity after the dissolution of the Syro-Egyptian union; he even discouraged any move toward unity and sought to obtain Arab support only for his foreign policy.[5]

Nasir's goals seem to have been the legitimate goals of any country aspiring to achieve independence and to occupy her deserved place in the comity of nations. But because his perception of Egypt's national security interests conflicted first with Western defense plans and then with Israel's security, Nasir was accused of being inspired by personal ambition. Propaganda attacks and counter-attacks exaggerated, if not misrepresented, Nasir's position as well as the position of his opponents, and Nasir often reacted indignantly because his opponents failed to appreciate his country's just claims to protect vital interests. There seems to be now a greater understanding of Nasir's pursuit of Egypt's national claims, because Egyptians continued to assert them after his death.

---

[5] Egypt's historical role in the Arab world from the time of the Mamluks to Muhammad 'Ali was to dominate rather than to unite the Arabs. The Arabs, for their part, have refused to be dominated. Nor did Egypt tolerate Arab unity without her participation, especially among the countries of the Fertile Crescent, because such a combination of states might weaken Egypt's preponderate position in the Arab world. For a discussion of Arab unity, see my *Political Trends*, pp. 262-65.

III

Some of Nasir's goals and ideas might be traced to certain facts and events connected with the social milieu in which he was raised. The first important fact is that Nasir was born to a relatively poor family, and he was deeply affected by the deplorable conditions in which the people of his neighborhood lived. He was born in Alexandria on January 15, 1918; three years later his father, a minor government functionary, was transferred to the postal administration of Asyut, a town in upper Egypt, where he had been born in 1888.[6] Before Nasir's father had entered government service, the family was not much better off than the rest of the villagers of his birthplace, who lived in abject poverty. These conditions aroused in Nasir a strong sense of sympathy for the poor; they also left him with the impression that the rich accumulated their wealth by exploiting the poor. When he later discovered the widespread corruption among well-to-do families, he equated richness with corruption and contended that wealthy people could not possibly be honorable or patriotic. After he seized power, he began to take pride in his humble origin and identified himself with the "common man," for whose welfare and dignity he dedicated his life. "I always glory," he said, "in being a member of a poor family . . . and I take an oath that I will continue to remain poor until death."[7]

The second important fact about Nasir's life was that he had no enduring family ties after early childhood. Because of his father's frequent transfers from one town to another, he was often sent away from home to continue his schooling. He went to live first with an uncle in Cairo to complete his primary education. When he was eight, his mother died, and he went to Alexandria to live with his mother's family to pursue his high school education. After he lost his mother, to whom he was deeply attached, his relations with his father became less affectionate, especially after his father remarried.

Away from home, nostalgia found a surcease and an exciting diversion in extracurricular activities and in student demonstrations.

[6]More specifically, Nasir's father was born in a village called Banu Murr, located about three kilometers northeast of Asyut.

[7]Nasir, "Man Ana" [Who Am I?], *al-Musawwar Yuqaddim Jamal 'Abd al-Nasir* [al-Musawwar Presents Jamal 'Abd al-Nasir], ed. Nasim Ammar (Cairo, 1957), p. 9.

During the 1930s, students, indoctrinated with nationalism, felt it was their patriotic duty to strike or to have street demonstrations (often in reality instigated by professional politicians). In 1933, Nasir participated in his first political demonstration in Alexandria. In 1935, he took a leading part in a demonstration in Cairo demanding the restoration of the Constitution of 1923. When the demonstration passed the old Shepherd's Hotel, Nasir, upon seeing British officers, shouted "Down with England." It is said that one of the officers fired at him and that he was hit by a bullet. His name was reported in the press on the following day, which gave him a sense of pride that his nationalist activities had attracted public notice. And this was not the only time that his patriotic feelings ran high.[8]

In his spare time, he read history and literature; he was particularly excited by the careers of historical figures—Alexander the Great, Julius Caesar, and others—who distinguished themselves in great events. When his school presented the play "Julius Caesar," he played the role of Caesar. He was particularly attracted to Voltaire's writings, about whom he wrote an article in his school's paper, and he also read some of Egypt's leading writers who criticized social conditions.[9]

Restless and not inclined to be scholarly or withdrawn, he saw in the army an opportunity to continue his studies after graduation from school in 1936. However, when he applied to the Military Academy, his application was rejected because of his record as a student agitator. Thereupon he entered the Law College, where he spent one term. He applied again to the Military Academy in March 1937. The Wafd Party was then in power and looked with favor on students who displayed nationalist feelings; he was admitted because he was *persona grata* to that party and also because, after independence, a greater number of young men were needed for the army. His admission also indicated that he had made a very favorable impression in the oral interview, since his school record was not very high and many other applicants had been refused. As a cadet, Nasir was in his element; he showed that he could maintain high discipline, he did his school work satisfactorily, and he passed his examinations.

[8] For student political agitation, see Joachim Joesten, *Nasser: Rise to Power* (London, 1960), Chap. 5; Stephens, *Nasser*, pp. 31-37.

[9] See n. 4 above. He also read Tawfiq al-Hakim, Taha Husayn, Khalid Muhammad Khalid, and others (see Stephens, *Nasser*, pp. 32, 33 and 40).

In July 1938, Nasir graduated as a second lieutenant and was posted first to Mankabad in the Asyut province and then to the Sudan for three years. His experiences as an officer confirmed his belief about widespread corruption and irregularities in government service, and he was determined to oppose these practices. At Asyut, he was able to resist some of his superior's orders which appeared to him partial and arbitrary. While still a second lieutenant, he fraternized with some officers—Anwar al-Sadat, Zakariya Muhyi al-Din, and others—and he cemented relations with some former classmates, like 'Abd al-Hakim 'Amir, who joined his secret revolutionary circle. These initial activities helped Nasir to become a leader.

When World War II broke out, Nasir was still in the Sudan. He began to follow the course of military operations and to speculate about their possible effects on the future of Egypt. He read the debates in the British Parliament about shortages in British military preparations and noted the reverses in the battlefields. From all this he noted England's weakening hold on an extended empire and concluded that there was an opportunity for Egypt to obtain national freedom if her leaders knew how to take advantage of it. He was in favor of quick action while Britain's position was still weak, but the Egyptian government showed no sign that it was prepared to move. He and his fellow officers were particularly irritated when the British Ambassador asked King Faruq to appoint Nahhas as Prime Minister to keep the country quiet—an action which they regarded as an affront to Egyptian dignity and independence. Nasir contended that Faruq should have abdicated; instead, he yielded to British pressure and poor advice from the politicians and agreed to entrust power to Nahhas on February 4, 1942.[10] As a result, Faruq lost the respect of his countrymen. When the officers seized power in 1952, they were determined to avenge the affront by forcing Faruq to abdicate, even though Faruq was prepared to accept the demands of the military, and they insisted on complete evacuation of British forces, even though Britain was ready to recognize Egypt's full independence.

In 1942 Nasir was promoted to the rank of captain; and in 1943 he was appointed an instructor at the Military Academy. Meanwhile,

---

[10] For a first-hand account of these events, see Muhammad Husayn Haykal, *Mudhakkirat Fi al-Siyasa al-Misriya* [Memoirs on Egyptian Politics] (Cairo, 1953), Vol. II, pp. 227-46.

he entered the Staff College and subsequently became one of the instructors. As a teacher he found an opportunity to intensify his efforts to win supporters and disseminate revolutionary ideas. He made it a regular practice to invite cadets to his home; on such occasions he came to know the political opinions of these young men while discussing national questions, and he would then invite some of them to join his secret military organization. It is exceedingly difficult to know the names of all of those to whom Nasir spoke his mind freely or when and how the secret organization began to develop; some of the officers seem to have joined Nasir's secret circle when he was still a cadet at the Military Academy; others joined when he was posted to Asyut. There is no doubt that an "organization" already existed when Nasir became an instructor in the Staff College and that he subsequently reorganized it as its numerical strength and scope were widened.[11]

Participation in war always tends to add prestige to a leader's stature, especially if he has won a battle or showed extraordinary courage. Nasir's opportunity came when Egypt participated in the first Palestine war of 1948-49. His experiences in this war proved invaluable to him in later life. His stubborn resistance in the Faluja battle, in which he repulsed Israeli attacks, showed that he possessed a tactical capacity and an ability to organize units and exercise command. This war, which Egypt and the other Arab countries lost, demonstrated the utter failure of Egypt's ruling class to defend the country and protect her national interests. After their return from Palestine, Nasir and his fellow Free Officers began to speed up the revolutionary movement. He said:

> It was in Palestine that the cells of Free Officers gathered together in trenches and at outposts in deep deliberations and study . . . . We used to sit, in total oblivion of the siege and with utter disregard to its end or outcome, completely absorbed in duty of saving the mother-country. . . . Faluja was then besieged and the target of a terrific and terrifying bombardment from land and air. . . . We have been duped—pushed into a battle for which we were unprepared. . . . Everytime I reached this stage in my flights of imagination, my thoughts would suddenly fly

[11] Cf. Stephens, *Nasser,* p. 49.

across the battlefields and borders to Egypt: There lies our
mother-country . . . a second Faluja on a large scale.[12]

Nasir had already laid down the plan of the revolution. Although
he was the acknowledged initiator and organizer of the movement,
he seems to have hesitated to come out in the open as leader. He was
not afraid to lead; but he preferred, for reasons not altogether clear,
to entrust leadership to a senior officer, as he had done in military
actions.[13] He naturally turned to 'Aziz 'Ali al-Misri, whom he had
admired as a revolutionary leader, but 'Aziz 'Ali pleaded ill-health.
General Najib, who had made a favorable impression on the officers,
was then entrusted with the command, although he did not become
a member of the inner circle until after Nasir assumed the premier-
ship in 1953. That Nasir would eventually come out in the open
and assume leadership was never in doubt; however, Najib, who
stood for liberal reforms through parliamentary democracy, made a
deep impression on the country and was a popular leader.[14] In his
bid for power, it was inevitable that Nasir's public utterances would
be highly pitched in order to sway audiences that had become wildly
enchanted with Najib's oratory and disarming manners.

From 1954 until his death in 1970, Nasir laid down no detailed
plans for future development. Of course, the ultimate goals had
evolved in Nasir's mind long before the Revolution; but they were
very vague and nebulous and they began to take shape only after he
seized power. He proceeded from one step to another in an experi-
mental—trial and error—method. He was successful in giving an impression that he was proceeding in accordance with a plan already
laid down, because the steps he took often seemed to follow one
another logically. In the final adoption of Arab socialism, he moved
gradually from free enterprise to collectivism.[15]

Nasir's actions seemed to be carried out without restraints or
remorse; this induced many writers to inquire into the secrets of his

[12] See Nasir, *Philosophy of the Revolution,* pp. 14-15.

[13] In military actions, Nasir thought it was prudent to entrust command to a senior officer in accordance with military discipline; but as a political leader, he had no inhibition
about taking command over superiors.

[14] For Najib's political ideas, see Mohammed Neguib, *Egypt's Destiny* (London, 1955),
Chaps. 5-6.

[15] See my *Political Trends,* Chap. 7; P. J. Vatikiotis (ed.), *Egypt Since the Revolution*
(London, 1968), Chaps. 1-4.

methods which apparently could often turn lost causes into victories.
Some sought an explanation in his charismatic leadership, others in
his ingenious political methods, and still others in the combination
of favorable circumstances. It is not the purpose of this essay to give
a narrative of Nasir's actions and achievements, which may be found
elsewhere,[16] but to study his methods, personality, and character,
to which we shall now turn.

IV

The armed forces were and remained in Nasir's eyes the principal
pillar of his regime. Egypt's independence and security naturally required the strengthening of the army, and Nasir, who carried out the
Revolution of 1952 by a military coup, keenly felt that in the last
analysis his power was dependent on the army. In a conversation I
had with him in 1955, shortly before the Soviet arms deal, he stressed
first the need for arms to enable Egypt to defend herself against sudden attacks, especially after the Israeli raids on Ghaza early that year,
but then he candidly admitted that weapons were needed to enable
fellow officers (whose support was necessary to achieve the Revolution's objectives) to reorganize and enlarge the army to their satisfaction. Soon after he seized power, the officers were treated as a
favored class and given special conveniences—houses, cars, and other
items—not always available to men of equal income. Officers close
to Nasir were at the outset given key positions in the administration
and later in the Cabinet. At first, the military was able to inspire
efficiency in the administration and to reduce corruption and irregularities, which enhanced the prestige of the new regime, but
later the new ruling class developed its own corrupt practices which
Nasir could not completely control despite attempts to reduce them
by transfers or dismissals.

Nasir did not think that the Egyptian people were yet capable
of governing themselves through democratic processes and held
that in free elections unscrupulous leaders would be able to manip-

[16] For a study of Nasir's career and achievements, see Jean and Simonne Lacouture,
Egypt in Transition (New York, 1958); Keith Wheelock, *Nasser's New Egypt* (New York,
1960); Robert St. John, *The Boss* (London, 1960); P. J. Vatikiotis, *The Egyptian Army
in Politics* (Bloomington, 1961); Anthony Nutting, *Nasser* (London, 1972); Muhammad
Hasanain Heikal, *The Cairo Documents* (London, 1972).

ulate the elections to their advantage. "If free elections were held today," he told me, "the professional politicians would return to power and undo what the Revolution tried to do."[17] Until the social structure was completely reorganized and the present generation, brought up in deprivation and servitude, was replaced by another more content and molded under the guidance of the regime's new leadership, the public would not be free or able to control democratic processes. At the beginning of the Revolution, Nasir thought that within a decade the Egyptian people might be able to develop a democratic system of their own, but later he doubted the feasibility of reform through democratic processes and began to think in terms of developing an alternative to democracy. For a long while he had deemed it necessary to rely on his personal authority to carry out reform plans, even by coercive measures if necessary, without regard to individual freedom, believing that the interests of the common man would be best served by these methods. Before the common man would be able to participate in political processes, Nasir maintained, he must be educated in the art of how to exercise his civil rights. He held that a single-party system might achieve this end. In practice, however, the one-party system—the Liberation Rally and the National and Socialist Unions—only provided legitimization for his authoritarian regime; it did not train the people in political participation or prepare the way for transfer of authority from military to civil hands.[18]

What rendered the task of developing free institutions more difficult was Nasir's involvement in foreign affairs. Shortly after he seized power, he became preoccupied with problems of national security and defense, which diverted most of his efforts from domestic to foreign affairs. Because the implementation of social goals often leads to domestic controversy while foreign policy objectives require national solidarity, Nasir was prepared to postpone or even abandon the former so long as he was preoccupied with the latter. To his surprise, he found that the achievement of some foreign policy objectives brought him more glory and prestige than the implementation of social goals: the Soviet arms deal, nationali-

---

[17] In 1956 Nasir told British Ambassador Humphrey Trevelyan, "Complete freedom would lead to a communist victory." H. Trevelyan, *The Middle East in Revolution* (London, 1970), p. 93.

[18] See R. H. Dekmejian, *Egypt Under Nasir* (Albany, 1971), pp. 144 ff.

zation of the Suez Canal company, and nonalignment aroused greater enthusiasm and excitement than the enactment of the Agrarian Reform Law, the socialist decrees, or even the completion of the Aswan High Dam. It is small wonder, therefore, that he often found himself compelled to pursue foreign ventures, especially in Arab affairs, which tended to enhance his prestige in his own country—as well as in the world—and bring the material advantages which he thought necessary to the achievement of ultimate social goals.

Nasir's ability to overcome internal opposition and defy foreign interventions with impunity confirmed his sense of "destiny"—that his role as a leader was determined by the historical process in which he was involved. This sense of destiny was demonstrated by his choice of reading material: biographies of great men who appeared to him to have been destined by historical processes to play a role in achieving national goals.[19] He felt that he himself had been drawn into such a historical role, whether by choice or accident, and he was determined to play it in order to carry out his country's cherished goals as he understood them. This sense of destiny, not unprecedented in Islamic tradition, often prompted him to take firm positions—even against decisions made at the Cabinet level—and when he succeeded despite overwhelming adverse circumstances, as in the case of nationalization of the Suez Canal, his sense of destiny was deepened and he was no longer prepared to listen to counselors. His major decisions, when they were announced to the people in public speeches, were often taken by the masses as prophetic utterances. He became so confident of his hold over the masses that he often warned opponents that if they opposed him he would bring the matter in question to the people, who would take care of them.[20]

Despite this messianic sense, Nasir was neither an abstract thinker nor a reformer who could design long-term plans. He possessed a practical turn of mind and sought to implement his goals by improvised methods. He admitted that he had no definite future plans. Instead, he applied himself to Egypt's immediate needs and showed remarkable skill in supplying them, with the resources

[19] It is said that Nasir was inspired with this "sense of a historical role" from his reading of Pirandello's *Six Characters in Search of an Author*.

[20] See the memoirs of one of the Syrian leaders who served in Cairo as Minister during the Syro-Egyptian union, Ahmad 'Abd al-Karim, *Adwa 'Ala Tajribat al-Wahda* [New Light on the Experience of Unity] (Damascus, 1962), p. 264.

available to him. His social goals, some of which may be traced back to childhood, were necessarily vague and very broad; they did not really begin to take concrete shape until he felt the time had come to carry them out. When he seized power, he asked himself, "What are our immediate objectives?"[21] Egypt's national demands then consisted mainly of liberating the Suez Canal Zone from British control and relieving the country from pressing economic needs by agrarian reform. He began to address himself to these basic immediate problems, not realizing that this was too simplistic an approach. As he passed from one issue to another, he began to realize the complexity of his country's problems and to learn how to tackle them by trial and error. Possessing both intelligence and the willingness to learn from experience, he improvised his methods and was prepared, if one experiment failed, to abandon it in favor of another. Thus, although ideologically committed to certain overriding objectives, he was not a utopian reformer for whom one simple solution would make everything come out right.

V

Like Nuri, Nasir was a man of action whose criteria of judgment depended essentially on concrete results; but while Nuri was prepared to compromise with reality, Nasir was not prepared to bend, especially on matters to which he was ideologically committed. Unlike Nuri, Nasir was a man who took pride in being a revolutionary leader and was not prepared to conduct himself as a professional politician.

Nasir not only held certain firm convictions about public affairs. He was also a confirmed believer in Islam and performed the essential religious duties—the daily prayers, fasting, the pilgrimage to Makka, and other rituals.[22] He seems to have been quite content with his family life. His wife, the daughter of a Persian carpet dealer,

---

[21] Nasir, *Philosophy of the Revolution*, p. 31.

[22] Conflict with the Muslim Brotherhood has raised doubt about Nasir's belief in Islam. As a modernist, Nasir held that religion was a matter of individual conscience; but he did not approve of religious fanaticism or of mixing political and religious issues. Consequently, he opposed the Brotherhood's interference in politics, especially after the attempt on his life by a member of the Brotherhood in 1954.

was devoted to him and his children, and he lived in a modest house without any desire to indulge in the material advantages which power brings. Nasir knew that mundane temptations cannot be kept long in secret from the public eye, and he tried to set an example of immunity from material rewards. He had a keen eye for corruption within his own ranks, which often helped him to control his fellow officers, for he consciously closed his eyes on occasion in order to expose them whenever they proved difficult in moments of disagreement.

Nasir possessed an ability to understand his followers, to size them up, and to assign suitable tasks to them. Jealous of his powers, he kept a vigilant eye on their movements. At the beginning of the Revolution, when some officers—'Abd al-Latif Baghdadi, Zakariya Muhyi al-Din, Salah Salim, and others—played an important role in revolutionary activities, he was very critical of their achievements and tried to play one against the other in order to keep them all under control. When he became secure in power, he treated them as almost equal subordinates.[23]

Not only did Nasir use these balancing tactics with fellow officers but also in his dealings with the Great Powers. His policy of positive neutrality did not mean a passive attitude in the East-West conflict, but an attempt to play one power off against another in order to obtain from each financial or moral support. There were always two schools of thought among the officers concerning Egypt's attitude toward the East-West conflict, one favoring the East and the other the West. Nasir shifted his support from one to the other depending on which policy he thought was more advantageous to Egypt at the time. 'Ali Sabri, well known at first as anti-British and regarded as anti-West in general, was entrusted with power to seek Soviet military assistance in 1955. Nasir again allowed 'Ali Sabri to seek Soviet assistance in 1964 and 1965, when the United States refused the renewal of food assistance. From 1959 to 1964, Nasir had leaned toward the United States, and he again wished to do so in 1966; he therefore replaced 'Ali Sabri with Zakariya Muhyi al-Din as Premier. He was prompted to make this shift not only to show that he was not completely dependent on

---

[23] For details of how he maneuvered fellow officers, see Ahmed Abul Fath, *L'Affaire Nasser* (Paris, 1962); Arabic edition, entitled *Jamal 'Abd al-Nasir* (Bayrut, n.d.), Vol. II, pp. 215 ff.

Soviet assistance but also to reduce 'Ali Sabri's influence, which had grown considerably. These tactics could not be used to Egypt's advantage indefinitely, of course, for the country might lose the support of both powers, but Nasir played the game with dexterous hands until the Arab-Israeli conflict of 1967 brought Egypt closer to the Soviet Union than ever before. However, Nasir's oscillations between East and West were never intended to mean an irrevocable commitment to either side.*

In his dealings with foreigners, Nasir possessed an ability to make them feel at ease. Tall, handsome, and powerfully built, he made a very good impression on them. He talked in a relaxed manner in fluent, though not perfect English, rarely raising his voice or losing his temper. He could be very charming and warm, and he often carried the conversations for hours, entertaining his visitors with anecdotes and witty remarks. But he could also be very arrogant and difficult to deal with when he was faced with an affront or suspected a plot, as in the case of Dulles' sudden withdrawal of financial assistance to the Aswan Dam or Ba'thist opposition to his Arab leadership.[24]

In public speeches, Nasir made a quite different impression: he raised his voice, spoke with emotion and often with indignation, and used strongly worded sentences—even harsh words—against adversaries. At first his speeches were dull, but after the Russian arms deal, he began to indulge in oratory, and he soon excelled in rhetorical speeches pregnant with colloquial phrases and sarcastic remarks about opponents. The manner in which he made public speeches was deliberately intended to excite the masses, who responded with great enthusiasm—often with wild applause—although most of his speeches were verbose and repetitious. After 1967, his addresses became shorter, more balanced, and directly to the point.

---

*This remark was written long before Egyptian-Soviet relations became strained after Nasir's death; indeed, the book was being set in type when President Sadat asked the Soviet government to withdraw its military advisers from his country on July 18, 1972.

[24] For Nasir's blunt words to Ba'thist leaders, see *Mahadir Jalsat Mubahathat al-Wahda* [Proceedings of Conversations on Unity] (Cairo, 1963).

VI

Of the three officers studied here—'Aziz 'Ali al-Misri, Nuri al-Sa'id, and Nasir—Nasir was the only military politician who possessed impressive charisma and was able to sway audiences, notwithstanding the fact that his regime depended in the last analysis on military support. His ideological commitments epitomized long-cherished popular demands, and he was able to achieve some of them by defiance, perseverance, and hard work despite unfavorable circumstances. His stature rose higher in the popular imagination when his refusal to bargain with national demands was crowned with success, as in the Suez crisis of 1956. So high did popular confidence rise in his ability to turn defeat into victory that when he decided to step from power in 1967, the public rose almost to a man to demand his continuation in office. Such public confidence has rarely been enjoyed by any other leader in the Arab world.

'Aziz 'Ali, it is true, was popular among the officers, but he failed to take advantage of opportunities which might have brought him to the highest political posts because he refused to subordinate ideals to realities. Nuri, a man of calculation and shrewd judgment, reached the highest positions of power, but as a leader he associated only with those in high military and civil ranks. Nasir, a revolutionary leader, sought the support of junior officers and young leaders whose interests lay in radical changes, and was suspicious of both the senior officers and the bureaucracy, whose loyalty lay with the status quo. He continued to keep his hold over the military and civil groups through these young intermediaries even at the height of his power.

Like 'Aziz 'Ali, Nasir's character possessed certain elements of adventurism, and after he seized power, he showed a readiness to take great risks—some said he took risks greater than they thought wise[25]—but he was not blind to the limits of his power. Before he seized power, he was prepared to resort even to assassination, because revolutionary leaders often deemed it necessary to crush opponents by violence if the ideal or ideological goals were ever to be

[25]Neguib, *Egypt's Destiny*, p. 216.

achieved.[26] Yet Nasir was perceptive enough to appreciate the power of opponents, as his struggle with Najib, to whom he deferred temporarily, demonstrated. 'Aziz 'Ali, on the other hand, was blind to the shape of things to come and often plunged into impossible situations. Nuri always warned against adventurism and warned against radical changes, thus revealing a conservative attitude, but he was not against social change in principle.

Nasir surpassed all contemporary Arab leaders in his readiness to take full responsibility for actions. If one experiment did not work, he never minded admitting failure and was prepared to try again, as his experiments with the Syro-Egyptian union and with political organizations to replace political parties demonstrated. At times of crisis, his high sense of responsibility often prompted him to take an obstinate position and to continue the struggle by any means; he probably felt that his historical destiny and his firm belief in the justice of his country's cause would bring ultimate victory. Nasir admitted failure on more than one occasion, although his failures were due as much to the nature of the society he was trying to reform as to his own personal limitations.

Yet Nasir's imprint as a leader should be sought neither in the specific projects he completed—some have yet to be completed—nor in the ingenuous methods he pursued to achieve them (some of which were shared by other leaders) but in something deeper, something that affected the way of life of his countrymen and their outlook. True, native Egyptians have often been accused of lethargy, inefficiency, and lack of responsibility, despite perseverance and hard work. Nasir tried to show the falsity of these accusations and to prove that his countrymen can do what other people do. The operation of the Suez Canal after nationalization is but one example of technical know-how which Egyptians demonstrated they could learn. The significance of the management of the Canal, as Chou En-Lai is said to have told Nasir, "is not important financially; it is important in proving that what they [Westerners] can do, we can do." At bottom, it was self-respect, defiance, and pride that Nasir's achievements symbolized. Nasir also tried to inspire loyalty to the fatherland and respect for—not fear of—authority, which native Egyptians lacked because of centuries of submission

[26] See Nasir, *Philosophy of the Revolution,* pp. 33-35; and Fath, *Nasir,* pp. 215-17.

and servitude. No one has depicted this new feeling more finely than Sir Walter Scott, who wrote:

> Breathes there the man, with soul so dead,
> Who never to himself hath said,
> This is my own, my native land!

PART TWO

THE MAN OF SKILLS
THE PROFESSIONAL
POLITICIAN

 "My master is trying to make his faults fewer,
but he has not yet succeeded," replied the messenger
[of one of Confucius's disciples] to the question as to
how he was doing.

Confucius

Al-Hajj Amin al-Husayni

CHAPTER V

The Traditional (Idealistic)
School – The Extremist
Al-Hajj Amin al-Husayni

Behind emigration to Palestine lies the hope which Jews have never relinquished: the domination of the whole world through this important strategic center—Palestine [from a letter to the Hungarian government in 1943].

Al-Hajj Amin al-Husayni (the Mufti)

Like the military politicians, the professional politicians were faced with essentially the same problems of a society undergoing rapid social changes. While the military leaders entered the political scene in most cases with a sword and sought to achieve reforms by revolutionary processes, the professional politicians ordinarily played the political game by peaceful methods and only a few achieved power by collaboration with the military.[1]

Five examples of professional politicians, each representing a different school of thought, will be studied here. First is the professional politician who tried to achieve by traditional methods the demands of Arab society. Al-Hajj Amin al-Husayni, a leader who grew up in a conservative environment and who was accustomed to traditional patterns of authority, is an extreme example of the tra-

---

[1] See Chap. XII.

ditional school of thought. The second type is a professional politician who used moderate methods in trying to meet the demands of a traditional Arab society. King Faysal of Saudi Arabia, exposed to new ideas and skills, is representative of this moderate school of traditionalist thought. The third is a professional politician who received Western training and tried by modern methods to achieve the demands of Arab society without abandoning its cultural identity. Habib Bourguiba, possessing modern skills and flexible methods, represents this pragmatic approach. The fourth and fifth types are professional politicians who grew up under the spell of either moderate or radical social thought and who pursued goals in accordance with a particular ideology. Chadirchi and Junblat, both of whom used essentially traditional methods in entering politics, represent a moderate ideological school—social democracy. Khalid Bakdash, seeking power through a proletarian revolution, represents a radical ideological school—communism.

II

As a professional politician, al-Hajj Amin al-Husayni represents a school whose adherents chose to play the political game in accordance with traditional methods. He possessed almost all the requisite qualities—personal and otherwise—which enable a leader to wield sufficient power and prestige to carry his country behind him. And yet the kind of leadership he offered his people failed to meet their new demands and expectations, despite the brilliance with which he played the political game and his longevity—over a quarter of a century—in power.

Why did al-Hajj Amin fail to achieve his ultimate objectives? Did he betray the trust of his people or did the people fail in their duties? Was he incompetent to provide the kind of leadership that would enable his people to stand up to new challenges? These and other questions should be scrutinized in the light of the encounter between two types of societies, each possessing different patterns of political behavior, if the role of traditional leadership is to be understood in its proper perspective.

Amin al-Husayni was born in Jerusalem in 1897 to one of the

leading families of Palestine.[2] He claims descent from an Arab ancestor, Muhammad al-Badri, who had taken residence in Jerusalem almost six hundred years ago. In 782, according to the hijra calendar (A.D. 1380), al-Badri had moved to Jerusalem from Wadi al-Nusur, a town situated to the southwest of Jerusalem on the road to Jaffa. His ancestors had lived for some two hundred years in Wadi al-Nusur after one of them, Muhammad ibn Badr, had migrated from the Hijaz in the twelfth century of the Christian era.[3] Since the seventeenth century, almost without interruption, a member of this family had held the position of Mufti, a scholar who gives an opinion on the sacred law (shari'a).[4] Before al-Hajj Amin al-Husayni became the Mufti in 1921, three members of his immediate family had held this prestigious post: his grandfather, Mustafa al-Husayni; his father, Tahir al-Husayni; and his elder brother, Kamil al-Husayni. Although the post of Mufti did not necessarily carry with it political influence, some members of the Husayni family managed to rise in social status and to acquire wealth, which enabled them to obtain high positions under the Ottoman administration. Thus Amin al-Husayni was born to a family which had already secured wealth, social status, and spiritual and political influence—qualities which would ensure anyone drawn into politics an important leadership role.

[2] Some writers give the date of birth as 1893 (see M. Pearlman, *The Mufti of Jerusalem* [London, 1947], p. 10); cf. "Safahat Mudi'a," *Filastin* (Palestine), Vol. VII (April, 1967), p. 10. In a letter to the writer, the Mufti confirmed 1897 to be his birth date.

[3] In a letter to the present writer (dated December 11, 1971), al-Hajj Amin al-Husayni, provided the following information about his family's background: Muhammad al-Badri, who settled in Jerusalem in 782/1380, was a descendant of Husayn, second son of the Caliph 'Ali (d. 661). The direct ancestors of Muhammad al-Badri, from his generation back to the Caliph 'Ali, are as follows: Abu al-Hasan 'Ali, son of Shihab al-Din Dawud, son of 'Abd al-Hafiz, son of Muhammad, son of Badr (who settled in Wadi al-Nusur), son of Yusuf, son of Badran, son of Ya'qub, son of Mutar, son of Zaki al-Din Salim, son of Muhammad, son of Muhammad, son of Zayd, son of Husayn, son of Sayyid 'Arid al-Murtada al-Akbar 'Awad, son of Zayd (known as the Martyr), son of 'Ali Zayn al-'Abidin, son of al-Husayn, second son of the Caliph 'Ali ibn Abi Talib (d. 661) and his wife Fatima, daughter of the Prophet Muhammad. This family pedigree may also be found in 'Abd al-Rahman al-Jabarti, *'Aja'ib al-Athar Fi al-Tarajum wa al-Athar* (Cairo, 1322/1904), Vol. I, pp. 374-75.

[4] In the eighteenth century, one Mufti of the Husayni family died without leaving a male heir. The post went first to the 'Alami family and then to the Jar-Allah family. However, the sayyid lineage and the title of al-Husayni were preserved by the descendants of some of the daughters of the Husayni family, even though these daughters had married into other families. For details about the Husayni family male interruptions, see Y. Porath, "al-Hajj Amin al-Husayni, Mufti of Jerusalem," *Asian and African Studies,* Vol. VII (1971), pp. 123-24.

But young Amin possessed some other personal qualities that enabled him to rise even further in status and eventually become his country's most powerful leader. From early childhood he displayed native intelligence, skillful manners, and vigor. Not inclined to be scholarly or detached by nature, his studies were short and not very profound. After completing primary education in a local school (including the study of the French language in a French school), he went to Cairo in 1912 to study at the Azhar University. He frequented the house of Rashid Rida, the great Muslim reformer and an active leader in Arab religious-political circles, under whose inspiration and guidance he came to appreciate the role of religion in politics.[5] While still a student, he made the pilgrimage to Makka in 1913 with his mother and returned to Jerusalem shortly before World War I began. Instead of completing his studies in Cairo, he went to Istanbul to study at the Military Academy. During the war, he served in the Ottoman army as an officer in Smyrna and in some other strategic centers on the Black Sea. These experiences opened his eyes to the realities of life and taught him how to endure hardships and escape dangerous situations. He also learned how to organize active groups of followers and to become a leader of men.

Returning to Jerusalem in 1917, Amin al-Husayni, a restless young man, at once became active in politics. During the period 1919-20, he participated with other young men in nationalist and cultural societies, and for a short time he taught at the Rawdat al-Ma'arif College (a Muslim educational institution) of Jerusalem. He took part in street demonstrations on the occasion of the visit of the King-Crane Commission to Palestine in 1919 and was arrested by the police for his role as one of the instigators. More significant was his part in the first uprising against the British Mandate over Palestine and British support of Zionism on April 4, 1920. The uprising lasted for four days and resulted in destruction of life and property in the Jewish quarters of Jerusalem. A British Military Court of Enquiry was set up to investigate the incident, and the trial focused on the two who were held responsible for the riots—'Arif al-'Arif, member of a notable family, who had personally

---

[5] Amin al-Husayni also attended the school of religious studies and guidance founded by Rashid Rida in Cairo before World War I (see C. C. Adams, *Islam and Modernism in Egypt* [London, 1933], pp. 197-98). For Rida's teachings, see my *Political Trends in the Arab World* (Baltimore, 1970), pp. 65-69.

commanded the attackers, and Amin al-Husayni, whose speeches and articles in the press had been incitements to violence. Both fled the country and were given sentences *in absentia* of ten years' imprisonment.

Amin al-Husayni spent the next year and a half in Trans-Jordan and Syria. A number of Palestinians there supported the Arab regime in Damascus (under Faysal's rule) because they regarded the lands on both sides of the River Jordan as the southern part of Syria. Amin al-Husayni, as well as other Palestinian leaders, hoped that if Palestine came under Faysal's control she might be saved from Zionist claims. The collapse of Faysal's regime in July 1920, resulting in the occupation of Syria by France, was a blow to Palestinian nationalists, since it left them to face Zionist pressures alone. Outside support for Arab rights in Palestine, however, continued to be al-Hajj Amin's goal throughout his life. For over a year, Amin al-Husayni was engaged in nationalist activities in Trans-Jordan, where some of the Arab nationalists from Damascus had moved after the French occupation of Syria. When Sir Herbert Samuel, the first British High Commissioner for Palestine, arrived in 1920, an amnesty for prisoners sentenced by the military court was issued. Sir Herbert, a Jewish High Commissioner, apparently deemed it wise to begin his administration of an Arab country by giving a gesture of friendliness and peace to the Arab community. When he visited Trans-Jordan later in the same year, Amin al-Husayni (and also 'Arif al-'Arif) was given a special pardon. Amin al-Husayni returned to Palestine early in 1921 to resume his political activities with more subtle methods.

A year after his return from exile, Amin al-Husayni was appointed to two positions which enabled him to play an increasingly important role in his country's politics—Mufti of Jerusalem and President of the Supreme Muslim Council. Since the first office was for life and the second almost as irrevocable, the manner in which he was installed in these two offices and the power he wielded through them call for an explanation.

Before World War I, Palestine was part of the Ottoman Empire, and its internal administrative system, though in theory controlled by the central government in Istanbul, was dominated in practice by Palestine's aristocratic houses. The two most prestigious offices were the posts of Mayor and Mufti of Jerusalem; the first was ordinarily held by one house and the second by another. However, shortly before World War I, both offices were held by the Husayni clan. After the British occupation, the Husayni Mayor was dismissed by the military authorities and a member of the Nashashibi house was installed in his place, partly because a Nashashibi was *persona grata* to the authorities and partly to maintain a balance between two rival houses.[6]

On March 21, 1921, Kamil al-Husayni, the Grand Mufti and President of the Court of Appeal, died and there arose the problem of choosing successors for the two posts. According to the practice in Ottoman times, a number of 'ulama (religious leaders) representing various parts of the country chose a panel of three men, from which the authorities selected one as the Mufti. The British authorities, unwilling to interfere in religious affairs, decided to follow the Ottoman practice in the appointment of the Mufti; but to fill the post of President of the Court of Appeal, the British, as a temporary measure, chose Shaykh Khalil al-Khalidi, member of another influential family, in order to keep the two offices of qadi and mufti separate.

Al-Hajj Amin al-Husayni, possessing the requisite qualifications (he had studied at the Azhar University, performed the pilgrimage, etc.), offered himself as a candidate for the post of Mufti. But the Nashashibi party, opposing his candidacy, secured the nomination of three candidates of its own house, and al-Hajj Amin's name appeared fourth on the list. Since the appointment of a Nashashibi candidate might have caused dissatisfaction among the Husayni party, one of the three chosen persons was persuaded by the authorities to withdraw in order to enable al-Hajj Amin to become the third candidate. Sir Herbert Samuel then appointed al-Hajj Amin Mufti of Jerusalem.[7] Subsequently, the followers of al-Hajj

[6] The Husayni Mayor had come into conflict with the British authorities, but the Husayni Mufti—Kamil al-Husayni—proved quite helpful by urging his countrymen to cooperate with the authorities for the maintenance of public order and security. He was rewarded by an appointment to the presidency of the Shari'a Court of Appeal, thus combining the offices of qadi and mufti, traditionally kept separate, and by becoming the head of the Waqf Committee—thereby exercising a greater influence in the country than any other religious leader. Following the example of Egypt, where the Mufti was appointed for the entire country, Kamil al-Husayni was called the Grand Mufti (al-Mufti al-Akbar), which meant that his post of Mufti of Jerusalem was superior to other muftis in the country.

[7] For conflicting views over the appointment of al-Hajj Amin as Mufti, see Porath, "al-Hajj Amin al-Husayni," pp. 128-37; and Elie Kedourie, *The Chatham House Version and Other Middle Eastern Studies* (London, 1970), Chap. 4.

Amin—indeed the entire press of Palestine as well as the press of other Arab countries—always called him either the Mufti of Palestine or the Grand Mufti. We shall hereafter refer to him as "the Mufti."[8]

But it was not only this office which enabled al-Hajj Amin to become a political leader; his subsequent election first to the presidency of the Supreme Muslim Council in 1922 and then to the chairmanship of the Arab Higher Committee in 1936 were in reality far more important than the post of Mufti. The Supreme Muslim Council, which was organized in 1921, had under its control the Awqaf (Muslim religious foundation) and Shari'a (religious law) courts, because these affairs were strictly Islamic and were deemed outside the jurisdiction of the British Mandate authorities. The Mufti, holding a supreme position among the 'ulama, was elected President of this new organization in 1922 despite the opposition of rival leaders, especially Nashashibi followers. In this new capacity he had the control of the Awqaf funds, appointments of qadis (religious judges), and supervision of orphans' funds. These sources brought under the Mufti's control over £50,000 a year (in some years a much higher amount) until he left the country in 1937; some of these funds may have been used for political ends. The prestige of the two religious offices extended beyond religious circles, since religion and politics were often hardly distinguishable in Islamic lands.[9]

No less significant was the Mufti's control of the Arab Higher Committee, which exercised supreme leadership over Arab political parties. It was organized as an executive committee in the early 1920s to coordinate Arab political activities and was headed first by Musa Kazim al-Husayni, a senior member of the Husayni family (who was once Mayor of Jerusalem), and then by the Mufti in

[8] As we have already pointed out, the title "Grand Mufti," as applied to al-Hajj Amin, was not unprecedented, since it had been used by his elder brother Kamil. However, the British authorities, especially after al-Hajj Amin left Palestine, always referred to him as the Mufti of Jerusalem, probably to remind the Arabs that he was not the spokesman of the entire country. It is true that a number of other towns in Palestine (as well as in other Muslim lands) had their local muftis, but since the Mufti of Jerusalem was appointed from among three candidates chosen by the leading 'ulama of Palestine and since he played a leading role in other Islamic and political activities, there was ample justification for him to claim the title of Grand Mufti of Palestine.

[9] For the structure and working of the Supreme Muslim Council, see *Palestine Royal Commission Report* [Lord Peel's Report] (London, 1937), Cmd. 5479, pp. 174-81; Porath, "al Hajj Amin al-Husayni," pp. 137 ff.

1936. The Mufti gradually brought the major organizations of the Arab community under his control and became the most powerful leader in the country. He wielded such immense power that the Peel Commission, in its report on the internal conditions of the country in 1937, described the Mufti's political machinery as a parallel government—an *imperium in imperia*.[10] For almost a decade and a half, until he left the country in 1937, he pursued his goals by all the means and resources under his control.[11]

Before his flight in 1937, the Mufti was involved in three popular uprisings—in 1920, 1929, and 1936. In the first, as noted earlier, he was charged by the authorities with incitement to violence; in the second, he was accused of being partially responsible for the disturbances; and in the third, he was declared to be fully responsible for the disorder. In the disturbances of 1936-38, which took the form first of a general strike and then a widespread revolt, the Mufti took an openly hostile attitude, which prompted the British authorities to order his arrest. He fled to Lebanon on October 13, 1937, having remained in the sanctuary of the Aqsa Mosque for some three months.[12]

The Mufti's political activities, though by no means ended, fall into three periods. The first began when he joined the Ottoman army and ended with his sudden departure from Palestine in 1937. During this period, his activities were essentially aimed at mobilizing the forces within his own country to achieve its national aspirations. The second began with his flight in 1937 and ended in 1946.

[10]*Palestine Royal Commission Report*, p. 181.

[11] For Arab sources on the life and activities of the Mufti until he left Palestine in 1936, see "Ma Yajib An Ya'rifah Kul 'Arabi 'An Jihad al-Filastiniyyin wa Thabat Za'amatuhum al-Wataniya" [What Every Arab Should Know about the Struggle of Palestinians and Their Confirmed National Leadership], *Filastin*, Vol. IV (March 1964), pp. 6-12; "Al-Sayyid Amin al-Husayni Intukhib Wa Lam Yu'ayyan Ta'yyinan" [Al-Sayyid Amin Was Elected and Not Appointed], *ibid.*, Vol. IV (August-September 1964), pp. 22-26; "Safahat Mudi'a Min Hayat al-Sayyid Muhammad Amin al-Husayni" [Some Pages from the Life of al-Sayyid Muhammad Amin al-Husayni], *ibid.*, Vol. III (April 1967), pp. 10-15. See also Muhammad 'Izzat Darwaza, *Hawl al-Haraka al-'Arabiya* [On the Arab Nationalist Movement] (Sidon, 1951), Vol. III *passim*.

[12] The story of how the Mufti sought refuge in the sanctuary of the Aqsa Mosque and then fled the country by secretly escaping from behind the mosque's walls is told in his *Memoirs*, which begins with this incident. These *Memoirs*, first published in *Akhbar al-Yawm* (Cairo), October 19, 1957-January 4, 1958, were reprinted with additions in the periodical *Filastin*, Vol. VII (May 1967) and later issues. Hereafter these will be referred to as the Mufti's *Memoirs*.

This period of exile was marked by attempts to achieve his country's political aspirations by enlisting outside support. The third began with his return to the Arab world in 1946 to resume the struggle against his enemies. This period is not yet over, though there has been a gradual transfer of his country's leadership to other hands.

III

From the time he left Palestine in 1937, the Mufti pursued his objectives by a variety of methods: first he enlisted the support of other Arab countries by identifying their national aspirations with those of Palestine; then, during and after World War II, he used secret diplomacy and war. After he arrived in Lebanon, he continued to encourage his followers to carry on the struggle until World War II broke out in 1939. During the war, when Britain brought reinforcements into the area and the country was rigidly governed under martial law, Palestinian leaders decided to suspend their activities until the end of the war.[13]

The Mufti saw in the war new opportunities which might be exploited to his country's advantage. Convinced that there was no hope that British policy might change in favor of Arab national aspirations as he understood them, he was almost instinctively inclined to rely on a possible Axis victory to achieve national objectives since German policy appeared to be opposed to the establishment of a Jewish National Home. He envisioned that if he, as the chief spokesman of his countrymen, entered into an agreement with Nazi leaders to guarantee essential Palestinian national aspirations, all his countrymen would be prepared to side with Germany in the event Palestine became part of the theater of war. Because other Arab countries, Egypt and Syria in particular, had already shown signs of pro-Axis feelings—in their opposition to England and France—he concluded that Arab public opinion would not look with disfavor on his dealings with Nazi leaders to achieve national goals.[14]

[13] See the Mufti's *Memoirs* (*Filastin*, Vol. II [June 1962], pp. 4-10; *ibid.*, Vol. VII [July 1967], pp. 36-44).

[14] For the Mufti's prewar contacts with Axis agents, see Lukasz Hirszowicz, *The Third Reich and the Arab East* (London, 1960), pp. 34 ff.

During the initial stages of the war, however, there were no clear indications that Britain might be defeated, and the Mufti did not want openly to take sides, although there was no doubt where his sympathies lay. When his movements in Lebanon were more strictly watched after the outbreak of the war, it seemed that 'Iraq might be the Arab country in which he could best achieve his purposes. Consequently, he suddenly disappeared from Lebanon and went to Baghdad in October 1939.[15] For almost a year, he and his entourage watched the development of the war with a keen eye and tried to keep out of domestic politics. However, disagreement among 'Iraqi leaders on the fulfillment of their country's treaty obligations to Britain prompted the Mufti to intervene in 'Iraqi affairs; some of those leaders appealed to him to seek Axis support against Britain. At the outset the Mufti counseled against premature action until the outcome of the war became fairly clear and his secret negotiations with the Axis powers were completed; but Britain's need for landing forces in 'Iraq brought matters to a head and the war with Britain broke out in May 1941, resulting in the overthrow of a nationalist regime before the Axis powers were prepared to lend it support. It is not our purpose to give an account of these events in which the Mufti participated or of his initial negotiations with the Axis powers, since these have been dealt with elsewhere;[16] but it is significant to note that the Mufti's presence in 'Iraq encouraged some 'Iraqi leaders to come into sharp conflict with Britain, which helped neither 'Iraq nor Palestine and compelled him to seek refuge in Axis lands before the outcome of the war became known.[17]

Before he went to Axis lands, the Mufti tried to reside in neutral countries—he enjoyed a temporary asylum in Iran, until that country fell under Anglo-Soviet occupation in August 1941; when he

[15] The Mufti's *Memoirs* (*Filastin*, Vol. VII [July 1967], pp. 40-41). The Mufti's secretary, 'Uthman Kamal Haddad, claimed that the Mufti left Lebanon because the French authorities asked him to issue a statement of policy favorable to the Allies. See 'Uthman Kamal Haddad's memoirs, *Harakat Rashid 'Ali* [The Rashid 'Ali Movement] (Sidon, 1950), p. 5.

[16] See my *Independent 'Iraq*, Chaps. 8 and 9. For the Mufti's account of these activities, see his *Memoirs* (*Filastin*, Vol. VII [August 1967], pp. 20-26; *ibid.*, Vol. VII [September 1967], pp. 16-20; *ibid.*, Vol. VII [October 1967], pp. 50-55). See also Haddad, *Harakat Rashid 'Ali*, pp. 100-126; and Hirszowicz, *The Third Reich and the Arab East*, Chaps. 5-7.

[17] See Appendix, pp. 236-46.

sought to reside in Turkey, he was denied permission even to enter that country. Escaping arrest in Iran, he passed through Turkey in disguise, met with his followers in Istanbul, and proceeded to the Axis capitals.[18] The doors had now been thrown open for full collaboration with the Axis powers and there was no retreat for the Mufti (as well as a few who followed him) from these new ventures, although some, after the Soviet Union's entry into the war, saw the futility of the Mufti's pro-Nazi policy and ceased to cooperate with him.

From the time he entered into secret negotiations with Axis leaders in 1940, the Mufti began to speak on behalf of not only the Arabs of Palestine but the Arabs of other countries as well. After he left Palestine in 1937, he had met leading Arab politicians who looked to him to be the spokesman for the right of all Arabs to achieve unity and independence. Consequently, the Mufti's political ambition no longer remained confined to Palestine: it gradually grew to encompass first the Arab East and then, after he went to Axis lands, North Africa.

But the Mufti was not the only Arab leader who sought Axis support for leadership; Rashid 'Ali al-Gaylani, the 'Iraqi Premier, followed him to Berlin to challenge his leadership. Because Rashid 'Ali was given asylum in Turkey on his way from Tehran, he was able to reach Istanbul before the Mufti; there he discussed future Arab policy toward the Axis powers with other Arab leaders. Those leaders were divided into two camps: some advocated full collaboration with the Axis powers as the only possible way to save Palestine from Zionist penetration and other Arab countries from British and French control; others, who saw grave dangers from an association with Axis policies, especially after Hitler's attack on the Soviet Union, preferred to wait for the outcome of the war and sought refuge in Turkey as a neutral country. In one of the meetings (October 1941), those who had decided to collaborate with the Axis powers formally entrusted Rashid 'Ali with a mission to negotiate with Axis leaders for Arab unity and independence on the basis of the Arab national demands already formulated in Baghdad and presented to the Axis government. Rashid 'Ali, accord-

[18] For the story of how the Mufti escaped arrests and passed in disguise across the Perso-Turkish frontiers and from Turkey into Europe, see his *Memoirs* (*Filastin*, Vol. VII [November 1967], pp. 14-17).

ing to my informants, agreed to proceed to Berlin and negotiate with Nazi leaders.[19]

Shortly after Rashid 'Ali left Istanbul, the Mufti arrived to find that some of his followers had already asked Rashid 'Ali to present Arab demands to the Axis leaders. Consequently, the Mufti hurriedly left Istanbul in disguise and arrived in Berlin via Rome before Rashid 'Ali on November 9, 1941. He was welcomed by the Nazi authorities and assigned a villa in a western suburb of Berlin. When Rashid 'Ali arrived, he at first shared the Mufti's villa, but after the arrival of his family he was provided with a separate residence. Personal relations between the Mufti and Rashid 'Ali remained outwardly correct and friendly, but rivalry over leadership had already begun to come to the surface notwithstanding their agreement on Arab national objectives in principle.

Even before he set foot in Axis lands, the Mufti was determined to play the leading role as spokesman for the Arab people. Both as a religious and Pan-Arab leader, he was very widely known in Arab and Islamic lands and had carried on extensive correspondence with Arab and Muslim leaders in Europe, Asia, and North Africa; Rashid 'Ali, on the other hand, though a former Prime Minister, was in reality only a local leader whose influence was essentially confined to his country and who was scarcely known outside 'Iraq. In Berlin Rashid 'Ali led a relatively quiet life with his family, while the Mufti, alone and restless, became very active. More astute and persuasive, he exerted greater influence on Nazi leaders, especially Himmler, with whom he seems to have gotten along very well, and Von Weizäcker, Deputy Foreign Minister, in the Foreign Office.[20] Nevertheless, Rashid 'Ali, though his political horizon was more limited, challenged the Mufti's leadership and claimed that, as head of the 'Iraqi government, he was formally entrusted by Arab leaders to speak on their behalf. He was not discreet about his wishes and often quarreled with his own followers, such as Naji Shawkat, a member of his own Cabinet, who supported the Mufti's leadership.

[19] Information on Arab meetings in Istanbul has been provided by Rasim al-Khalidi, who advocated collaboration with the Axis Powers, and Akram Zu'aytar, who preferred non-cooperation and remained in Turkey to the end of the war. Both were active in the Mufti's circle in Baghdad.

[20] See the Mufti's *Memoirs* (*Filastin*, Vol. VIII [March 1, 1968], pp. 30-32; *ibid.*, Vol. VIII [August 1968], pp. 12-15); and Ernst Von Weizsäcker *Erinnerungen* (Munich, 1950), p. 33.

Differences between Germany and Italy about their respective positions in Arab lands may have been reflected in the conduct of the
two Arab leaders, notwithstanding the fact that Italy and Germany
had agreed earlier that the Mediterranean would be an Italian sphere
of influence and the area beyond in Asia and Africa a German
sphere of influence.

In his relations with Nazi leaders, there was no doubt that the
Mufti made a greater impression than Rashid 'Ali—he saw Hitler in
November of 1941, long before Rashid 'Ali was able to see him in
1942. Although the Mufti failed to induce Hitler to make an immediate public statement in favor of Arab aspirations, he was as-
sured of Axis sympathy with the Arabs and that a public statement would be made when German forces crossed the Caucasus.[21]
However, since the Nazi leaders could not afford to ignore the
wishes of a man whose country was expected to fall within the
German sphere of influence, they continued to deal with Rashid
'Ali, formally acknowledging him as the Premier of 'Iraq in a letter
from Von Ribbentrop on December 19, 1941, even before he met
Hitler. This prompted the Mufti to seek Italy's support, and shut-
tling between Berlin and Rome, he made greater headway than
Rashid 'Ali.

In their efforts to secure Axis support of essential Arab aspirations, on which Rashid 'Ali and the Mufti were agreed, the two
leaders presented proposals for a joint statement to be issued by
the Axis powers, including a request for a specific reference to
Palestine. Both Count Ciano and Von Ribbentrop, on behalf of the
two Axis powers, were authorized to reply to Rashid 'Ali and the
Mufti in an identical letter; the text of the letter to the Mufti,
dated April 28, 1942, follows:

> Eminence,
> In response to the letter sent today by you and by His
> Excellency the President of the Council, Rashid 'Ali al-Gailani,
> and in confirmation of the conversations with you, I have the
> honour to communicate the following:
> The Italian Government fully appreciates the confidence
> placed by the Arab people in the Axis Powers and in their ob-

[21] For the Mufti's conversation with Hitler, see his *Memoirs* (*Filastin*, Vol. VIII [April
1968], pp. 12-17); and my *Independent 'Iraq*, p. 239.

jectives, as well as their intention of participating in the fight against the common enemy until final victory is achieved. This is in accord with the national aspirations, as conveyed to you, of the Arab countries of the Near East at present oppressed by the British. I have the honour to assure you, in full agreement with the German Government, that the independence and freedom of the Arab countries, now suffering under British oppression, are also the objectives of the Italian Government.

Italy is therefore ready to grant to the Arab countries in the Near East, now suffering under British oppression, every possible aid in their fight for liberation; to recognize their sovereignty and independence; to agree to their federation if this is desired by the interested parties; as well as to the abolition of the Jewish National Homeland in Palestine.

It is understood that the text and contents of this letter shall be held absolutely secret until such time as we together decide otherwise.

Please accept, Eminence, the expression of my highest consideration.[22]

This was perhaps the climax of the two Arab leaders' achievements in Axis lands, since at last they had obtained a commitment to Arab independence and unity, vague as it may have been, as well as recognition that both were the principal spokesmen for Arab lands. However, Italy supported the Mufti's claim for precedence, presumably for his tacit support of Italian claims to North Africa, since the letter deliberately confined the reference of independence to Arab countries of the Near East and left the matter of federation or unity to the future.[23]

The shifting fortunes of the Axis powers put an end not only to the struggle for precedence between the two Arab leaders, but also to the achievement of Arab national aspirations through Axis support. As the war dragged on and the bombing of German and Italian cities continued, the two leaders were bound to look to their own safety and to seek refuge in places unlikely to be bombed. During the latter days of the war, they moved quickly from one place to another (with the help of the German authorities), flying before the

[22] See my *Independent 'Iraq*, pp. 240-41.

[23] In a letter to the writer, the Mufti denied his acquiescence to Italian claims to North Africa and asserted that he supported the Libyan demand for independence in particular.

rapid advance of Western and Soviet forces. Disguised and unnoticed, they reached the Swiss border when the armistice was signed in May 1945. Rashid 'Ali was not admitted;[24] the Mufti, who managed to reach Berne, was informed that he would not be given asylum and that he would have to leave. While crossing the frontier, he was arrested by the French authorities and taken to the French capital.

In a suburb of Paris the Mufti resided in a guarded villa for over a year. Although his movements were restricted, he was able to receive visitors and often visited Paris under police supervision. He heard that his name had been mentioned as a possible war criminal, and some members of the British Parliament asked the government to extradite him, but no action was taken. It was alleged that while he was in Germany he gave his blessing to the "final solution" of the Jewish question through his personal relations with some Nazi leaders, especially with Himmler. More specifically, it was reported that he had written to the German Foreign Office protesting a contemplated plan to send some 4,500 Jewish children to Palestine in exchange for German prisoners, and that he had written to the Hungarian government demanding an end to the immigration of Jews to Palestine in 1943. It was also alleged that he advised the authorities that, in order to control the Jews in the Balkans and to prevent them from escaping to Palestine, they be sent to Poland; presumably this would have come within the plan of the "final solution."[25]

When the Mufti became aware of these charges he began to make preparations to escape from Paris. Relaxation of the orders restricting his movements were interpreted to mean that he could escape; accordingly, he left Paris in disguise in May 1946 under the name and passport of Ma'ruf al-Dawalibi, the well-known Syrian nationalist (who was then studying law in Paris), and went to Cairo via Rome and Athens on board an American military aircraft. For almost a decade Cairo became the headquarters of his political

[24] In disguise Rashid 'Ali went first to Belgium and then to France. Still in disguise, he left for Bayrut, and then Damascus and Riyad, where he stayed until 1954. Between 1954 and 1958 he was in Cairo, returning to Baghdad after the Revolution of 1958. He died in 1964.

[25] An objective study of the Mufti's involvement in these activities has yet to be made. The Mufti once told me that all accusations against him concerning his involvement with the "final solution" were unfounded, since the Nazi leaders needed no encouragement about a plan which they had already laid down before he took residence in Axis lands. For some light on this issue, based in part on the German documents, see J. B. Schechtman, *The Mufti and the Fuehrer* (New York, 1965).

activities, although he traveled without restrictions to several other Arab and Islamic countries. Because of strained relations with the Egyptian military authorities he moved to Bayrut in 1959, for Lebanon, as he once told me, provided the only neutral atmosphere in the Arab world.

Had the Axis powers won the war, the Mufti would have returned to preside over a "new order" in the Arab world. Since his Axis allies lost the war, he returned to play an ever diminishing role in the unfolding events of the Palestine tragedy. Although the Arab League had taken full responsibility for defending Arab rights in Palestine, at the outset no action was taken without prior consultation or approval of the Mufti, since he was still acknowledged as the leading spokesman for the Arabs of Palestine. For two or three years after the war, until the Arab governments intervened militarily in the conflict, the Mufti's opinions provided guidelines for the positions taken by the official Arab representatives in the negotiations with the British government (in 1946) and in the discussions at the United Nations (in 1947 and 1948).

Fully convinced of the justice of his people's cause, the Mufti demanded full independence for Palestine and refused to accept any compromise which would recognize Jewish claims beyond the rights enjoyed by Jews who resided in the country before World War I. In taking this extreme position, which was indeed supported by many other influential leaders, Arab representatives in the London conferences and at the United Nations were bound to insist on independence and self-determination for Palestine. If moderate views had been presented, the Great Powers might have supported a compromise plan that would have preserved the country's unity under a regime (federal or unitary) in which Arabs and Jews would live together as equal Palestinian citizens.[26]

From the time the Arab governments decided to intervene by collective action to protect Arab rights in Palestine, leadership began to slip from the Mufti and his influence diminished considerably. He continued to speak on behalf of the Arabs of Palestine and to issue policy statements, but since the conflict had shifted from

[26] I have it on the authority of 'Abd al-Razzaq al-Sanhuri, who attended the London Conference in 1946, and Muhammad Husayn Haykal, who attended the United Nations meetings in 1947 and 1948, that they had to reject compromise plans because they were unacceptable to the Mufti, even though such plans might have received the support of the Great Powers.

the domestic to the international level—from a conflict between Arabs and Jews to a conflict between Israel and the Arab states— the Mufti's role, even as head of an Arab organization—the Arab Higher Committee—no longer remained relevant. His influence declined sharply after the first Palestine war of 1948-49 and was exercised indirectly through the Arab governments with whom he was able to maintain friendly relations. Since his position had become merely symbolic, no Arab state deemed it necessary to restrict his activities, except 'Iraq and Jordan—the first because of his activities during the war against the lawful regime, and the second because of his opposition to King 'Abd-Allah's moderate policies and also his role in the annexation of Arab Palestine to Trans-Jordan (renamed Jordan).[27]

The spread of the revolutionary movement throughout the Arab world early in the 1950s contributed to the decline of the Mufti's influence. The ideals of this movement, claiming to be opposed to traditional goals, were naturally unacceptable to the Mufti, although he tried to keep on friendly terms with its leaders. These relations became strained when the revolutionary leaders became involved in a power struggle first in Egypt and then in Syria with religious groups, especially the Muslim Brotherhood, with which the Mufti, as a religious leader, was intimately connected. Had the religious groups won the struggle the Mufti might have been able to recover lost prestige and influence. When Nasir won the first round against the Brotherhood early in the 1950s, the Mufti was at first permitted to remain in Egyptian territory, but later, when the Brotherhood continued its subversive activities, his presence in Egypt could no longer be tolerated and he was asked to leave the country in 1959. Since that time he has resided in Bayrut, and has often paid occasional visits to countries still opposed to revolutionary ideas. Despite financial support from these countries, the spread of the revolutionary movement has considerably restricted his movements, and he has often been compelled to take sides in the rivalry among leaders with whom he shares no common objective save the hope of recovering his lost country.

[27] Before its annexation to Jordan, the Mufti paid a quick visit to Palestine in 1948. He went to Ghaza to serve as speaker of a national convention when the short-lived all-Palestine government was established, but he soon returned to Cairo when it became clear that the all-Palestine government was merely a symbolic regime. He visited Jerusalem shortly before the June war of 1967—the first time since his departure thirty years earlier.

The breakup of the Syro-Egyptian union in 1961 and the
failure of Nasir to transform the United Arab Republic into a true
Arab union created frustration in Pan-Arab circles, especially
among Palestinians, who hoped that the United Arab Republic
might eventually recover Palestine by war or diplomacy. The establishment of the United Arab Republic, especially its socialist system, became the cause of discord rather than of unity and diverted
attention from the common enemy. Palestinian leaders, though
scattered and disunited, began to agitate for action, calling for
guerrilla (fida'iyin) warfare to recover their country, since Arab intervention had brought no positive results.[28] In this new atmosphere, the Mufti found an opportunity to raise his voice again for
unity and direct action under his leadership. While there was a favorable response to the Mufti's call among some followers, the majority
preferred to organize themselves under the direct or indirect
guidance of one of the revolutionary regimes rather than under the
Mufti's traditional leadership.

IV

What were the Mufti's political objectives and methods?

Arab leaders in the countries that had fallen under British or
French control after World War I had as their immediate political
objectives the elimination of foreign domination and the achievement of independence, even though they differed on the ways and
means of achieving these objectives. In Palestine, Arab leaders
pursued the same goals, but their task was complicated by Zionist
aspirations to establish in their country a Jewish National Home,
and by British support of these aspirations against their wishes. All
Arab leaders, whether Husaynis or Nashashibis, were in agreement
that foreign control should be superseded by independence and
that the Jewish National Home should cease to exist. But the Mufti,
in his drive for power, insisted on pursuing these goals by his own
methods and sought to give the effort a sacred outlook in which

---

[28] For the nature and drives of the Palestine Movement, see my *Political Trends,* pp. 205-9;
and Hisham Sharabi, *Palestine and Israel: The Lethal Dilemma* (New York, 1969), Chap. 8.

no compromises are tolerated regardless of how long, in his words, the struggle may take or how high the sacrifices may be.[29]

It is true that the Mufti has often been able to carry the country in his unrelenting struggle, but his negative and extreme methods have been pursued to the point of diminishing returns. And yet despite one failure after another, he has shown no sign that he is prepared to change or modify either his goals or his methods. The reasons are not as simple as the Mufti's critics contend; they accuse him of subordinating public to personal interests. The reasons actually lie deep in the social milieu in which he grew up and in the complex forces of Arab politics.

To begin with, the Mufti's early life was molded in an atmosphere of a traditional society. When he went to Egypt for study, his college education was charged with emotions and with a feeling of aversion to foreign influence. While in Turkey, where he had gone for further study, he fought with the Turks against Britain when the war broke out and shared Ottoman admiration for German military discipline and German support for Pan-Islamism. After the war, he pinned his hope on the Arab regime in Syria, but he was disappointed when that regime was overthrown by another European power—France. These adverse experiences were not very helpful for a young man who returned to live under the newly established British Mandate over Palestine whose task was to help develop a Jewish National Home in his country.

Even if he had been willing to accommodate his objectives to his country's new authorities, domestic political forces apparently would have conspired to force him to take a position opposed to those authorities. Although Palestine was a very small country, Arab society was so fragmented along social and confessional lines that it was exceedingly difficult to create cohesion and social solidarity even when

---

[29] In a letter to the writer (dated February 2, 1972), the Mufti made the following comment:

"As to the question of extremism, I still hold the same position as before, because men of principles should always remain loyal to their people's rights and should continue to do so if their people were to support them. . . . I am convinced in my belief that the question of Palestine cannot possibly be solved by a partial settlement, because Zionism, exceeding colonial objectives, is based on far-reaching and grandiose plans. It aims by all possible means at the eventual destruction of Arab existence not only in Palestine but in all other lands in accordance with an already laid down plan. For this reason the Palestine question should remain alive in the hearts of all Arabs regardless how long the struggle for its settlement may take or how high the sacrifices may be."

a common danger threatened its very existence. Because the rival Nashashibis received support from the British authorities—a Husayni Mayor had been replaced by a member of the Nashashibi house and the office of Mufti almost fell into Nashashibi hands—the Husaynis, led by the Mufti, were bound to depend on popular support. In his drive against the Jewish National Home, to which both Nashashibis and Husaynis were opposed in principle, the Mufti chose to hold both Britishers and Jews equally responsible on the ground that the latter were entirely dependent for support on the former; the Nashashibis, on the other hand, deemed it in the Arab interest to win over the British rather than to antagonize them. Even when Arab leaders finally agreed to organize the Arab Higher Committee, the leadership of which eventually devolved upon the Mufti, some leaders were opposed to the Mufti's use of indiscriminate violence and were ready to come to terms with the British authorities when the general strike of 1936 was called off. Thus, Arab opposition to the Jewish National Home was diverted by side issues which weakened the Arab leadership vis-à-vis Zionist leadership.

The Mufti, afraid that leadership might slip from him, denounced opponents for their readiness to accept compromise, and his followers, not without his knowledge or approval, often accused opponents of treason and threatened them with violence.[30] Because extremism has for long been more popular than moderation in traditional Arab society, the Mufti was bound to follow extremist and negative methods in order to win popular support against the British authorities and his political opponents. Thus the Mufti's methods appeared to outside observers as almost criminal acts; but to the Mufti they were the only means available to him to bring pressure on the British authorities to stop Jewish immigration to Palestine and to prevent the sale of Arab lands to Jews. In exile, the Mufti's cooperation with opposition groups seemed surreptitious to the authorities and resulted either in his expulsion or in his being declared *persona non grata.* But in all his actions, he has always been motivated by deep convictions and a sense of justice for his people; indeed he has often endured hardships and personal discomfiture in order to achieve the national goals for which he has

---

[30] Fakhri al-Nashashibi, one of the Mufti's opponents, was assassinated by extremists in 1941 because he was prepared to compromise with the British authorities, and King 'Abd-Allah of Jordan was assassinated in 1952 because he was prepared to negotiate with Israel.

worked so assiduously during his entire public life. Prudent and calculating though he may have often appeared, the Mufti falls, in the final analysis, in the category of idealist leaders because he put justice and legal rights above political realities over which he had no control. Such leadership, the product of traditional upbringing, may be useful in a society that honors traditional norms and values, but it proved inadequate for one undergoing rapid social change and a challenge from another more dynamic and progressive society.

CHAPTER VI

The Traditional (Idealistic) School—The Moderate King Faysal of Saudi Arabia

> The important thing about a regime is not what it is called but how it acts. There are corrupt republican regimes and sound monarchies and vice versa. The only true criterion of a regime—whether it be monarchical or republican—is the degree of reciprocity between ruler and ruled and the extent to which it symbolizes prosperity, progress and healthy initiative. . . . The quality of a regime should be judged by its deeds and the integrity of its rulers, not by its name.
>
> *Faysal*

As the third son of a reigning monarch, Faysal was destined neither to become the head of state in accordance with the line of succession established by his father, 'Abd al-'Aziz Ibn Sa'ud, nor necessarily even to play an important role in his country's politics. In a traditional society, political processes are relatively fixed, and there is little for public men to do outside the bounds set for them by custom or prescription. And yet from early life, Faysal was given the opportunity to play a significant role in public affairs and to help his countrymen cross the threshold into modern life—a step which eventually led to his assumption of supreme power a decade after the death of his great father, the founder of the modern Saudi state. Is Faysal's role as a leader the product of his country's new conditions or is it the creation of his own personal qualities? A

King Faysal of Saudi Arabia

study of Faysal's role in politics and an assessment of the elements of his leadership may throw light on the relationship between personal qualities and the circumstances favorable for the emergence of leadership.

II

Faysal was born in 1906, five years after his father had captured Riyad—the seat of government his grandfather, 'Abd al-Rahman, had lost in 1890 to Ibn al-Rashid, the chief of a rival house—and had begun to reestablish Saudi rule in central Arabia. Thus, from his early years, Faysal's career coincided with the rise of the modern Saudi state, and the experience he gained under his father's benevolent rule proved invaluable for the responsibility that eventually fell upon him.

Two significant events had far-reaching effects on both his early upbringing and his public life. The first was the premature death of his eldest brother Turki, who had been born in 1901 while his father was still in exile; he died in 1918 just when he had begun to exercise some authority delegated to him. Like his father, Turki was tall and handsome; he was very promising as a leader and had shown ability in commanding successful campaigns. Sa'ud, the next son, born in 1902, lacked his father's prudence and strength of character, although he possessed some of his physical attributes. Faysal, though delicate and less impressive than Sa'ud in physical appearance, possessed a far more receptive and discriminating mind, and his father was not slow in perceiving and exploiting his abilities in the service of his kingdom. He was entrusted with duties which would have been the privilege of the eldest son, had he been alive, or of the second after the death of the first, had he shown equal competence.

The second event was his mother's early death,[1] which brought Faysal under the care of his maternal grandfather—a man known for his piety and learning. This grandfather was a descendant of Shaykh Muhammad b. 'Abd al-Wahhab, a Muslim reformer and founder of the Wahhabi order, who had entered into an alliance

---

[1] She was his father's second wife and died soon after he was born.

with the Grand Sa'ud, founder of the dynasty.[2] It was in the tradition of this family that Faysal grew up—he learned to recite the Qur'an before he could read well, and he studied the Prophet's Traditions. In addition, he read Arabic literature and composed poetry.

However, it was from his father that he received his training for public life. Asked by the present writer as to whom he owed his apprenticeship in statecraft, Faysal replied without hesitation, "To my father." "I have not received formal education in school," he added, "but I was brought up under the direct influence and guidance of my father, and I have tried to follow in his footsteps." While still a child in his maternal grandfather's house, his father would send for him and talk or play with him; he also would take him out with him on some small outings. Remarks about men and public affairs opened his eyes, and he began to mature early in life. Above all, he learned the manners of great men from association with a great man—patience, self-possession, and the ability to handle men. From early childhood, Faysal combined an appreciation of Islamic values and a sense of reality about human affairs.

Before his mid-teens, Faysal was too young to be given any official duty, real or nominal, although he was taken on some excursions and had a glimpse of the fighting with Ibn al-Rashid toward the end of World War I. A year after the war, when King 'Abd al-'Aziz was invited to London to discuss border questions that had arisen between him and King Husayn, ruler of the Hijaz and an ally of Britain in the war, Faysal was given the opportunity to represent his father as head of a delegation. The king, being unable to leave his country, informed His Majesty's Government that he would send one of his sons. Since Turki, his eldest son, had died a year before, he named Faysal rather than Sa'ud to represent him.

The selection of Faysal may be regarded as a sign of his father's appreciation of his potential capacity—his dignity, manners, and self-possession—to act as his representative in a foreign country. Since Faysal was then only thirteen years old, King 'Abd al-'Aziz appointed Ahmad al-Thunayyan, who had traveled abroad before

[2] For an account of the founding of the Saudi dynasty, see Amin al-Rayhani [Rihani], *Tarikh Najd al-Hadith wa Mulhaqatih* [The History of Modern Najd and Its Dependencies] (Bayrut, 1928); H. St. John Philby, *Sa'udi Arabia* (London, 1955); R. Bayly Winder, *Saudi Arabia in the Nineteenth Century* (New York, 1965).

and spoke French and Turkish, to accompany him.[3] Both went to London wearing Arabian dress and the party caught public attention. It was announced that the object of the mission was to offer Ibn Saʻud's congratulations on the victory of the Allies in the war, and Faysal, in an audience with the King, presented two swords and a letter from his father. But political questions were also discussed with Lord Curzon, Foreign Secretary, in which Ahmad al-Thunayyan took an active part. No agreement on the border dispute seems to have been reached; but Ahmad al-Thunayyan promised on behalf of his master that "there shall be no war for three years." Ibn Saʻud honored the word of his representative, for the war that broke out and led to the occupation of al-Hijaz by Ibn Saʻud took place in 1924. Before his return, Faysal met in London and Paris with high officials concerned with Arabia and learned at first hand some realities about foreign affairs.[4]

Faysal's next assignment, which gave him an opportunity to learn about military operations, was to command a force sent to ʻAsir, a territory between the Hijaz and the Yaman, under the rule of the ʻAyid dynasty. ʻAsir had long been a bone of contention between the rulers of Najd and the Hijaz, and Faysal went in 1922 to support tribal chiefs who owed allegiance to Ibn Saʻud and who were opposed to ʻAyid rule. Faysal's expedition, a great achievement for a young man at the age of 16, gave him prestige and self-confidence. His father, impressed by Faysal's signal success, went in person to meet him and his army on their return from the campaign. A year later, in 1923, the entire territory passed under Saudi control, and it was incorporated into Ibn Saʻud's kingdom in 1930. As a military commander, Faysal took to the field again in 1934 to repulse a Yamani attack on a region considered to be within Saudi territory. In winning, Faysal might have penetrated deep into Yamani territory, but the Imam Yahya, King of the Yaman, sued for peace, and Faysal was instructed to withdraw, thus deprived of the fruits of victory. "I obeyed my father against my wish," he said,

---

[3] Ahmad al-Thunayyan, a member of the Saudi dynasty and a descendant of a former ruler, had lived in Istanbul and married a Turkish woman. He returned to Arabia and fought with Ibn Saʻud before World War I.

[4] For an account of the mission by one of the liaison officers, see Major N. N. E. Bray, *Shifting Sands* (London, 1934), pp. 296-98; de Gaury, *Faisal, King of Saudi Arabia* (London, 1966), pp. 22-31.

"but I realized later how right he was, since peace and friendly relations were maintained between the two countries ever since." In
1962 when civil war broke out in the Yaman, it was to Saudi
Arabia that the Imamic government of Yaman appealed for support,
and Faysal was not slow in extending assistance. In both 'Asir and
the Yaman, Faysal gained invaluable experience in war and diplomacy.[5]

Another important task given to Faysal, which was to last over
thirty years, was political and administrative—Viceroy of the Hijaz
and Minister of Foreign Affairs. The annexation of the Hijaz in
1925, without fully incorporating it under Ibn Sa'ud's administrative system, left the country's highest political post vacant after
the abdication of the King of the Hijaz. Ibn Sa'ud appointed
Faysal to govern as his deputy, and thus the Hijaz was maintained
as an autonomous entity within his dominion. A certain amount
of jealousy became apparent between Faysal and his brother, Sa'ud,
over the Hijaz, especially when Sa'ud expressed a desire to command the campaign in the Hijaz; but the king resolved the matter
by appointing Sa'ud as heir and deputy in Riyad, the capital, and
Faysal as deputy and Viceroy in the Hijaz. When a Ministry of
Foreign Affairs was created in 1931, Faysal was also appointed
Foreign Minister since his diplomatic ability had already been widely noticed. He proved equal to the dual task: aided by a Consulta-
tive Assembly, he dealt with the people of the Hijaz not as con-
quered people but as equal partners in his father's kingdom; and
he resided in Makka, the country's holy capital. As Foreign Minister, he often visited Jidda, a more cosmopolitan center, to receive
heads of foreign diplomatic missions; in this he was assisted by a
few Arab experts in foreign service recruited to carry out Saudi diplomatic missions. Before as well as after he became Foreign Minister,
he traveled to Europe (in 1926, 1932, and 1939), including an official visit to the Soviet Union. Since World War II his foreign
travels, both before and after he became king, have become more
frequent, covering almost all important regions of the world. There
was no doubt, even before the death of his father in 1953, that

---

[5] For an account of the wars in 'Asir and the Yaman, see Philby, *Sa'udi Arabia*, Chaps. 10-
11; de Gaury, *Faisal*, Chaps. 4-5; A. J. Toynbee, *Survey of International Affairs, 1934*
(London, 1935), pp. 310-21.

Faysal had become the most experienced member of the Saudi house.[6]

III

Until his death in 1953, supreme authority was held in Ibn Sa'ud's hands, and there was no question of division of powers. Shortly before his death, when poor health prevented him from exercising direct control, Ibn Sa'ud delegated powers to a Council of Ministers, to be presided over by his eldest son. The Council was established by a decree issued on October 9, 1953, and it was the first occasion in the history of Saudi Arabia that authority was exercised by someone other than the King. The component bodies of the Council had begun to evolve under the King's authority as early as 1931. In that year the Ministry of Foreign Affairs, as noted before, was established and the Viceroy of the Hijaz became its head. Other ministries followed, such as Finance (1932), Defense (1944), and Interior (1951).[7]

The question of the succession seems to have been very much on the King's conscience long before his death. The great man was very uneasy about Sa'ud, the Crown Prince, who lacked not only experience but prudence. It became clear that Faysal had overtaken Sa'ud in maturity and the King did not conceal his admiration for Faysal; Hafiz Wahba, one of the King's advisers, told me that he had heard the King saying on more than one occasion: "I wish I had several Faysals."[8] However, Sa'ud was the eldest son and he did not think it was proper to exclude him from succession.

Rumors about differences of opinion began to circulate long before Ibn Sa'ud's death, although the existence of such differences were always denied, and the two sons were called in by the great man to discuss the question of succession. The King pointed out the dangers of disagreement and asked the two sons to swear to him

---

[6] For Faysal's career as viceroy and foreign minister in the Hijaz, see Amin Sa'id, *Faysal al-'Azim* (Bayrut, 1385/1965), pp. 29-49; de Gaury, *Faisal,* Chap. 6; Fu'ad Hamza, *al-Bilad al-'Arabiya al-Sa'udiya* [The Saudi Arabian Lands] (2nd ed.; Riyad, 1968), pp. 84-96.

[7] For an account of the evolution and structure of these departments, see Hamza, *al-Bilad al-'Arabiya al-Sa'udiya,* pp. 114 ff.

[8] De Gaury reports the same remark from another adviser as follows: "I only wish I had three Faysals" (de Gaury, *Faisal,* p. 78).

that they would never quarrel after his death. It was agreed that Sa'ud would succeed and Faysal would be the Crown Prince. After Ibn Sa'ud's death (November 9, 1953), the princes, including Faysal, went to Sa'ud in person and formally gave their allegiance to their eldest brother.[9]

One of Sa'ud's first acts was to confirm Faysal's appointment as Viceroy of the Hijaz and Foreign Minister, retaining for himself the position as head of the Council of Ministers. Thus the new King became his own Prime Minister. Faysal, who may have expected to become head of the Council of Ministers, showed no sign of discontent, but disagreements between the King and the Crown Prince were often discreetly expressed on foreign affairs. Faysal showed a favorable attitude toward the new revolutionary regime of Egypt and voiced critical remarks about the Baghdad Pact and other matters—views which were not altogether in accord with Sa'ud's attitude. Thus the King departed from the foreign policy of his Foreign Minister. More dangerous was Sa'ud's vacillation in his attitude toward Nasir—siding with him on one occasion and then turning against him on another. He attacked the Baghdad Pact but approved of the Eisenhower Doctrine. Moreover, his quarrel with Nasir degenerated to the personal level—it was rumored that Nasir was involved in an alleged assassination plot against Sa'ud, and that Sa'ud tried to disrupt the Syro-Egyptian Union by offering bribes to Syrian leaders. Above all, the deficit in the Saudi treasury, resulting from the squandering of public monies and extravagant spending, brought the country to the verge of bankruptcy and alarmed many Saudi leaders.

The first move to limit Sa'ud's powers and bring Faysal to a position of greater responsibility took place in 1958. Faysal went abroad for medical treatment in 1957 and returned early in 1958. On his way back, he stopped in Egypt and talked with Nasir about foreign policy, which had been handled in his absence by Sa'ud, and discovered that Sa'ud had been negotiating with Nasir's Arab opponents. In protest, Faysal retired to a camp in the desert in March, giving recuperation as his reason. Sa'ud, absorbed in foreign intrigues, let the internal affairs of the country deteriorate.

[9] In Arab tradition the ruler need not necessarily be the oldest son, but Ibn Sa'ud decreed that Sa'ud, his oldest son, should succeed in order to avoid a family quarrel. He made all his sons promise solemnly that Sa'ud would succeed.

The princes, who had sworn allegiance to Sa'ud, became worried not only about the country but also about their own future. Some of them, led by Fahd, moved to stage what might be called a palace revolt. On March 24, 1958, twelve princes suddenly appeared before Sa'ud at a Ramadan breakfast, where he was sitting with an elder member of the family who was a great supporter of Faysal. They told Sa'ud that the princes had met and discussed the internal situation of the kingdom. "We decided," it is reported that they told the King, "to demand your abdication, but your brother Faysal opposed the idea and asked that you remain on the Throne. We have accepted on one condition, that you hand over all your power to Faysal."[10] Sa'ud, faced with formidable opponents, accepted the arrangement and a decree to that effect was issued on the same day. Faysal immediately assumed power, and began to deal with the pressing financial problems and to normalize his country's foreign relations with its Arab neighbors.[11]

A year later, when Sa'ud found he was not satisfied with being king in name only, a difference of opinion recurred. Faysal left the country for medical treatment, at least so it was announced, and returned toward the end of the year and submitted his resignation as Prime Minister. Sa'ud recovered all powers and ruled as his own Prime Minister for the next four years. Internal conditions again deteriorated while Sa'ud's mind was fully preoccupied with foreign affairs. A greater number of princes than before became worried about the situation, but they moved slowly now since Sa'ud began to rally supporters and became more difficult to influence.

In 1961, Sa'ud's health began to fail, and he went abroad several times for medical treatment during 1962 and 1963. In 1964, by which time Sa'ud's incompetence had exposed the country to real danger, the princes became restless and began consultations with Faysal about a possible transfer of powers to him. One of the

[10] De Gaury, *Faisal*, p. 93.

[11] Faysal's quick action to restore normal conditions is attested by Anwar 'Ali, the Pakistani Governor of the Saudi Arabian Monetary Agency, who helped Faysal with the task of reestablishing the country's financial position. "In 1957," he said, "we had an inflation that drove the cost of living up by 90 per cent. The finances were then reorganized and proper management introduced, the budget was put on a sound basis, the royal allowances sharply reduced, and the country began to live within its income. Of course, none of this could have been done without King Faisal. He carried out the painful economies and faced up to their social consequences" (Judith Listowel, "Saudi Arabia," *The Listener* [June 1, 1967], pp. 705-6).

princes, Tallal, who had been Sa'ud's most influential minister, defected and began to criticize him in the foreign press. This move
encouraged the other princes to put pressure on Sa'ud to invite
Faysal to become Prime Minister. In 1963, Faysal agreed to take
over control, and he issued a statement of policy intended to inspire confidence and improve conditions.[12] The war in the Yaman,
which brought Egyptian forces nearer to Saudi lands, aroused concern, since it was feared that the fall of the Yaman into Nasir's
hands might bring the revolutionary movement to Saudi Arabia.
Faysal, who was on good terms with Nasir, again became active in
an effort to save the Saudi monarchy. Since Sa'ud had proved totally incompetent, the princes pursued their efforts to induce him to
abdicate in favor of Faysal. The 'ulama, in concert with the princes,
discussed the matter in order to legitimize the action. Meanwhile,
Faysal felt bound to consult the leading tribal chiefs about his succession in order to obtain their support.

On October 29, 1964, the 'ulama formally met and issued a
fatwa (legal opinion) to proclaim Faysal king. Faysal, while accepting the offer in principle, made it clear that Sa'ud must first abdicate, by persuasion if possible, to relieve him of the oath of allegiance and to legitimize the succession.[13] On November 1, Sa'ud,
realizing the futility of resistance, agreed to abdicate. He left the
country immediately afterward.[14]

Faysal, on becoming King and Prime Minister, formed a new
Council of Ministers, composed of new and competent men in
whom he had confidence to run the government in a businesslike
manner. Khalid, a younger brother, was appointed Crown Prince
in 1965. A decade after Ibn Sa'ud's death the country was once
again in competent hands. It is abundantly clear that Faysal's
elevation to the throne was the culmination of a long career in
which he made his imprint on the country and not merely the
product of coincidental events. Had he not possessed a combination of suitable qualities and experiences, the country's challenge
of development would not have been met by wise leadership.

[12] For a summary of the statement, see p. 98, below.

[13] "Because he [Faysal] kept his promise," one Saudi said, "we have lost eleven years and
a mountain of gold."

[14] See texts of the fatwa and other relevant documents in al-Watha'iq al-'Arabiya, 1964,
pp. 136-37, 533-35; and Amin Sa'id, Faysal al-'Azim, pp. 73 ff.

IV

Faysal's ideas about social reform, though conservative in the eyes of Arab revolutionary leaders, are progressive for a traditional society. His ideas have been made known to his people in public statements and in press interviews, but they have never been spelled out in an elaborate program or in a blueprint, as have those of his contemporaries among Arab leaders. Perhaps the nearest approximation to a program is the ten-point statement of policy which he issued when he formed his Cabinet on October 31, 1962. The ten points may be summed up as follows:

1. Inasmuch as the system of government should be a reflection of the development achieved by the community . . . the government is prepared to develop the community educationally, culturally and socially so that it might reach the level that would be truly represented in the form of a unified system of government calculated to achieve the ideals embodied in the sacred law (shari'a). . . . It is believed that the time has come for the promulgation of a Fundamental Law for the Government, drawn from the Qur'an and the Prophet's Traditions and the conduct of the Orthodox Caliphs that will set forth explicitly the fundamental principles of government and . . . the basic rights of citizens, including the right to free expression of opinion within the limits of Islam and public policy.

2. The Government will also undertake to draw up legislation that will regulate local government in the provinces in order to improve the administrative system and achieve political and social development.

3. The Judiciary shall enjoy immunity and respect. . . . To achieve this purpose, a Ministry of Justice will be created to supervise the administrative affairs of the Judiciary and a Public Prosecutor to protect the individual's rights and interests.

4. Since the texts of the Qur'an and Traditions are fixed and the country's conditions are changing, it is imperative to consider important matters of state in the light of these changes and in accordance with the sacred law. For this purpose it has been decided to create a Judicial Council consisting of twenty members chosen from well-known jurists and 'ulama and whose functions will be advisory on all matters referred to it by the state or individuals.

5. The Government will continue its duties to uphold the principles of Islam, spread its call and protect it by word and by deed.

6. In order to achieve these duties, the Government has decided to reform the Committee for Public Morality, designed for moral guidance, so as to conform to the goals for which it was created.

7. One of the Government's most important functions is to raise the nation's social level. It has therefore decided to continue its work to provide free medical treatment and education at all levels. Social security, for which regulations have just been issued, will provide support for the aged, disabled, orphans and women without means for livelihood. Soon all the needy will have similar support as well as unemployed workers.

8. The Government will issue laws which will regulate the economic and social development in accordance with the country's needs and aspirations.

9. The financial and economic developments are the Government's prime concern at the present. Reform programs will be laid down to encourage initiative and private enterprise, to raise the standard of living, and to improve communications and transportations. Studies of water resources for drinking and agricultural purposes will be undertaken. It is hoped that Saudi Arabia will soon become an industrial and agriculturally self-sufficient country possessing adequate sources of revenue . . . . An industrial and an agricultural bank will soon be established as well as the General Petroleum and Mineral Agency. These and other agencies will undertake to develop the country's resources and exploit its minerals and other riches.

10. Slavery is absolutely prohibited and penalty will be imposed on those who are still engaged in this traffic.[15]

These points, to be sure, do not include all that the country needed or all of Faysal's views about reform; but they certainly point to the direction of his thoughts and the practical methods he would pursue in achieving the material progress of his country. Although he grew up in the desert, he appreciated the fact that his people could not remain much longer without the benefits of progress, and his ultimate goal is unmistakably to transform his

[15] For full text, see de Gaury, *Faisal*, Appendix I, quoted from Saudi Arabic Radio Broadcast, November 7, 1962.

country into a modern state. "Like it or not," he once said, "we must join the modern world and find an honorable place in it."

After his accession to the throne in 1964, one of Faysal's prime concerns, second only to national security, was to speed up the country's economic development and to increase social services. Since this essay is intended essentially to study Faysal as a political leader, it is impossible to examine Saudi Arabia's contemporary social and economic development;[16] I have therefore tried to discuss only his goals and methods and his role in Arab politics. Much of my material is based on personal interviews with him as well as with other public men who have served the country for over fifty years.[17]

Faysal is not a revolutionary leader by temperament or upbringing. He has studied the Islamic religion and Arab tribal and customary lore and takes pride in this heritage. He is also aware that he is the leader of a country that reveres religious values and still regards itself bound by the sacred law. He is therefore not prepared to break completely with the past or to accept purely secular legislation which would replace the sacred law and traditional polity. He has shown grave concern about the methods pursued by Arab revolutionary leaders, because these methods have often proved destructive and failed to achieve the progress promised to the people. He feels it is ironic that though the military denounce civilian leaders as reactionary, there is ample evidence to indicate that greater prosperity and stability have been achieved in the countries pursuing slow progress than in the revolutionary countries. Nor does he believe in the ability of the military to govern. They are fit for army command, not for civil government, he has said, and their attempts to involve the army in politics have corrupted both the military and governmental processes and have diverted the army from its primary task of defending the country against foreign attacks to the pursuit of internal quarrels.[18]

---

[16] For a survey of the social development of Saudi Arabia in recent years, see Hermann F. Eilts, "Social Revolution in Saudi Arabia," *Parameters,* Vol. I (Spring 1971), pp. 4-18; (Fall 1971), pp. 22-33.

[17] I had the pleasure of meeting him first in 1945 when he was the head of his country's delegation to the United Nations Conference on International Organization at San Francisco and I was a member of the 'Iraqi delegation.

[18] The writer's interview with King Faysal.

Nor has Faysal been impressed with the ideological orientation of Arab leaders. He believes their slogans are empty of content, since they have promised much more than they have been able to deliver to their people. While these leaders have talked about social justice and the rights of the people, they have done little to achieve real progress. Thus, Faysal's methods are manifestly realistic—he endeavors to deal with practical matters and to proceed from one problem to another. He is not prepared to replace religious by secular values—since the former are still valid in Arab eyes—but has addressed himself directly to social and material problems. Consequently, his reform program is not intended to initiate a religious revolution—a Reformation—but a "developmental" or industrial revolution. In an audience with King Faysal following the opening of the Kuwayt University in 1966, the Rector of the University of Riyad[19] and I were asked by the King: "Of what colleges is the Kuwayt University made up?" "Of the colleges of arts and sciences" I answered. "What we need," said the King, "is not a college of arts, but colleges of engineering and medicine since we have enough poets and writers." This and other remarks about the Arab need for scientific and technological skills indicate Faysal's concern about his country's immediate needs for material progress before its moral and religious values are reconsidered.

As to personal freedom, Faysal earnestly maintains that there is a great deal more freedom in his country than in other Arab lands. "Every one is free to say what he believes in Arabia," he asserted, "and there are no restrictions on the free expression of opinion." Censorship, as practiced in some Arab countries, does not exist in Saudi Arabia since Saudi citizens feel relatively free to speak out their minds about public affairs provided their opinions do not run contrary to social morality. However, there is undoubtedly greater relaxation of social morality and religious practices in some of the so-called revolutionary countries than in Saudi Arabia.

Faysal maintains that each Arab country should be fully sovereign and that no country should interfere in the domestic affairs of another, least of all in the political system which each is entitled to choose for itself. Faysal, it is true, seems to have been unhappy

[19] Dr. 'Abd al-'Aziz al-Khuwaytar.

about the spread of revolutionary ideas into Arab lands; but he felt
it was Egypt's own business whether a republican system was
adopted when the monarchy was overthrown in 1952, and he even
maintained friendly relations with Nasir. When the 'Iraqi monarchy
was destroyed by a military uprising in 1958, Faysal's government
waited a week to recognize the republican regime, while Egypt and
some other Arab countries extended immediate recognition, because,
as King Faysal told me, the Saudi house did not want to give the impression that it was pleased with the downfall of the rival Hashimi
house. But when the revolt in the Yaman failed to eliminate royal
rule in 1962 and Egypt sent a force to help Yamani republicans
against royalists, Faysal protested on the ground that the choice of
government was the privilege of the Yamani people. When Nasir continued to help the Yamani republicans, Faysal came to the support
of the royalists, and the civil war continued until the Arab-Israeli
war of 1967 forced Egypt to withdraw her forces from the Yaman,
leaving the two factions to reach a *modus vivendi* about the internal
regime. Had Faysal not protested against intervention in the domestic affairs of the Yaman, the revolutionary movement might have en-
gulfed Arabia and spread further to other Arab lands. As a positive
step to counteract the spread of revolutionary ideas, Faysal called on
Muslim heads of state to cooperate on a regional basis to protect
their independence and territorial integrity. Since he called on Islamic as well as Arab countries to cooperate, he invoked Islamic
principles as the common ground for cooperation among them.
This neo-Pan-Islamic policy, designed to align Muslim nations
against foreign aggression, came to be known as the policy of Islamic "solidarity." Although denounced as a reactionary policy by
most of the revolutionary leaders because of its opposition to
communist activities, it was in fact opposed to any form of foreign
intervention in Islamic lands. When Egypt, Syria, and Jordan were
attacked by Israel in 1967, Faysal was moved by the same spirit of
Islamic solidarity to lend political and material assistance to these
countries, notwithstanding the fact that their leaders had criticized
him for advocating an Islamic policy. And again in 1969 when the
Aqsa Mosque in Jerusalem was partially destroyed by fire, he called
an Islamic summit conference at which a resolution censuring Israel
for failure to protect Islamic sacred shrines was adopted (Jerusalem

has always been held in highest reverence by Muslims, second only to Makka and Madina).[20]

V

"King Faysal says very firmly," writes de Gaury, "that he learnt politics from his father and his father used to say equally firmly that there was one thing he knew better than all others and in which he had no rival and that was in the handling of the bedouin."[21] Faysal may not have become a master in the handling of Baduins to rival his father; he learned just enough to understand their problems. He also learned some other skills which his country needed when it had just begun to change under the impact of the sudden flow of new riches. His father's contribution to internal stability and unity were indeed invaluable, but these achievements had to be carried to their logical conclusion if the country was to survive after him.

Possessing leadership qualities as well as the intent to achieve reforms, Faysal succeeded just in time to continue his father's constructive work. Unlike the Mufti, who was a strict traditionalist, Faysal's long experience, patience, and discretion enabled him to pursue practical methods which would keep a nexus with the past and provide the necessary reform to bring his country into the modern world. Unlike Sa'ud, whose preoccupation with foreign ventures resulted in his neglect of internal affairs, he tried to pay increased attention to domestic problems. Because he possesses a high sense of duty and consciously tries to devote most of his time to official work, he perhaps has overworked himself by looking into all matters of detail. Although he has a number of able men around him—competent Cabinet ministers, palace counselors, and assistants—he tries to take up every matter himself and to make the final decision. This procedure might seem tedious and slow, but his meticulousness and his desire to do the right thing according to

[20] For Faysal's views on foreign policy and the political system, see *al-Watha'iq al-'Arabiya,* 1963, pp. 683-86; 1964, pp. 467, 537-38; 1965, pp. 127-28; 1967, pp. 76-77, 100-102, 111-12, 171-72, 308, 619-21, 713-14. See some of Faysal's speeches in Amin Sa'id, *Faysal al-'Azim,* pp. 351 ff; and a translation of some of these speeches in de Gaury, *Faisal,* pp. 152 ff.

[21] De Gaury, *Faisal,* p. 57.

his lights have induced him to undertake an even greater amount
of work and responsibility than his father, who often distributed
work to others to enable them to learn from experience. Faysal is
a demanding person and can be a difficult master for those who
work with him; but he is also fair, straightforward, and considerate.
He also keeps his promises, and reproaches others for failure to do
so.

Faysal, considering his primary duty to serve his countrymen,
has followed his father's example of simplicity and accessibility. He
is willing to see his subjects and to discuss with them some of their
problems.[22] This method of keeping in touch with his countrymen,
if a ruler can afford to maintain it, certainly endears him to them
since it shows a personal interest in their affairs and enables him to
know at first hand what they want. In Arabia, it is a tradition that
tribal chiefs should attend to the needs of their followers themselves,
a tradition that Ibn Sa'ud strictly adhered to and expected his sons
to follow. Despite pressure of work, Faysal is still available to hear
directly his subjects' complaints or requests.

To this day, Faysal still looks like a tribal shaykh; he has kept
his Arab dress and manners without adopting the styles of monarchy.
True, he is officially the King of the country and the press refers to
him with honorific words, but tribal shaykhs still address him as
they used to address his father, because he is one of them: *primus
inter pares.*[23] In foreign countries, he has traveled in Arab dress
and has carried on conversations with foreign heads of state and
government with ease and dignity. From early times he has maintained naturalness, patience, and discretion during foreign visits,
which make him not only a good representative for his country but
also a good diplomat.

Faysal's moderation—in word and deed—has proved to be his
greatest asset. It is true that both extreme traditionalists and radical
modernists have been impatient with his methods—the first have
denounced him as easy with the licentious and the second as too

[22] "If anyone feels wrongly treated," he often said, "he has only himself to blame for not
telling me."

[23] King Faysal told me that his father did not like to be called king; this title was thrust
upon him by notables when they gave him the *bay'a* (fealty) as ruler of Najd and the Hijaz
after the two countries were united. To the puritanical Baduins in particular, the words
"His Majesty" were foreign, and in a remark to one of them Ibn Sa'ud confessed that he
did not want or like to be called "His Majesty."

slow in carrying out reform; but these form a relatively small section of society and do not really represent the prevailing opinion. And yet the danger has often come from a small and active minority which presses hard to impose its views on the majority, as the puritanical Ikhwan (the extreme Wahhabis) tried to do under Ibn Sa'ud's rule and the revolutionary leaders are doing today in some other Arab countries. Faysal has not been unaware of these dangers and has tried to avoid them by giving some concessions to extremists. Actions taken to pacify the traditionalists, who often insist on the observance of strict religious practices, are carried out under the supervision of the Committee on Public Morality; and to appease the modernists, he has offered some high governmental posts and control over the newly established institutions of higher learning to young men anxious to carry out rapid reform.

Faysal has been fortunate in that the country's resources are fairly adequate to meet its fundamental demands, at least on the material level, without burdening the country with foreign debts which might carry in their train foreign influence. It is, indeed, Faysal's moderation in foreign and domestic policy that saved the country from overcommitting itself in foreign ventures, on the one hand, and from overspending on development and reconstruction, which might create internal social upheavals, on the other. Witnessing the extravagant spending in some rich Arab countries, Faysal, by cutting his own expenditures, set the example of moderation for others. True, the pace of his country's development is relatively slow, but it may well be in the long run the safest method, if Saudi Arabia is to remain immune from military uprisings.

Faysal's fundamental task, as he sees it, is to consolidate a relatively moderate social polity which will insure progress, stability, and relative prosperity. He is not concerned, as he has often reiterated in public, about what particular form of government his people, or indeed the people of any other Arab country, should choose. His view about government is, as Alexander Pope put it, that

> For forms of government let fools contest;
> Whate'er is best administered is best.

CHAPTER VII

The Realistic School
Habib Bourguiba

C'est le role difficile du chef responsable de voir plus loin que les militants, d'avoir *une échelle des valeurs juste,* de sacrifier le secondaire au principal, de sacrifier même ses préférences ou ses rancunes personnelles en vue d'assurer la durée, la force, et partant, *l'efficacité* d l'ensemble.

Bourguiba

Habib Bourguiba (Abu Ruqayba) stands almost unique among contemporary Arab leaders because of his use of political methods which, though acceptable to his followers, have aroused grave concern in other quarters. These methods have brought him into sharp conflicts with other Arab leaders, despite the fact that the goals which he sought to achieve for his country were not essentially different from the goals of other Arab countries. He was denounced by Arab nationalists, including even some moderate leaders, as a tool of imperialism, and by revolutionary leaders as a traitor to Arab nationalism. However, if his methods are weighed in terms of the realities of life, it is clear that they enabled him to achieve his country's independence before other French North African dependencies and to put his country peacefully along the path of progress and stability, including the adoption of radical reform measures.

Why, it may be asked, was Bourguiba's image so tarnished in contemporary Arab eyes and what was the real man? What were

Habib Bourguiba

the essential elements constituting his political methods, often summed up as the doctrine of Bourguibism, and what were the drives and circumstances which shaped them? In an effort to assess his leadership, we shall address ourselves first to the origins and development of Bourguiba's methods, and then to his role in pursuit of his country's national goals and the national goals of other Arab lands.

Bourguiba's political approach has been to achieve national goals by the method of "gradualism," a step-by-step process in which each step is designed to break new ground and lead to the next logical step until his countrymen are eventually set along the path of normal progress that has been established by advanced nations. This method, according to Bourguiba, is a perpetual "struggle for positions." As he explained it to me, when the first position is won, it must be consolidated before the next is undertaken; then other positions may be taken and in turn consolidated. Thus the perennial struggle toward national goals must proceed.

This method, simple though it may seem at the outset, is a complicated process in practice. It presupposes the existence of a set of favorable conditions: a common belief in the justice of the cause for which the nation is struggling, the requisite qualities of leadership, and the nation's response to the leader's call to carry on the struggle as he moves from one position to another. Bourguiba believed that his countrymen, though seemingly submissive to foreign control, possessed the essential qualities necessary to embark on a national struggle, such as the awareness of their own distinct national character, their unique religious and cultural values, and the existence of an underlying bitter feeling of humiliation and injured pride generated by foreign rule. Bourguiba was able to offer the kind of leadership that would bring these vital elements into operation so as to achieve his country's national aspirations. Aware of the dangers of power politics, he relied at the outset on his country's national potentials without exposing his people to conflicts among the Great Powers. He possessed firmness and perseverance combined with optimism and hope in the ultimate victory of the national cause and was able to commit his country to achieve national goals step by step regardless of how long this struggle might take. He was not unaware of the dangers of this long and protracted process. The struggle for a single position could take a very long time, and before it was finally achieved and another struggle begun, some of his followers, disheartened and despairing, might falter and desert him. He made these possibilities crystal clear to his countrymen in order to avoid frustration, and he constantly reminded them that conviction of the justice of the national cause would bring about ultimate victory. His optimism was an unfailing source of inspiration for a generation of crusaders whom he inspired to carry on the struggle from one position to another.

By relying on the national potentials and mobilizing public support in the struggle for positions, Bourguiba did not necessarily mean that he should come into conflict with his country's rulers; rather he argued that the door should always be thrown open for conciliation and cooperation in order to press for the next step. He consciously tried to avoid deadlocks, unless his opponents reneged on an already won position or denied a concession already promised. Otherwise, Bourguiba would never shut the door for negotiation. Like Mu'awiya, the Arab Governor of Syria and the founder of the Umayyad line of caliphs in the seventh century of the Christian era, he would never interrupt a dialogue with an adversary. Mu'awiya is reputed to have said: if there existed between my adversary and myself even a camel's hair, I would not cut it off; if he pulled the hair, I would loosen it; if he loosened it, I would pull it. In like manner, Bourguiba never consciously tried to interrupt a dialogue with the French, even when they imprisoned him; he always pressed for negotiation, knowing well that whenever the French were ready to negotiate, they would give a concession which he would accept and consolidate as a stepping stone in preparation for the next.

Perhaps Bourguiba favored a dialogue with the French because he felt that France was and would remain the natural friend and ally of Tunisia; Tunisia needed France far more than France needed Tunisia. Much as he sought to bring pressure on France to give concessions, he tried to avoid going so far as to break relations with her. Convinced that the rational and logical argumentations characteristic of the French people would prevail in the end, he strove to reason with them and to prevail on their leaders to concede some of Tunisia's national demands on the ground that cooperation between the two countries would bring advantages to both.

He was, however, well aware that occasionally the French, like other nations, might not react favorably to reasoning and might not concede even a small advantage. Resort to some pressure might then be necessary. Under these circumstances, he would turn to world public opinion—to Arab and Asian nations, to the United States and Great Britain, and finally to the United Nations. But these were always tactical moves, since he invariably returned to direct negotiations whenever France showed herself amenable to them. He realized that France's readiness to recognize Tunisia's national demands would be the direct way to ultimate independence. But he did not entirely exclude the use of pressure to influence France to negotiate, since, to Bourguiba, agreement to negotiate meant that France was ready to concede a national demand.

The strength of Bourguiba's position lay in his flexibility and readiness to compromise. He did not deny essential French interests in matters of defense or foreign policy. Believing that Tunisia's interests were closely tied up with French—and Western—interests, he was quite ready to allow France to preserve her right to defend his country against foreign aggression and to orient the foreign policy of his country toward French (and Western) foreign policy. Bourguiba has always been a firm believer in a pro-Western policy, because French and Western policies coincided with his own views on foreign policy and the Cold War. For this reason he was able to win not only the support of liberal elements in France for his country's national goals but also the support of Great Britain and the United States.[1]

Bourguiba maintained that he derived his political methods from his own political experiences and from a critical study of the methods of former and contemporary Tunisian leaders who had engaged in a futile national struggle with impractical methods. But Bourguiba's methods were not unprecedented in the Arab world. In 'Iraq, King Faysal I, who was able to achieve his country's independence in 1932 by peaceful methods, thought it more prudent to follow a flexible policy with Great Britain and accept what Britain was prepared to concede through negotiations, always continuing to press for further concessions as circumstances would al-

---

[1] Bourguiba's political views and methods are to be found expounded in many of his published articles and public speeches before and after independence. See Habib Bourguiba, *La Tunisie et la France* (Paris, 1954); Bourguiba, *Hadith al-Jum'a* [Fridays' Talks], ed. Ahmad al-Ratimi (Tunis, 1957); and other speeches, published separately in booklets in Arabic, French, and English. See also Bourguiba, "The Tunisian Way," *Foreign Affairs*, Vol. 44 (1966), pp. 480-88.

low, until he obtained independence for his country and membership in the League of Nations.[2]

No less important were Bourguiba's own temperament and upbringing, which were well suited to the role he was called upon to
play in the struggle for national liberation. These qualities as well
as the circumstances and favorable opportunities that he fully exploited helped him to achieve national goals beyond the expectations of many of his followers, and he has lived long enough not
only to occupy the highest position in his country after independence but also to preside over the shaping of future policies.

II

Bourguiba's doctrine of gradualism was not a set of abstract
principles laid down before he entered politics in 1929 but a
flexible political method the constituent elements of which evolved
in his mind as he became involved in his country's struggle for national freedom. This method has been continuously refined and
improved by Bourguiba as he gained experience from his successes
and frustrations. Not unnaturally, the horizon of national objectives widened as Bourguiba and his followers advanced from one
position to another. The outcome of this pragmatic approach justified Bourguiba's commitment to it, as it demonstrated to the satisfaction of Tunisian nationalists that it achieved substantial national
goals.

From the very beginning, when Bourguiba entered politics, he
was struck by the chasm between the two extreme demands which
were driving his countrymen apart: the Tunisian nationalists' insistence on independence and the French pursuit of a policy of coloniza-
tion and steadily increasing control. True, he noted, France was still
in law only a protecting power and Tunisian sovereignty was recognized under the Bardo and La Marsa treaties (1881 and 1883). But
the extent to which French domination had penetrated during the

---

[2] "He followed a policy aptly called in Arabic 'take and ask,' or, in Western terminology,
'step by step.' This moderate approach to Anglo-'Iraqi relations proved not only more advantageous to 'Iraq, but it also fitted well into the pattern of British colonial policy, which
allowed dependencies to develop toward self-government by a slow and peaceful method"
(see my *Independent 'Iraq* [2nd ed.; London, 1960], p. 5). See also Sati 'al-Husri, *Safahat
Min al-Madi al-Qarib* [Pages from the Recent Past] (Bayrut, 1948), pp. 16 ff.

span of a half century rendered the power of Tunisia's head of state and its ministers merely nominal; real power rested in the hands of the French proconsul and his staff. It became abundantly clear to Bourguiba that while the nationalist leaders continued merely to stress Tunisia's legitimate claim to sovereign independence (Istiqlal), which the French had never contested in principle, the country was gradually slipping from Tunisian to French hands. French control of the country was implemented by a policy of gradual assimilation. The French authorities not only imposed their language and culture on the Tunisians but also encouraged them to opt for French nationality, since the French colonizers—the colons— were relatively few and could not possibly dominate the country until a substantial number of Tunisians had become French both in culture and in nationality. The ultimate aim of this policy in Tunisian eyes was to extinguish Tunisian national identity as a step toward the country's becoming part of France. Bourguiba realized the futility of the extremist demands for independence and argued that the immediate aim of nationalist activities should be the reversal of the process of assimilation. He urged his fellow nationalists (leaders of the Dustur Party) to insist that France honor her obligations under the Bardo Treaty and protect the fundamental rights of Tunisians under the protectorate and not to indulge in fruitless agitation for independence. The first step in this practical approach, Bourguiba pointed out, was to ask the French authorities to stop their discrimination between Tunisians and the French colons and to abandon their endeavors to lure Tunisians to opt for French nationality. He naturally realized that unless Tunisians themselves refused to become French nationals he could not possibly prevent the French authorities from granting French citizenship if it were demanded. To achieve this practical step, Bourguiba and his followers began to write in their party's organ, *L'Action Tunisienne,* articles stressing the cultural and national identity of their country which would inspire pride in its history and traditions.

However, the French offer of French nationality carried with it certain privileges, essentially financial, which not all Tunisians were prepared to turn down.[3] Some had already become French

---

[3] French citizens were entitled to the so-called *tiers colonial,* which meant an increase of some 30 percent of the salary of Frenchmen serving abroad. Consequently, anyone who became a French citizen (even if he was born in Tunisia) would be eligible for this privilege.

citizens and showed readiness to renounce their national identity after the French authorities issued decrees in 1920 extending to Tunisians the opportunity of becoming French nationals with all the rights and privileges of the colons. This action caused commotion in nationalist circles, but no serious step was then undertaken to discourage those who were prepared to cross nationality barriers.

In 1932 there seemed to have been an increasing number of Tunisians who were prepared to give up their nationality when the French authorities intensified their activities to win them over. The Italian, Greek, and Maltese residents in Tunisia had already become French citizens, and now Tunisian intellectuals and government functionaries were encouraged to share the privileges of this new status without changing their religion on the strength of a *fatwa* (legal opinion) given by one of the pro-French religious shaykhs. To counter this, Bourguiba and his party secured a *fatwa* from another learned shaykh who opined that any Muslim who died as a French national had lost his right to be buried in a Muslim cemetery because, by changing his nationality, he had forfeited his religious privileges. The indignation and public controversy which Bourguiba and his followers were able to stir up among the people induced the French authorities to modify their position and to accept an agreement to the effect that Tunisians who had opted for French nationality would be buried not with other Muslims but in a special corner of the same cemetery. Bourguiba regarded this compromise as a victory for his party since it demonstrated that nationalist stirrings could influence France to grant concessions. Insignificant as this gain may seem, it is precisely what he sought to achieve—the winning of one step at a time.

This "victory," for which Bourguiba congratulated himself, failed to impress the leaders of the Dustur Party, who doubted the real value of his political method. Some were disappointed with the compromise because it still permitted Tunisians who had become French nationals to be buried within the compound of the Muslim cemetery. In January 1934, Bourguiba was taken to task by the Dustur leaders in the town of Qasr Hilal (Ksar Hellal) because he had taken unilateral action in reaching agreement with the French authorities. He was denied even the right to defend himself, and it was decided that he had either to abandon his fruitless political methods or to part company with the Dustur leaders. From January to March controversy raged between the older and younger

Dustur leaders, ending only when the younger leaders decided (March 2, 1934) to organize a new political bureau of the Dustur Party under the leadership of Bourguiba; this became the nucleus of the Neo-Dustur Party.

This incident, which marked the transfer of leadership from inflexible to dynamic and dexterous hands, proved to be the turning point in Bourguiba's political career and gave him the opportunity to regenerate Tunisia's national struggle with new and vigorous methods. Released from the ties of older leadership, Bourguiba had no inhibition against embarking on a direct appeal to the Tunisian people and arousing their indignation against discriminatory actions. He inspired them with confidence and national pride to demand equality of opportunity with the privileged colons. Strikes and demonstrations against specific incidents of persecution and injustice necessarily led to clashes with the police, although Bourguiba always warned his countrymen against the use of violence. However, whenever violence was committed, Bourguiba never disclaimed responsibility, even though it might have been instigated by extremists, but he put ultimate blame on the French authorities themselves because of their denial of legitimate and just national demands. Under the laws and regulations of the protectorate, Bourguiba was liable to arrest and banishment, but he seems to have welcomed exile, as it enhanced his prestige and renown among his countrymen. Of the twenty years spent in the struggle for national freedom, from the time of his entry into politics to his last imprisonment in France in 1952, he is reputed to have spent almost half in detention or exile.

In September 1934, Bourguiba experienced the first of a series of arrests and exiles following a clash between a band of demonstrators and the police. He was banished to a village in the southern part of the country, where he spent the next two years. But he was not out of touch with his followers, especially Salih Bin Yusuf and other young leaders, who continued to inspire protests and demonstrations against French actions. The exile of two years, as Bourguiba told the present writer, was a period of "rupture" (al-Qati'a) of contacts between nationalist leaders and the French authorities, but he was determined to discontinue negative maneuvers whenever the French were ready to compromise and negotiate with him. On June 10, 1936, he published a set of proposals, declared to be minimum national demands, which the Dustur Party had laid down and presented to the French; they consisted in part of the rights of the Tunisian people to determine their national budget and to enact laws by a representative assembly within the framework of the protectorate's constitutional regime. They also included requests to issue a new nationality law for Tunisians and to release political prisoners and several other items relating to financial, judicial, social, and educational reforms.[4] In October 1936, Bourguiba went directly to the French capital to present these demands to Pierre Viénot, Under-Secretary of State for Foreign Affairs in the newly formed government of the Popular Front of Leon Blum, with whom he seems to have come to an understanding on the future relationship between France and Tunisia within the framework of the protectorate.[5] The Blum government was then engaged in negotiations with nationalist leaders of the Levant countries with a view to granting them independence and was considering the possibilities of granting some similar liberal concessions to Tunisia and Morocco. It was in accordance with these liberal promises that Bourguiba returned early in September to call with enthusiasm upon his countrymen to cooperate with the French authorities. This step, in Bourguiba's calculations, was another newly won "position" on the basis of which he and his party were to open a new chapter in French-Tunisian relations.

However, this was a short-lived French promise. The fall of Leon Blum from power in 1937 resulted in the breakdown not only of negotiations for the independence of the Levant countries but also of the rapprochement with Tunisian leaders. On his part, Bourguiba considered the French reluctance to pursue the negotiations (which he had become aware of even before the fall of Leon Blum) a breach of faith which justified a rupture in the dialogue that had just been initiated. The break in negotiations resulted in renewed strikes and demonstrations, which continued for the next two years and eventually provoked the French authorities to punitive measures. They ordered the arrest not only of Bourguiba but also of a number of other leaders, including Bahi al-Adgham and al-

[4] For a summary of these demands, see Tunisia, Department of Information and Guidance, al-Habib Bourguiba: Hayatuh, Jihaduh [Habib Bourguiba: His Life, His Struggle] (Tunis, 1966), pp. 62-63.

[5] For an account of the Bourguiba-Viénot conversations and text of the proposals submitted to Viénot, see Bourguiba, La Tunisie et la France, pp. 77-83, 83-90.

Munji Salim (Mongi Slim).[6] After this arrest, Bourguiba was to
spend the next five years in detention or exile in Tunisia, France,
and Italy, but he did not remain completely idle. In 1942, after his
capture by the Germans, he was handed over to the Italians in the
vain hope that he might be a quisling.

Exile and internment, uncomfortable though they may have
been, made no change in Bourguiba's conviction that his country's
ultimate freedom would depend on cooperation with France rather
than secret dealings with France's enemies regardless of his political
convictions. Despite lavish Axis promises, which might have tempted
lesser leaders to collaborate, Bourguiba remained faithful to his conviction that democracy rather than dictatorship was the answer for
his country, and he instructed his followers in secret dispatches to
lend their support to the democratic rather than the Axis powers.
It is to his credit that not only did Bourguiba pin his hopes on the
ultimate victory of the democratic countries, as he stated in one of
his letters to a nationalist leader in 1942, but also that his personal
convictions were based on democratic rather than totalitarian principles.[7]

No sooner had Bourguiba returned to his country on April 7,
1943, after an Allied victory over Axis forces in Tunisia, than he
resumed the struggle for national freedom by cooperating with
France to form a Franco-Tunisian bloc.[8] But despite his willingness
to cooperate, he was rebuffed by the Free French desire to reestablish France's hegemony in his country. He and his followers continued their internal resistance, and he also foresaw the value of
bringing the Tunisian question to the attention of the world and to
the United Nations in which the new countries of Asia and Africa
had begun to exert an increasing influence. For this reason Bourguiba
left his country reluctantly in 1945 for an extended tour of the
Middle East, Western Europe, and the United States, during which

[6] See *ibid.,* pp. 106 ff, 168-72. Reasons for the arrest of other leaders varied from political
agitation in support of Bourguiba to underground activities prohibited by law.

[7] See the text of the letter sent by Bourguiba to Habib Thamir, leader of Tunisia's underground resistance movement, dated August 8, 1942, in Bourguiba, *La Tunisie et la France,*
pp. 177-82.

[8] *Ibid.,* pp. 184-87. Bourguiba was released from French military detention by the Germans in November 1942, and was handed over to the Italian authorities in the hope that
he might collaborate with them. He returned to Tunisia on April 7, 1943, a month before
the Axis defeat in North Africa.

he was in constant touch with Arab, European, and American political circles in an effort to bring pressure on France to negotiate
with Tunisian nationalist leaders. Nor did he fail to appeal directly
to French public opinion. After his return to Tunisia in 1949, he
went to Paris in 1950 and established contact with French political
leaders, the Socialist Party in particular, who received him and gave
him a sympathetic hearing. The Socialist leaders apparently promised support of Tunisian demands to terminate the protectorate
regime and to replace it with a Franco-Tunisian treaty of alliance
in which the two countries would cooperate in defense, financial,
cultural, and foreign affairs. These efforts, coupled with continuous
pressure from nationalist circles, inspired France to meet some of
Tunisia's national demands. But it was not until Mendes-France,
leader of the Radical Socialist Party, had come to power in 1954
that negotiations between the French government and nationalist
leaders were resumed. After long negotiations followed by a visit
of Mendes-France to Tunisia in 1954, a treaty was finally signed on
June 3, 1955, giving Tunisia home rule, or full control of internal
affairs. This was another step toward final independence in which
Bourguiba demonstrated the practical value of his step-by-step method. Nevertheless, the new French agreement was criticized by none
other than Salih Bin Yusuf, a great supporter of Bourguiba, on the
ground that the agreement did not recognize Tunisia's right to independence. Bin Yusuf, who enjoyed a considerable following in the
country, seems to have contemplated a bid for power and therefore
to have tried to discredit Bourguiba for failure to press for immediate
independence. The rivalry between the two leaders was finally settled
by a vote of confidence in Bourguiba's favor, and Salih Bin Yusuf
left the country to resume the personal struggle against Bourguiba,
in the course of which he was brutally assassinated. Further negotiations in 1955 and 1956, in which Bourguiba pressed for the
abrogation of the protectorate agreements, resulted in France's
final recognition of Tunisia's independence (March 20, 1956),
which again proved the value of his gradualist method. The height
of his political career was reached when he became the head of government in 1956 and the head of state in 1959—worthy rewards
which he could scarcely have dreamed of a decade before.

After independence, when French domination no longer remained the concern of national struggle, Bourguiba's doctrine of

gradualism was completely vindicated, especially inside his own country. He began to encounter disenchantment in other circles, however, entirely different from the criticism he had known before. Bourguiba had no difficulty in persuading his own followers to pursue the same methods in the internal reorganization and development of the country after independence, but he was not able to persuade the Arab leaders in other Arab countries to accept his methods. In addition, the rising tide of the Arab revolutionary movement began to affect the new generation in Tunisia, which questioned the validity of his methods for achieving social reform. Before we assess these new social forces, let us discuss Bourguiba's personality and character as related to his leadership.

III

Countries undergoing rapid social change afford an opportunity to potential political leaders to play a role in politics if they possess the qualities necessary to appreciate the working of underlying forces. Before French occupation, Tunisia was governed by dynasts and legionnaires who, when the country passed under French control, found it in their interest to seek an accommodation with the French rather than to oppose them. Religion and tribalism were the major elements of North African culture; in time they were crushed by foreign forces and thus became an ineffective base for leadership. It was from the rising force of nationalism that new leaders appeared. Bourguiba, possessing the requisite qualities for the new leadership, succeeded where the old leaders failed because he epitomized hopes and expectations which had been suppressed since his country passed under foreign influence.

Bourguiba was born in Munastir on August 3, 1902, in a home quite modest in means. Though respectable in social status, the family was not regarded as middle class even by local standards. The place of birth, family background, and the social milieu in which Bourguiba grew up had an impact on his life and helped in no small measure to shape his future political career and orientation.

Bourguiba's parentage belonged neither to a class whose fortune was closely tied to the French authorities and the colons nor to the workers and peasants who formed the lower and dissatisfied strata of society. Thus, Bourguiba owed no patronage to the French, nor did he look upon those in authority, especially the Bey, with favor. In fact, his grandfather took part in a rebellion against the Bey, although it must also be remembered that his father, 'Ali, who was recruited into the Bey's small armed force, participated in the suppression of that rebellion in 1865. 'Ali's services earned him promotion to the rank of second lieutenant before he retired in 1881, following the establishment of the French protectorate and the disbanding of the native army. In 1893, he served again under the Bey's administration as an agent in one of the villages, but he resigned four years later for reasons not altogether clear. Needless to say, the Bourguiba family, though humble in status, could feel relatively secure with its meager income and an association with the native authorities. Seven children, including two girls, were born to the family. Habib Bourguiba was the youngest.

A second significant influence was Bourguiba's birthplace. He was born in a town in the Sahil, the seaboard extending from the northeast to the south. The Sahil has provided its inhabitants with a fairly fertile land and commercial ties with the outside world since ancient times, which enabled them to develop a relatively advanced way of life. The urban centers of the Sahil, essentially small towns and villages, may be regarded as the backbone of the country and the source of its ruling elite. Life in the Sahil manifested greater family solidarity than in the interior desert area, where tribal traditions had presented a challenge to local authorities for centuries. Bourguiba, though not really a member of the well-established families of the Sahil, grew up with the traditions of family solidarity that characterized the region; when he entered the political scene he was imbued with a sense of loyalty not only to the coastal region but, more important, to the country as a whole.

The traditions of self-help and family solidarity enabled Bourguiba first to enter school in the country's capital, where one or two of his brothers were making a living, and then to pursue his studies in France. After his return to Tunisia, Bourguiba began to climb the social pyramid on his own, armed with a solid French education.

Before he went to France, Bourguiba received his primary education first in the Sadiki School, established by the Bey, and then in the Carnot Lycée, a school based on the French system of education. His mother, to whom he was devoted, died in 1913 while he was studying in the Sadiki School. Homesickness, hard work under the strict surveillance of an older brother, and inadequate nourishment in school during World War I resulted in the boy's contracting tuberculosis. He spent a short time in the hospital and some two years in a small town in the south where one of his brothers was practicing medicine.

During recuperation, Bourguiba's national pride was aroused by a volume entitled *La Tunisie Martyre,* published by 'Abd al-'Aziz al-Tha'alibi, leader of the old Dustur Party, in which Tunisia's aspirations for freedom and independence were vividly expressed. Thus, at a tender age, Bourguiba was awakened to the hopes of the national movement, and he was determined to return to school to prepare for his own future participation. Bourguiba's patriotic feelings were further stirred when he directly experienced discrimination against Tunisian students in school, although by native intelligence and hard work he was able to demonstrate that a Tunisian could attain as high a scholastic standing as any European student.

While still in school, Bourguiba experienced his first excitement in nationalist activities when, on April 5, 1922, he participated in a popular demonstration organized by the Dustur Party in support of the Bey's powers against French encroachments. Nevertheless, this event proved frustrating for Bourguiba because the demonstration produced no change in Franco-Tunisian relations, although it did arouse French concern. On the same day of the demonstration, Bourguiba is said to have registered his name as a member of the Dustur Party and to have begun to observe the internal affairs of his country with a keen eye. He was impressed in particular with the success of Muhammad 'Ali of Qabis in mobilizing the labor force of his country to form an independent Tunisian labor union and thought that such a force could eventually be directed against French domination in the country. Although Muhammad 'Ali's efforts were frustrated by the French authorities, Bourguiba learned how to stir and organize Tunisian workers and other popular forces.

No less important a set of influences, though having an entirely different effect on Bourguiba's upbringing, was the French environment where he spent three years in college. Until he went to France, Bourguiba's education was essentially traditional, stressing religious and literary subjects, although he did study French and some modern disciplines at the Carnot Lycée. But these disciplines were taught in Tunisia by French teachers who were disdainful toward Tunisian students, as were the colons toward the native Tunisian people. In Paris young Bourguiba found the French people quite different from the colons in Tunisia; he was attracted in particular to the liberal atmosphere of the University of Paris, where he enrolled for study, and to the Quartier Latin, where he lived. He found his professors, as well as some French writers and politicians with whom he had come into contact, quite willing to listen to his account of French actions in Tunisia and was able to arouse their sympathies for his country's national aspirations. Bourguiba's early experiences in Paris were essential for his later career as a political leader when he tried to appeal to French public opinion, since he was convinced that France was ready to listen to his country's national demands.

In the second year of his life in the French capital he met Mathilde Lorrain—a woman sympathetic toward Tunisian nationalist aspirations; they married and had one son, Habib Bourguiba, Jr., who was brought up in the family's tradition of loyalty and who rendered invaluable services first to his father and later to his country. Bourguiba's marriage to a French woman and his French education helped to form an image of France different from that created by his early upbringing—not of an enemy but of a potential friend and ally.

Before Bourguiba resumed his political activities after his return to Tunisia in 1927, he spent two years as a legal apprentice, during which he watched the political scene closely. He noted how weak his country's position was after half a century of foreign domination and realized that it would be impossible for his country to regain independence by a quick and easy method, whether by an uprising or by direct confrontation, since France had established firm control over the country and its resources. Nor was the Tunisian nation yet ready for concerted action, since nationalist leaders possessed neither the will nor the ability to mobilize public opinion, even though the people were quite ready to be stirred against discrimination and injustice. It was precisely for these reasons that Bourguiba and some of his followers revolted against the futile and impractical methods of the old Dustur leaders and were ready to offer their countrymen a new and more aggressive leadership that would champion the cause of the country's needs and aspirations by more effective methods.

Bourguiba was by temperament as well as by upbringing prepared to assume the new leadership. He was full of vitality and dash, but his dynamism and romantic outlook were tempered by academic disciplines and by the rigor of legal training and apprenticeship. While he was a student at the Sorbonne, he once told the present writer, he chose to write papers on Rousseau and Claude Bernard; from each he learned something which improved his training: the first stirred his romantic love for freedom, and the other sharpened his rational, systematic approach to practical problems.

His adoption of the gradualist method in politics was, therefore, the product of both training and experience. Not only did he see the futility of putting forth extreme national demands without the ability to pursue them, as the experiences of the old Dustur leaders demonstrated, but he also well understood the character of the Tunisian people, who preferred peaceful to violent methods. True, the rank and file might often be stirred to strike or demonstrate against authority, but a full-scale uprising, which might receive tribal support, was not a Tunisian way of action. Bourguiba did often stir the public into expressing specific grievances, but he never relied solely on violence, save to display public dissatisfaction. He never professed to be a revolutionary leader; he took pride in the fact that he always sought to negotiate with French leaders.

Bourguiba possessed two other qualities which were well fitted to his political methods. First, he was dedicated to the national cause and convinced of the justness of its claims. This almost instinctively induced him to pursue the national struggle regardless whether the goals for which he worked would be realized in his lifetime, though believing firmly in ultimate victory. Second, he had a realistic and pragmatic approach which qualified him to become a better spokesman for his country's national demands rather than other leaders, although all were agreed on the gradualist approach to national goals.

After independence Bourguiba met no initial opposition to his political methods either in the decolonization of his country or in the pursuit of social and economic development. Given the limited resources of Tunisia, Bourguiba may well be congratulated for obtaining economic assistance from Western countries without binding his country with obligations which would encroach on her independence or sovereignty. His avowed pro-Western orientation in foreign affairs did not prevent the Neo-Dustur Party from adopting socialist measures in 1964 and transforming the economy of the country from a wholly free enterprise system to one based on collectivism and planning. Even the name of the Dustur Party, which in the past emphasized national values, was changed to the Socialist Dustur Party. These gradualist changes were designed to provide incentives for economic expansion and to meet the needs of peasants and workers, who form the bulk of the population, without hurting landowners and small capital investors, whose interests were protected by the maintenance of a private sector. In the late 1960s when Ahmad Bin Salih, in a drive for power, pursued further socialist measures to win support of wage earners, Bourguiba's prudence prompted him first to restrict Bin Salih's actions and then to drop him from power in order to keep a balance between socialism and free enterprise. Thus the principle of gradualism prevailed over radical actions.

In his effort to insure that his ideas would continue to reign after him, Bourguiba, together with Dustur leaders, completely reorganized the internal structure of the state to insure the monopoly of power by one party, presided over by the all-powerful Bourguiba. These authoritarian trends left no room for opposition and virtually brought all national institutions under direct or indirect state control, although Bourguiba often allowed—some say even encouraged— "loyal opposition" within the Dustur Party. Once the party decided on the measures to be adopted, they were carried out without opposition in the legislative and executive branches of the government. These actions, although regarded as essentially in accordance with gradualist methods, have aroused criticism among liberal elements and caused widespread disenchantment among the new generation.[9] No less trenchant criticism has been directed against Bourguiba's policy toward the other Arab countries, especially his quarrels with the revolutionary Arab leaders over Arab national and international problems. These issues have tended to isolate Tunisia from the so-called procession of Arab nationalism and have reflected on the

[9]Criticism of authoritarian trends led to public debate in June 1970 with a view to limiting presidential powers. In 1971, Bourguiba, owing to poor health, actually handed over much of his power to his First Minister.

validity of the Bourguiba doctrine for domestic affairs by stressing its personal and parochial orientation.[10]

IV

In his relations with other Arab countries, Bourguiba tried to urge upon Arab leaders the pursuit of the same realistic and gradualist methods which he had applied to Tunisia. His brilliant success in the service of his country naturally merits consideration by other Arab leaders. However, his counsel and admonitions were often either bluntly rejected or ignored, a fact which reflected on his image in Arab lands and his prestige in Tunisia itself. Bourguiba reacted either by boycotting Arab summit and regional meetings or by recalling his senior diplomatic representatives from major Arab countries. These moves, though often intended only as warnings, had at least two unfavorable effects.

First, Bourguiba's actions tended to break the solidarity among Arab leaders and to isolate his country from the rest of the Arab world. His policy appeared to be too parochial and tended to subordinate Arab collective interests to Tunisia's particular interests. Second, Bourguiba's conflicts with other Arab leaders unavoidably tended to undermine Bourguiba's own position in his country and encouraged critics, especially the intelligentsia and younger leaders, to become more vocal in their opposition to the growing authoritarian tendencies of the one-party system and to Bourguiba himself as the all-powerful leader. As a result, an intense struggle for power within the party ensued, in which each leader tried to discredit the other because of an increasing dissatisfaction in the country with government policies. Bourguiba could not avoid being involved in this struggle, which adversely affected his influence and his health as he grew older.

It may seem surprising to outside observers that Bourguiba, who had succeeded more than many other Arab leaders in achieving his country's fundamental national goals, should be discredited and his image tarnished in Arab eyes. Bourguiba may eventually be

[10] For studies on Bourguiba's life, see Felix Garas, *Bourguiba et la Naissance d'une Nation* (Paris, 1956); Jean Rous, *Habib Bourguiba* (Paris, 1969); W. K. Ruf, *Der Burgibismus und die Aussenpolitik des unabhängigen Tunesien* (Germany, 1969).

seen in a good light again; at this juncture, however, an explanation of his image in Arab eyes is called for.

Perhaps by coincidence, Bourguiba achieved his country's independence and entered into an alliance with France in 1956, the very year in which the tripartite attack on Egypt took place and in which Arab feeling against France and England for their collusion in the Israeli attack ran very high. While some of the Arab countries, Egypt and Syria in particular, severed diplomatic relations with England and France, and some, like 'Iraq, broke off relations only with France, Tunisia did neither. At the same time that Nasir was launching a campaign against Western influence in Arab lands, France was allowed to continue enjoying her privileges in Tunisia. As a result, Bourguiba appeared to Arab eyes to be ready to subordinate Arab rights to his country's interests and to fraternize with the enemies of the Arabs. Whatever Bourguiba's inner feelings and sympathies with Arab nationalism may have been, his failure to join with the rest of the Arab world against France and England was a telling point against him—indeed, his action appeared as treason in the eyes of Arab nationalists.

In the years that followed the tripartite attack, efforts by moderate Arab leaders were made to bring Bourguiba into the Arab fold and to patch up differences. For his part, Bourguiba made it clear that his real feelings were with the Arabs, not with the foreigners, and that the special circumstances which necessitated the alliance with France to obtain his country's freedom did not blind him to the fact that France had committed aggression against a sister Arab country—Egypt. He pointed out that he was bound to honor Tunisia's obligations to France until his country's independence was consolidated, as demonstrated in his subsequent support of Algerian nationalists to obtain their country's independence. Although there had never been close cooperation between Bourguiba and other Arab leaders, especially Nasir, relations among them became on the whole fairly amicable, and formal declarations of support in favor of Arab rights against Western claims were often made.

In 1965 Bourguiba embarked on a tour of eastern Arab countries during which he gave the impression that his initial talks with Arab leaders produced salutary effects among them. But this was to be short-lived. When he visited refugee camps in Jordan in the spring of that year, he made a speech in which he ascribed the misery and sorry plight of the refugees to Arab failure to grasp the reality of their position vis-à-vis Israel and suggested a temporary peaceful arrangement with Israel to alleviate refugee conditions.[11] The somewhat vague and casual remarks about peace with Israel and the fact that he made his feeling public without notifying Arab leaders produced a wave of fire and fury against Bourguiba.[12] Though he spoke candidly and bluntly, Bourguiba did not really call for a final peace settlement with Israel, nor indeed did he call for recognition of Israel or for an acknowledgment of her de facto occupation of Arab territory. He merely suggested a temporary peaceful arrangement to settle the refugee question. In accordance with his gradualist doctrine, Bourguiba's suggestion was only a step or a "position" which might be superseded or replaced by another whenever the Arabs were strong enough to impose their terms on Israel. Long accustomed to a complete defiance of Israeli attacks even if they led to de facto occupation of Arab lands, the Arabs construed Bourguiba's words to mean a surrender to Israeli demands, since any temporary peaceful arrangement with Israel would legitimize her usurpation of Arab lands and property. Bourguiba's call, plausible and realistic though it may seem, especially in Western eyes, was an anathema to the Arabs.

In the light of events subsequent to the Arab-Israeli war of 1967, Bourguiba's warning proved almost prophetic. Nevertheless, Bourguiba was not unsympathetic to his Arab adversaries when they suffered defeat. Not only did he issue statements denouncing Israeli aggression, but he also pleaded for Western support for the Arabs.[13] He thus demonstrated that the ultimate goals of his policies were not essentially different from the goals of other Arab leaders but only that he disagreed with them on the ways and means of achieving them.

[11] See Bourguiba's speeches at Jericho and Jerusalem on March 3 and 4, 1965 (al-Watha'iq al-'Arabiya, 1965, pp. 87-89).

[12] Although Bourguiba had communicated his views about Arab relations with Israel both in private talks and official meetings (see Bourguiba's speeches in Tunis on May 21, 1965, and in Carthage on September 13, 1965), Arab leaders apparently did not expect him to make his views public. For Bourguiba's defense of his position, see his speech in Carthage on March 15, 1969. Bourguiba's speeches are published by the Tunisian government, Department of Culture and Information.

[13] See Bourguiba's speeches on the Arab-Israeli conflict on June 13, 1967; and his interview with a Swedish correspondent on April 16, 1969 (Tunis, 1967 and 1969).

Bourguiba, realizing the weakness of the Arab position, counseled caution and suggested cooperation with friendly Western powers. He was always in favor of pursuing flexible policies and urged Arab leaders to follow similar policies in the hope that they would achieve greater advantages for their peoples. He was, of course, fortunate in leading a people who preferred on the whole peaceful over violent methods and who accepted the slowness of gradualism. Other Arab leaders, especially in the so-called revolutionary countries, were operating on entirely different levels and leading peoples who by their very nature had always tended to be more violent in action.[14] Believing that the human and material resources of their lands could provide the requisite strength for a struggle against the enemy, they were not prepared to wait but threatened to strike at the enemy even under unfavorable circumstances. By a policy of playing off one Great Power (or more) against another, which often did yield some material advantages, they hoped to achieve national goals more quickly than Bourguiba. But in the long run no leader could claim to have achieved for his people more than Bourguiba did—some have even brought disaster and heavy losses to their people. Thus Bourguiba's Arab adversaries proved to be short-run politicians who sought immediate results, while Bourguiba proved on the whole to be more successful in the long run.[15]

[14] See my *Political Trends,* pp. 24-25.

[15] For a defense of Bourguiba's policy toward other Arab countries, see Mahjub Bin Milad, *al-Habib Bourguiba fi Subul al-Hurriya al-Tunisiya* (Tunis, 1968), pp. 9-25.

CHAPTER VIII

The Ideological School—
The Moderates
Kamil al-Chadirchi
and Kamal Junblat

KAMIL AL-CHADIRCHI

The philosophy which I propose to my party is democratic socialism.
Chadirchi

Kamil al-Chadirchi and Kamal Junblat stand unique among professional politicians because they possessed in varying degrees certain aptitudes which might qualify them to be regarded as intellectual politicians. However, during most of their lives, they were so involved in the activities of political parties and in pursuing political objectives that goals were often subordinated to methods—a common characteristic of professional politicians; therefore, they appeared to differ but little from other politicians.

Chadirchi and Junblat possessed many qualities in common, intellectual and otherwise, which might help one to generalize about their political roles, although they operated in two somewhat different social environments and the impact of each on his country may be clearly distinguished from the other. Each will be discussed separately, but their ideas, methods, and imprints will be compared and assessed on the same scale.

Kamil al-Chadirchi

II

Kamil al-Chadirchi was born in 1897 to a well-to-do family and belonged to what may be regarded as an aristocratic house, since his father served in the Ottoman administration and was mayor of the city of Baghdad. The Chadirchis claimed descent from Ottoman stock, but they were assimilated, since they had resided in 'Iraq for some three centuries, and had come to be regarded as indigenous and were as fully identified with the religious and social traditions as any native family. Since religion was the primary loyalty, they professed Sunni Islam, the faith of the ruling class. Possessing ample wealth to afford a decent living, Chadirchi suffered neither depriva-tion nor social insecurity—indeed he made use of some of the estate he had inherited to promote his political activities.

After World War I, when nationalism began to supersede reli-gious loyalty, many Arab leaders became staunch advocates of Pan-Arabism, and some of them claimed Arab tribal origins, real or imaginary. Chadirchi did not adopt the fashionable Pan-Arab ideal, although he and his family had just as much right to claim pan-Arabism as their mode of loyalty as other local leaders.[1] Like some other young men who had fallen under the spell of liberal doctrines, he chose a liberal symbol of loyalty rather than a traditional sym-bol, religious or national, and advocated socialism, which distressed some members of his family.

Chadirchi's early education was neither systematic nor very profound; he received his primary and high school education before the British occupation and served for a short while in the Ottoman army during World War I. After the war, 1919-20, when 'Iraq passed under British occupation, his father apparently took part in some anti-British activities and had to flee the country with his family to escape trial or imprisonment. The Chadirchis spent the next two years in Turkey. Young Chadirchi entered the Istanbul Medical Col-lege, but before completing his studies, he returned to Baghdad when a national regime was established in 1922. He then entered the Baghdad Law College, graduating with a law degree after three years of study.[2] Thus Chadirchi's formal education provided him

---

[1] For Chadirchi's views on Sami Shawkat's claim to Pan-Arabism (Shawkat being of non-Arab origin), see Kamil al-Chadirchi, Ba'th al-Fashiya fi al-'Iraq [Resurrection of Fascism in 'Iraq] (Baghdad, 1946), p. 18.

[2] In 1935 the period of study was extended to four years.

with little more than professional training to serve at the bar or the bench, but his self-education made him quite familiar with most of the books that were then published in Cairo and Bayrut. Although his knowledge of English was at first elementary, he pursued his study of English works with the assistance of friends, especially works dealing with contemporary social and political problems.[3]

Before he entered politics, Chadirchi worked for a short while in the Municipality of Baghdad where his father had served as Mayor and then in the Department of Finance, in charge of the parliamentary division, during 1926-27. This short administrative experience gave him a certain insight into governmental processes, and it opened his eyes to his country's bureaucratic practices and abuses. It also gave him an opportunity to meet some members of Parliament, with whom he was later to be involved in political activities, when he acted as liaison between the legislature and the Ministry of Finance.

In 1927, Chadirchi entered Parliament when he was barely thirty years old. He won the election (which at that time was held under complete governmental control, as were all elections) because his older brother was then a member of the government, not because he espoused a particular political philosophy. In the 1930 elections he lost his parliamentary seat. He did not enter Parliament again until 1936, after independence. At that time he crossed to the left and participated in the coup d'état of 1936, which brought to power the members of his newly adopted political group. He held a Cabinet post for some eight months but resigned in protest against the army's interference in the business of government and remained in relative solitude until World War II. In 1954 he entered Parliament for the last time, only to lose his seat after one meeting of Parliament. To the end of his life, he never again held a public post, even when his party cooperated with other groups to form coalition governments. He preferred to delegate his party's representation to other members of the party—Muhammad Hadid and Husayn Jamil—rather than to take direct responsibility.[4]

Neither in his position in the Cabinet nor in his membership in Parliament should we seek Chadirchi's role in political activities—his

---

[3] For Chadirchi's own account of his early upbringing, see Kamil al-Chadirchi, *Min Awraq Kamil al-Chadirchi* [Some Papers of Kamil al-Chadirchi] (Bayrut, 1971), pp. 16-60.

[4] For an account of Chadirchi's participation in those events, see my *Independent 'Iraq* (2nd ed.; London, 1960), Chap. 9; and my *Republican 'Iraq* (London, 1969), Chap. 6.

impact on his country's politics must be sought first in his leadership of the Ahali group and the National Democratic Party, to which he devoted the best part of his life, and then in the editorship of *Sawt al-Ahali* (Voice of the People), his party's organ, in which he expounded his ideas and carried his party's message to the people.

III

Before he entered Parliament in 1927, Chadirchi had been watching the political scene with a keen interest, and once he became a member, he decided to join Yasin al-Hashimi's opposition party, which was demanding immediate independence. His decision to work with the opposition was indicative of the fact that he did not expect an immediate return from participation in politics. He stood for certain nationalist demands which were then shared by most young men of his generation. He remained loyal to Yasin al-Hashimi for some six or seven years before he crossed party lines. During the first three or four years after he entered politics, Chadirchi's chief preoccupation was with such questions as British control of domestic affairs and the ways and means of achieving independence. Intellectual curiosity led him to read some works on political thought, and he became fascinated with the idea of democracy, which he adopted as a political creed. In one of his articles on sovereignty and democracy, he advocated the need for public participation in a truly parliamentary democracy in order to achieve progress.[5]

Two years after independence, the party to which Chadirchi belonged began to compromise with the 'Iraqi rulers. One of the leading members, Rashid 'Ali al-Gaylani, became Chief of the Royal Palace in 1933, and the leader of the party, Yasin al-Hashimi, became Prime Minister in 1934 after tribal uprisings.[6] In protest, Chadirchi along with several others left the party in 1934.

It may seem strange indeed that Chadirchi should leave a party in the aftermath of victory when he, with other leaders, could have shared the spoils. But Chadirchi was thinking about other things. He felt keenly that his party had abandoned its opposition

---

[5] Kamil al-Chadirchi, "al-Siyada wa al-Dimuqratiya" [Sovereignty and Democracy], *al-Bilad* (Baghdad), August 28, 1931.

[6] For an account of these events, see my *Independent 'Iraq,* pp. 37 ff.

to the Anglo-'Iraqi Treaty of 1930, which in his opinion compromised 'Iraq's sovereignty and violated the party's promise to the public that its members would not accept government posts unless that treaty was revised in 'Iraq's favor. Apart from that, the party had no plans to deal with the country's social and economic problems after independence. Nor could Chadirchi influence older leaders to make such plans since he was a relatively young member, and he despaired of changing their outmoded methods and self-seeking motives.

In 1931 a band of young men who advocated liberal reforms had organized the Ahali group, and their views had excited many younger political figures.[7] They appeared to be the promising leaders of the future, but they had not yet been able to entrust leadership to experienced hands. Chadirchi, impressed by the ideas of this group, aspired to play the role of leader of young men rathei than that of junior partner among older politicians. He joined the group in 1934, two years after independence. Very soon, Chadirchi proved to be the most outstanding leader of the Ahali group and became editor of the party's paper. More experienced in politics, he reorganized the group and gave it a sense of cohesion and direction, although in the process he came into personal conflict with one of the founders, who left the group in protest.[8] Under his influence, a number of older politicians, who had become disillusioned with the ruling oligarchy, joined the group in order to enhance its prestige and spread liberal views in wider circles. This quick enlargement of the group induced army officers to give it their sudden and unexpected support; they promised to carry out the Ahali ideas by overthrowing the ruling oligarchy and entrusting power to Ahali hands. Resort to the army as an agent for reform brought disastrous results and distorted the group's goals, but it did teach the Ahali leaders a lesson—to pursue peaceful methods. Chadirchi began to urge the founding of a political party which would advocate reform through legal channels, but political parties were not permitted by 'Iraqi rulers until after World War II.

---

[7] For the Ahali movement and its political ideas, see my *Independent 'Iraq,* pp. 96 ff; and *Political Trends in the Arab World* (Baltimore, 1970), pp. 105-7.

[8] 'Abd al-Fattah Ibrahim, an outstanding member of the Ahali group and author of some of its publications, left it shortly after Chadirchi had become the dominant leader. See my *Independent 'Iraq,* p. 73.

Before the Ahali leaders were able to organize a political party, they held several meetings during 1942 to reformulate political goals. They learned that Sir Stafford Cripps, a member of the Labour Party and the newly appointed Viceroy of India, was to stop in Baghdad on his way to India. They prepared a memorandum to be presented to him, hoping that he might be interested in their proposals for democratic freedoms and the establishment of a political party advocating liberal views and that he might pass it on to the British government for possible consideration. Sir Stafford never stopped in Baghdad and the memorandum was never presented,[9] but the meetings of the Ahali leaders were not in vain, for they resulted in a decision to resume the publication of the Ahali paper. Under the name *Sawt al-Ahali,* it was issued on September 23, 1942. It asserted the people's constitutional rights—the rights to free expression of opinion, free elections, and the organization of societies, trade unions, and political parties. The Ahali leaders hoped eventually to create an enlightened public which would respect the laws and maintain internal stability. Perhaps more important was their decision to discuss in the paper the country's principal problems, especially those related to land, health, and economic, social, and educational matters.[10] These problems were discussed by a number of Ahali members, especially by Chadirchi, who contributed in no small measure to efforts to arouse public interest in political activities after the war.[11]

Some of the Ahali leaders urged the resumption of political activities in spite of war restrictions and censorship, but Chadirchi could see no real gain from open or clandestine activities which might end in arrests, imprisonment, or detainment. He therefore suggested they first prepare the public for liberal views and awaken it to its responsibility before political activities were resumed. This suggestion, although adopted by the majority, alienated some extremists who left the group to join communist organizations.

In 1945, when the war was over, the Ahali group as well as others favoring democratic freedom often met in Chadirchi's house

[9] For the text of the memorandum, see Kamil al-Chadirchi, *Mudhakkirat Kamil al-Chadirchi* [Memoirs of Kamil al-Chadirchi] (Bayrut, 1970), pp. 78-83.

[10] For these aims, see Chadirchi, *Mudhakkirat,* p. 55.

[11] For a summary of the leading articles, see Fadil Husayn, *Ta'rikh al-Hizb al-Watani al-Dimuqrati* [History of the National Democratic Party] (Baghdad, 1963), pp. 15 ff.

to discuss ways and means for organizing a political party which
would include all persons desiring to work through democratic
processes. They were all agreed on their opposition to the ruling
group; but they failed to agree on a common platform. Some desired to adopt radical social and Marxist doctrines while others insisted on moderate views. No common ground could be found despite Chadirchi's suggestion that they work to carry out only the
views agreed upon collectively. 'Abd al-Fattah Ibrahim, though a
radical, agreed with Chadirchi, but personal conflict over leadership prevented the two men from working together and he left the
group.[12]

When the organization of political parties was again allowed in
1946, three political parties rather than one were founded, resulting
in the weakened position of all democratic elements. Chadirchi's
group, holding moderate views, stressed democracy and economic
planning but fell short of asserting socialist principles, even though
Chadirchi himself was in favor of socialism. As a result, many young
men either organized other left-wing parties or joined the unlicensed
Communist Party.[13]

A year after political parties were reorganized, Chadirchi submitted a memorandum to his party embodying specific socialist
proposals for possible adoption. Chadirchi pointed out three fundamental reasons that prompted him to present these proposals. First,
apart from the unlicensed Communist Party, there were four other
political parties which formally asserted liberal principles like those
of their party, especially democracy; two of them were in reality
Marxist and did not seriously believe in democratic processes, while
the other two parties were essentially nationalist and not really interested in social reform. Nevertheless, Chadirchi said, all of these
parties declared similar programs and, therefore, appeared in the
public eye to hold the same principles. Because their party had certain leanings toward socialism—some members were more outspoken about it than others—Chadirchi argued that the time had
come to adopt socialist principles formally, and that this would distinguish their party, the National Democratic Party, from the others.

Second, there was a need to point out the differences between

---

[12] For the conflicting views, see Chadirchi, *Mudhakkirat,* pp. 72-76.

[13] For an account of the new political parties, see my *Independent 'Iraq,* pp. 299-302.

methods used to implement socialism which are democratic and peaceful and the revolutionary methods of communism. Chadirchi, who had accepted democracy early in his political career, had begun to see its shortcomings without an association with other principles. After he had joined the Ahali group, he had sought to institute by peaceful methods a combination of democratic and socialist doctrines, which he called democratic socialism (al-Dimuqratiya al-Ishtirakiya), a form of social democracy comparable to the program of the British Labour Party.

Third, Chadirchi stated that his experiences in 'Iraqi politics had taught him that young men were often attracted to nationalist symbols used to disguise reactionary trends. He had witnessed how the Ahali movement itself was eclipsed by the upsurge of Pan-Arabism when Fascist and Nazi ideas invaded nationalist circles before World War II, and that only after the victory of democracy over dictatorship did Arab nationalists dissociate themselves from Fascist ideas. In 1946, when the ruling oligarchy began to resist liberal ideas, Chadirchi had again become deeply concerned about the possibility of a reactionary revival under the guise of some form of Arab nationalism. More specifically, he was alarmed when Sami Shawkat, a former Minister of Education and leader of the Futuwwa (militant youth) movement, whose activities prompted many young men to participate in the Rashid 'Ali uprising in 1941, reappeared to organize a new National Resurrection Party.[14] Chadirchi, in an article entitled " 'Iraq's Mosely"[15] and then in a series of articles on "The Resurrection of Fascism in 'Iraq," had launched an attack on Shawkat and warned against a reactionary movement which, he said, might impede the development of democratic institutions and enhance the power of the ruling oligarchy. Meanwhile, Chadirchi's own views had undergone some changes and he had moved further toward the left when fascist ideas were discredited after the war. His name had become closely identified with socialism—indeed, even with communism—in conservative circles. By 1947 Chadirchi thought that the time had come for his party to adopt socialist principles.

Chadirchi's memorandum to the Executive Committee, dated

[14] For Shawkat's youth movement and "integral nationalism," see my *Independent 'Iraq,* pp. 166-68; and *Political Trends,* pp. 177-79.

[15] "Mosely al-'Iraq," *Sawt al-Ahali* (Baghdad), January 2, 1946.

August 15, 1947, therefore proposed socialism as a basic principle. This "philosophy," he said, should be called democratic socialism to distinguish the party from Marxists and communists, on the one hand, and from other right-wing political parties, on the other. There were other circumstantial reasons, he added, which prompted him to propose this philosophy. One of the leftist parties, headed by 'Abd al-Fattah Ibrahim, had decided to dissolve itself, and he hoped that his party might attract its members if socialism were formally adopted. Another reason, he said, was the need to acquaint liberal and socialist parties in other countries with his party's role, which could be done only if it stated its aims clearly and had a well-defined philosophy of its own. Specifically, he had in mind the British Labour Party, which was then in power in England. He suggested that his party establish close contact with some British Labour leaders who might inform British representatives in 'Iraq about his party's concern for democratic freedoms and influence 'Iraqi rulers to remove restrictions on his party's political activities, since the 'Iraqi rulers were in close alignment with the British government.

Chadirchi did not spell out fully in his memorandum what he meant by democratic socialism, but both from conversations with him and from published works, it is possible to sum up his views about it. Chadirchi made it clear that he was neither a communist nor a Marxist. Nor did he believe in class struggle, though he did recognize the existence of a class structure in 'Iraq and consciously tried to secure public support from both the middle and the lower classes. Workers and peasants, he said, were not sufficiently organized to form the backbone of his party. Its appeal, therefore, should be to the people in general and to the intelligentsia, the lower middle class, and the workers and peasants in particular. Its principal opponents, he held, were tribal chiefs and landowners. Just as the British Labour Party derives its support from labor and the lower middle classes, so, he thought, should his party in 'Iraq.[16]

Committed to peaceful methods long before he joined the Ahali group, toward the end of his life Chadirchi's belief in democratic processes grew stronger, and he repudiated the use of force

[16] Toward the end of his life, Chadirchi tried in a memorandum intended to be circulated among supporters to lay down further details about democratic socialism, but he died before it was completed. See Chadirchi, *Min Awraq,* pp. 103 ff.

in principle. I had put to him on more than one occasion the question: How would he justify support given by his group to the military uprisings of 1936 and 1958, in which two former regimes were overthrown by force? Chadirchi invariably replied that force was justified only to overthrow regimes that crucified freedom. In a memorandum of August 1947, he stated his position briefly as follows: We pursue democratic procedures to achieve democracy, but if 'Iraqi rulers should obstruct democratic processes, resort to force would then be justified. Earlier he had expressed himself in this cryptic phrase: the "revolutionary right to achieve democracy."[17] These views were reiterated in his memorandum with the warning that force should be used only when all possible means to achieve democracy were denied by 'Iraqi rulers.[18]

The principles of democratic socialism recognized private ownership and limited free enterprise, but they also espoused the nationalization of industry and government ownership of essential utilities. Chadirchi expressed no opinion on the banking system, but Muhammad Hadid, second in command of the party, stated that banks should remain in private hands. Limited free enterprise should be encouraged, said Chadirchi, because 'Iraq needed economic development by private initiative, provided it took place under government supervision. It is clear that Chadirchi wanted a moderate brand of socialism which would neither impede economic development nor limit the rights of workers and peasants.

When Chadirchi's memorandum was scrutinized at a meeting of the Executive Committee (November 8, 1947), it was accepted in principle, and not without reservations, by only two members— Muhammad Hadid and Husayn Jamil, respectively Vice-President and Secretary of the Party—and was rejected by all others, most emphatically by Zaki 'Abd al-Wahhab and Tal'at al-Shaybani, two right-wing leaders. These opponents argued that 'Iraq's social and economic conditions were at such a backward stage that socialism would be inadequate to cope with development. What 'Iraq needed, they held, was to restrict landownership and the power of tribal chiefs in order to relieve workers and peasants from oppressive conditions. Chadirchi's proposal that the support of British Labour leaders

[17]Chadirchi, *Ba'th al-Fashiya*, p. 40.
[18]Chadirchi, *Mudhakkirat*, p. 210.

should be secured to influence 'Iraqi rulers to give concessions was rejected on the ground that the British Labour Party was just as imperialistic in foreign policy as the Tory Party. It was not realistic to maintain that Labour leaders would approve of the just demands of an 'Iraqi party, Chadirchi's critics contended, since British interests were best protected by the present 'Iraqi rulers. The only way to achieve their party's aims, they added, was first to reduce British influence. Hadid and Jamil, in support of Chadirchi, proposed that democratic socialism be accepted as a guiding principle without formal adoption, but their compromise was rejected.

On the following day, November 9, 1947, Chadirchi submitted his resignation from leadership of the party because his proposals had been rejected. The resignation was not accepted. Zaki 'Abd al-Wahhab and Tal'at al-Shaybani then submitted their resignation, because it became clear that Chadirchi would have no confidence in them if he continued as leader of the party. After these two opponents had left the party, Chadirchi felt free to give more liberal (i.e., socialist) interpretations to the party's program; indeed, the unofficial socialist stamp continued as long as Chadirchi remained leader of the National Democratic Party.

In 1948 and 1952, when liberal and nationalist elements publicly challenged the ruling oligarchy, they were joined by the National Democratic Party. These groups were ostensibly seeking to induce the government to relax restrictions on free expression of opinion, but their activities culminated in the overthrow of the government by popular *coups d'état*. In 1958 Chadirchi was unwittingly drawn into supporting a military uprising on the ground of defending free expression of opinion. To the end of his life in 1968, he continued to preach democracy and socialism, notwithstanding the fact that he often supported leaders whose objectives ran contrary to these principles.

IV

No less significant than Chadirchi's leadership of the Ahali group for his political career was his editorship of the Ahali paper and the articles he contributed to it. He followed his country's politics closely— indeed, he was well informed about almost all that went on behind closed doors in Baghdad's political circles—and wrote commentaries on questions of the day which were widely read. He wrote critical remarks about premiers when they were in and out of office—these were often so blunt that they led to judicial proceedings and imprisonment. Perhaps Chadirchi's most trenchant attack was made against Arshad al-'Umari—an engineer whose brilliant work as Mayor of Baghdad elevated him to a Cabinet position. When 'Umari became Premier in June 1946, he tried to govern in a high-handed manner, and this brought him into conflict with political parties. Soon after 'Umari had formed a government, Chadirchi wrote a leading article in which he said:

> Many 'Iraqi citizens are aware that Arshad al-'Umari's actions are carried out too quickly, almost on the spot—because he is an unbalanced and erratic person—and therefore they never believed he would ever become an important figure in politics, regardless of how high the position he may occupy. Consequently, when they learned that he formed a government, they received the news with obvious coolness—indeed, with cynicism—especially when they heard how quickly he formed it. It is said that he ostentatiously declared that he was able to form his government by telephone calls within half an hour [after the royal summons]![19]

These uncomplimentary words having been said, Chadirchi went on to explain that 'Umari, a product of Ottoman despotism, had been entrusted with power by the ruling oligarchy to enforce restrictive measures against the newly formed political parties. The purpose of his government, therefore, was unworthy, and it was the duty of all democratic elements to oppose it. Because of this and several other articles,[20] Chadirchi was brought to trial on the ground that his articles were seditious, intended to create dissension and disturbances among the people. He was condemned to imprisonment for six months; however, by an appeal to higher courts and by

[19] Chadirchi, "al-Ghaya al-Khafiya Wara' Khittat al-Hukuma al-Hadira" [The Hidden Motive behind the Plan of the Present Government], Sawt al-Ahali (Baghdad), July 10, 1946, pp. 1 and 4. See M. Hadid, "Conditions in 'Iraq," New Statesman (London), September 4, 1946, p. 186.

[20] See Sawt al-Ahali (Baghdad), July 15 and 18, 1946.

a subsequent change of government,[21] in which Chadirchi's party was represented,[22] the case was finally dropped by the government.[23] After 'Umari had fallen from power, Chadirchi labeled him as the "pocket dictator," because 'Umari pretended to play the role of a dictator but failed to carry out dictatorial orders![24]

But this was not the only instance in which Chadirchi tried to debunk political figures who appeared to him to be vain and self-seeking. He called Shawkat, as we noted before, the Mosely of 'Iraq and General Nuri al-Sa'id the Smuts of 'Iraq, presumably on the ground that General Nuri was an ally of the British Empire. He also nicknamed several others with such undignified labels that he appeared to be seeking not merely to debunk but to undermine political opponents by resorting to character assassination.[25]

Some of Chadirchi's writings and commentaries were constructive and quite suggestive, although they were not always welcomed by the authorities.[26] When publication of the Ahali paper was suspended, he either published his commentaries in other daily papers or distributed them in pamphlets or mimeographed circulars.[27] All his writings were taken very seriously, and his views were commented upon both in official and nonofficial circles.

Chadirchi's own "salon," frequented by friends and visitors, provided a forum for remarks and commentaries on questions of the day which spread beyond the walls of his house and often embarrassed men in high authority. Some of his remarks described brilliantly the personality and character of political figures, but

[21] A new government was formed by General Nuri al-Sa'id in November 1946.

[22] Muhammad Hadid, Vice-President of the National Democratic Party, became Minister of Supply.

[23] For the documents relating to this case, see Chadirchi, *Muhakamat Kamil al-Chadirchi* [Trials of Kamil al-Chadirchi] (Baghdad, 1946).

[24] The author heard Chadirchi on more than one occasion using these words. See Chadirchi, *Ba'th al-Fashiya*, p. 529; and "Bayan al-Hizb al-Watani al-Dimuqrati Bimunasabat Istiqalat Wazarat al-'Umari," *Sawt al-Ahali* (Baghdad), November 27, 1947. For an account of 'Umari's Cabinet and the country's reaction to it, see my *Independent 'Iraq*, pp. 256-58.

[25] Chadirchi's sarcastic criticism of Rafael Butti, editor of *al-Bilad* and fellow member of a former political party, incited Butti to reply in seven severely, often profanely, worded articles which exposed Chadirchi's early career. For Chadirchi's article on Butti, see *Sawt al-Ahali* (Baghdad), December 13, 1946; and for Butti's reply, see *al-Bilad* (Baghdad), December 26, 1946-January 10, 1947.

[26] See *Sawt al-Ahali* (Baghdad), December 2 and 20, 1946, February 9 and 21, 1947, December 2, 1948; and *al-Hiyad* (Baghdad), December 28, 1953.

[27] See my *Republican 'Iraq*, pp. 227, 231.

others were often harsh, unfair, and undignified.[28] While his polit-ical satire often amused foreign visitors, it angered native citizens when the unfriendly remarks were directed toward political op-ponents.

Effective in journalism and political pamphleteering, Chadirchi did not like to appear in public to address a public meeting or harangue a crowd. True, he gave speeches in party congresses, but these were reports given to party leaders and could hardly be re-garded as addresses to sway audiences. Chadirchi was not a good public speaker; therefore he tried to rely on individual and private conversations to influence followers rather than on public speeches.

Nor was Chadirchi a flexible man. From the very beginning when he joined the Ahali group he came into conflict with other members; he refused to enlist in his party leaders of other political parties even if they were prepared to cooperate with him. Had he agreed to form a broader political organization, the ruling oligarchy would perhaps have been unable to suppress political parties, as it did by dealing with them separately. Chadirchi, keen on maintaining firm control over his party, preferred cohesion and solidarity within a smaller body to toleration of differences among many followers. As a result, Chadirchi's influence was confined to a relatively small group and could hardly have been expected to achieve power by peaceful methods. In moments of despair, when his own freedom was restricted, he allowed his party to participate in two military coups—in 1936 and 1958. The first undermined his party and the other destroyed it. Nevertheless, the principles for which Chadirchi stood remain unchallenged as watchwords of moderate and liberal groups to this day. Above all, the strength of his character and loyalty to his party make him unique among the professional politicians of his generation. Had he been endowed with flexibility and popular appeal he might have been able to overcome solitude and lead his party in pursuit of popular support.

[28] For remarks about King Faysal II and Brigadier Qasim, see my *Republican 'Iraq,* pp. 46 and 185.

KAMAL JUNBLAT

> In my opinion progressive parties will eventually succeed to create a
> new society . . . by an active cooperation among workers, peasants
> and educated young men. . . . Socialism will then emerge as the only
> system capable of superseding feudalism, confessionalism and
> partisanship, and the [Lebanese] people will become a nation in the
> modern sense of the word.
>
> *Junblat*

Junblat and Chadirchi share many qualities as well as a fundamental political orientation. Both received initial political support from their family background, but they differed considerably in their political methods. Like Chadirchi, Junblat was born to a well-to-do family; indeed, the Junblats were much wealthier and played a far more important role in politics than the Chadirchis. Junblat was born in al-Shawf (Chouf), in central Lebanon in 1917. His ancestors, the Janbuladhs—now corrupted into Junblats and pronounced Jumblats—had come to Lebanon from the region of Killis and 'Ayntab in southern Asia Minor, and were known to have been originally Kurds. They had accepted the Duruz faith, an offshoot of the Fatimi Shi'i religion, long before they moved into southern Lebanon over three and a half centuries ago.[29] They may have been driven out by sectarian strife then in progress in Asia Minor, either when this new faith began to spread in that region or later when the Ottoman Empire extended its control into eastern Asia Minor.[30] In their new home, the Junblats in time acquired large estates and became feudal lords. Some members of the family became very prominent both as spiritual and as secular leaders, and a few even became rulers of the country, either as Ottoman governors

---

[29] The Junblat family claims descent from Salah al-Din (Saladin), who is known in history to have been a Kurd, although the Durzi people as a whole are of Arab descent. For a brief account of the origin and faith of the Duruz (Druzes), see G. S. Hodgson, "Duruz," *Encyclopedia of Islam,* Vol. II (n.d.), pp. 631-34.

[30] For the history of the Junblat family, see Tannus al-Shidiaq, *Akhbar al-'Ayan fi Jabal Lubnan* [Chronicles of Notables in the Mountains of Lebanon] (Bayrut, 1954), Vol. I, pp. 144 ff.

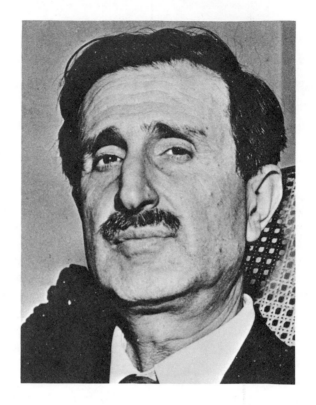

Kamal Junblat

or semi-independent princes. To this day, the leading members of
the family enjoy feudal privileges.[31]

Like Chadirchi, young Junblat suffered no deprivation or social
insecurity; indeed, he relied on his family's wealth and prestige to
achieve his political ambition to a larger extent than Chadirchi could
have done. Younger than the latter by some twenty years, Junblat
received a more solid education in Lebanon and Paris than was available to Chadirchi. Junblat's mother, Nazira, who was deeply attached to her son, gave him his first informal instruction at home
and then, ten years later, sent him to the Lazarist School at 'Ayntura,
where children of prominent Lebanese families studied. In 1936,
Junblat went to Paris and studied literature and philosophy at the
Sorbonne, although his mother wanted him to study law. In 1938,
fearing the outbreak of war, his mother called him home, and he
entered the St. Joseph University School of Law, graduating in 1942.
He was called to the bar and practiced law as an apprentice for a
year; however, his heart was in literature and philosophy, and his
self-education in the humanities deeply influenced his views about
social and political questions.

Like Chadirchi, Junblat entered politics when he was elected to
Parliament in 1943. His victory at the polls had nothing to do with
his personal political views, however, since the constituency he represented always elected a member of the Junblat family. His cousin,
Hikmat Junblat, who had held the parliamentary seat for al-Shawf,
died in 1943 and Kamal Junblat was elected to fill this vacancy. For
a short time, Junblat played an independent political role, not joining any of the then existing political parties, but cooperating with
certain groups from time to time. He continued to hold his parliamentary seat on the strength of his family's traditional role as Durzi
leaders. He ran for Parliament in all general elections; he was re-
elected in 1947 and 1953, but defeated in 1957 because of his opposition to the Camille Sham'un regime. He returned to Parliament
in 1960 and also won in the two subsequent elections of 1964 and
1968. Junblat first entered the Cabinet in 1946 as Minister of National Economy. Since then he has frequently held the portfolios

---

[31] For a discussion of the character of feudalism and confessionalism in Lebanon, see
Michel Ghurayyib, al-Ta'ifiy wa al-Iqta'iya fi Lubnan [Confessionalism and Feudalism in
Lebanon] (2nd ed.; Bayrut, 1964); and Samir Khalaf, "Primordial Ties and Politics in
Lebanon," Middle Eastern Studies, Vol. IV (1968), pp. 243-69.

of Agriculture, Education, Public Works, Planning, and Interior under various prime ministers who either formed coalition governments or with whom he had entered into an alignment against previous regimes.

In 1949, Junblat founded the Progressive Socialist Party and published *al-Anba'* (News), its official organ. The program of this party, embodying his social and political goals, indicated not only what Junblat stood for as a politician but also his political and literary propensities, for he is a frequent contributor to the press. However, for a study of Junblat as a politician, one would have to look beyond his party's activities and political writings.[32]

II

Before he organized his political party in 1949, Junblat joined no particular party even though he shared the principles of some and may even have contemplated joining one of them. On more than one occasion, he aligned himself with some groupings and agreed to cooperate with a few leading politicians; but in the last analysis, he proved to be a lone wolf and preferred to organize his own party when he realized that none of the existing parties held a similar outlook to his and that his views would not enjoy strong enough popular support to form a government except in coalition.

Under the influence of postwar social and political trends, Junblat adopted the principles of socialism and democracy mixed with religious and ethical values which he derived from his reading of European and Oriental religious writings. Some of his ideas, like collectivism, which have become popular among young men, were adopted from European thought, but his ethical and religious ideas were derived from his study of Hindu, Buddhist, and other Oriental religions. Three or four years before he organized his party, he began to put into practice his socialist doctrines by distributing among peasants some of his own personal landed estate against his mother's protest. This action, whether intended for publicity or as a mani-

---

[32] For a brief account of Junblat's political activities, see Lucien George and Toufic Makdessi, *Les partis Libanais en 1959* (Beirut, 1959); and M. W. Suleiman, *Political Parties in Lebanon* (Ithaca, 1967), pp. 213-27.

festation of genuine belief in social justice, made Junblat's name popular and contributed in no small measure to the support his party received from peasants in certain rural districts and the intelligentsia in big towns and cities.

The party which Junblat founded—*al-Hizb al-Taqaddumi al-Ishtiraki* (the Progressive Socialist Party)—is fully identified with his own personality and leadership. The powers entrusted to him as leader of the party are indeed very extensive—he appoints all party officials, supervises their work, and assumes responsibility for all activities. Although he is ordinarily guided by decisions of the party's Council of Directors, Junblat often exercises autocratic powers and his orders are carried out without prior consultation with other party leaders.

Junblat subscribes to several doctrines, derived from diverse social and political systems, which are not always easy or possible to reconcile. The assumption that the individual is the object of all social and political organizations, Junblat maintains, stems from the philosophy of individualism. "Society," he asserts, "is only a means to enable the individual to develop." To achieve this end, society must be democratic so that peace, freedom, welfare, and security may be insured for the individual. This liberal philosophy, however, must be tempered by collectivist doctrines, according to Junblat, in order to prohibit exploitation and excessive profit by a few individuals. Thus socialism, in Junblat's eyes, is not an over-riding but a corrective principle—it is a means to an end, not an end in itself, although it is one of the basic principles. This combination of individualist and collectivist principles is viewed as dynamic and not as static in character; the principles are bound to change and develop in accordance with the growing needs and expectations of the individual. For this reason, Junblat characterized his social philosophy as continuously changing and called his party "progressive" in order to distinguish it from other doctrinaire and dogmatic parties, whether communist or otherwise.[33]

But that is not all. Junblat tried to infuse into his social philosophy and consequently into his party's teachings, certain spiritual and religious values, reflecting his own preoccupation with religious

---

[33] See *Mithaq al-Hizb al-Taqaddumi al-Ishtiraki* [Platform of the Progressive Socialist Party] (Bayrut, 1949).

problems. His writings stress religious experiences, and he often quotes from the Prophet Muhammad and other Western and Oriental teachers.[34] These spiritual injunctions are perhaps intended to temper the materialistic character of modern individualism and socialism, although it is not clear whether Junblat is prepared to subordinate secular to spiritual doctrines.

Junblat's ideas are not to be found systematically spelled out in any single treatise; they are scattered in a number of speeches and essays and have apparently not yet evolved into a coherent system. Nor is he always consistent about basic principles. In some of his writings, he has stressed individual freedom, democracy, and spiritual values; in others he has complained about the inadequacy of democratic processes to achieve progress and called for the limitation of personal freedom. Such inconsistencies are scattered in his writings and in public speeches; some of them are perhaps prompted by the vagaries of the occasion and the mood of audiences to which they are addressed.[35]

What are Junblat's goals and methods?

In most of his writings, Junblat is inclined to state his views about the individual and society in abstract terms, but there is no doubt that at the back of his mind these views are to be applied to the practical problems of Lebanese society. Nor are Lebanon's problems discussed in isolation—they are always discussed in relation to Lebanon's Arab neighbors and, indeed, to the world at large. Aware of the weak position of his country as a small state and her dependence on the good will of other nations, especially the Arab world and the Great Powers, he has often stated his views about Lebanon in her regional and world setting. More specifically, he has stated that Lebanon, though a separate political community having its own distinctive character, is an Arab country which shares with other Arab countries a common cultural heritage and similar national aspirations. Arab countries, Junblat has said, are also aware that they are members of a larger community of nations

---

[34] Among Western Christian writers, Junblat often quoted Teilhard de Chardin, to whose writings he seems to have been attracted. He also read the literature of Islamic and other Oriental religions.

[35] Both in his published works and in private discussions, Junblat reiterated his belief in democracy and other liberal principles, but he complained that the requisite conditions for realizing them did not yet exist.

whose survival depends on the maintenance of peace, stability, and cooperation among themselves to achieve national interests. However, as a politician whose objective is to achieve goals in his own country, Junblat has endeavored first to transform Lebanese society in accordance with his goals before looking beyond Lebanon's frontiers, although on more than one occasion he has tried to link his political activities in Lebanon with political movements in neighboring countries.[36]

In founding his political party, Junblat considered it not merely as a political organization which would seek representation in Parliament and government but also as an instrument which would achieve social reforms by holding conferences and rallies and by propagating his own ideas. Junblat's appeal is not confined to a particular class or confessional community but includes the nation at large, although he pays particular attention to the intelligentsia and to the new generation as a whole. His stress on freedom, socialism, and democracy have undoubtedly impressed young men, and although he is no longer the only leader who uses these slogans, his voice carries perhaps more conviction than many others, because he was one of the leaders to speak earnestly on the matter early in the postwar years.

As a thinker and a writer, Junblat has been able to influence his country's young men more than any other politician. In books, pamphlets, and public speeches dealing with theoretical as well as practical political questions, he has demonstrated that he is a profound thinker and an impressive speaker, especially on international and interregional questions. His style, though often vague on abstract subjects, is on the whole clear and lucid. He writes both in Arabic and French and can address an English-speaking audience.[37]

Finally, by participating in election campaigns, in parliamentary debates, and in the executive branch of government, Junblat has been able to influence policies and political processes in which he was directly involved. Nor has he shrunk from taking part in revolutionary activities when public policy ran contrary to his convictions, but has sought by an alliance with opposition parties to achieve power

[36] See Kamal Junblat, *Fi Majra al-Siyasa al-Lubnaniya* [On the Course of Lebanese Politics] (Bayrut, n.d.).

[37] I had the pleasure of introducing Junblat to an American audience during his visit to Washington in 1954, when he gave a speech in English and answered questions on Lebanon and the Arab world.

through violence. By resorting to these methods, however, Junblat failed to rise above the level of other professional politicians who often subordinate principles to convenience.[38]

III

Junblat's ultimate goal, if the intent of his teachings were to be carried out to its logical conclusion, would be to establish a new social polity in which his social and political ideas would be given full expression. Although Junblat has often expressed himself in general terms without reference to a particular country, the test of his principles is their relevance to a specific community—Lebanon. But Lebanon in reality is not a cohesive community with which one can experiment with relative ease; it is an aggregate of communities, gathered together by diverse local, feudal, and confessional loyalties, some of which cut across one another. In order to establish a new system, Junblat realized that he had first to change Lebanon's traditional social order and create a new one. For this reason, he called for the abolishment of the operating—often unwritten—rules of the existing political structure. More specifically, Junblat demanded that the heads of state, government, and Parliament, not to mention other offices in lower echelons of the political system, should not be elected or selected on confessional grounds but in accordance with secular laws under which all citizens would be eligible to hold public offices regardless of creed or status.

In theory, Junblat's basic views seem plausible and are indeed acceptable to almost all political leaders; but the methods by which he has tried to carry them out are unacceptable to many citizens.

To begin with, Junblat entered politics, as we have already had occasion to notice, in accordance with traditional practices, feudal and confessional, before he became known as a national figure even in his own community. His subsequent re-elections to Parliament and his elevation to Cabinet posts were also determined by essential-

[38] For Junblat's political writing, see *Democratie Nouvelle* (Bayrut, 1950); *Adwa' 'Ala Haqiqat al-Qadiya al-Qawmiya al-Ijtima'iya al-Suriya* [Light on the Reality of the Syrian Social National Party's Question] (Bayrut, n.d.); *Haqiqat al-Thawra al-Lubnaniya* [The Reality of the Lebanese Revolution] (Bayrut, 1959); *Fi Majra al-Siyasa al-Lubnaniya; Thawra fi 'Alam al-Insan* [A Revolution in the Realm of Man] (Bayrut, 1967); *Fima Yata'ada al-Harf* [Beyond Words] (Bayrut, n.d.).

ly traditional loyalties, even though he had become the leader of a
political party and a well-known national figure. Thus, if he were to
be taken at his word, Junblat should have followed methods consistent with his declared principles and party platform rather than
pursued political objectives in accordance with traditional methods.
This is perhaps the fundamental weakness in Junblat's leadership—
the contradiction between his uttered words and actions, between
theory and practice.

It may be argued, however, that before Junblat could achieve
basic change in the social order, he was bound to resort to traditional methods and continue his participation in politics on the
parliamentary level, or even in the Cabinet, in order to achieve immediate objectives necessary for ultimate goals. The weakness of
this argument lies in the fact that, unless Junblat committed himself to his declared principles, his call for reform could not be taken
seriously. In fact, resort to traditional methods has often prompted
him to cooperate with leaders with whom he had little or nothing
in common save a desire to defeat an opponent or opponents in
power. Such methods have given the impression that he differed
but little from other professional politicians whom he denounced
as opportunistic and ready to subordinate principles to questionable
methods.

Junblat has not been unaware that this juxtaposition would remain awkward if he were to continue the struggle to put words into action by peaceful methods. Consequently, he has often talked
about the need for revolutionary change in order to destroy traditional loyalties and create new ones consistent with his social and
political creeds. He has not only subscribed to revolutionary change
in principle but has also participated twice in popular uprisings—in
1952 and 1958—in which he resorted to force to destroy "old
regimes" that were to be replaced by new ones which would assert
new loyalties. In pursuit of these methods, Junblat has utterly
failed to carry the country behind him. He has often realigned himself with professional politicians whom he previously denounced as
corrupt and self-seeking and thus has undermined his efforts by the
very methods he disapproved in others.

Leadership of a political party remained the only instrument
by which Junblat could participate in politics on the popular level
and appeal for support of a platform essentially embodying his own

social and political ideas. True, this method, in a country where public opinion has not yet sufficiently developed, is not effective enough to achieve reform, but it is the only democratic method consistent with the ideas which he had proposed to the public. In the ninety-nine member Parliament, those from Junblat's party usually number between three and five, but even these are not all elected on party lines, which reflects the relative weakness of Junblat's party in comparison with its opponents.[39] Needless to say, the existence of a multiple-party system in any country makes it exceedingly difficult for any party to obtain a majority in Parliament without an alignment with other parties. However, Junblat's error seems to be that he has often shifted his alignments. To obtain public confidence in his party, Junblat needed to persuade his countrymen to accept its platform, which would be a long-range proposition. But he has seemed to be too impatient to follow this slow and tedious process, which his 'Iraqi counterpart decided to pursue. Consequently, Junblat improved but little on the skills and methods of other professional politicians.

IV

Junblat received more solid modern education than Chadirchi and possessed certain intellectual qualities which might well have qualified him to become an intellectual politician; but Chadirchi, despite certain intellectual limitations, proved more consistent in his actions than Junblat and preferred to maintain a relatively untarnished image in the public eye by subordinating immediate returns to long-term goals. It is true that Chadirchi was unable to formulate as elaborate and sophisticated a platform as Junblat, but he proved on the whole more faithful to his declared ideas by avoiding erratic actions in carrying them out. Even when he supported revolutionary movements—which ran contrary to his principles, as we noted earlier—Chadirchi was prepared to change his mind if the results were unsatisfactory; but Junblat showed no

[39] Among Junblat's opponents, Pierre Jumayyil has a following of nine, and Camille Sham'un, perhaps the strongest, of thirteen in the present composition of the House. The whole party membership barely exceeds eight or nine thousand, although Junblat claims a much larger following.

readiness to stop even if his actions produced negative results, which reflected on his fidelity to principles.

However, Junblat has shown greater flexibility in his relations with other leaders and proved a far more able leader in keeping party members working together—indeed, to win a few more party supporters—than Chadirchi, whose personal quarrels with other party leaders prompted them either to leave the party or caused serious splits within it. Thus, Junblat may well be regarded as a greater leader than Chadirchi, although his flexibility often compromised cherished values and gave the impression that he was more interested in winning supporters than in pursuing ultimate goals.

Despite these occasional vagaries and vicissitudes, Junblat has shown greater moral courage, vigilance, and perseverance in pursuing objectives than perhaps all his political opponents; in some of these qualities he is even superior to his 'Iraqi counterpart. In intellect as well as in the ability to articulate his thoughts and the aptitude for languages, he certainly ranks higher than Chadirchi, but it is doubtful that he could surpass him in dedication and strength of character.

Khalid Bakdash

CHAPTER IX

The Ideological School –
The Radical
Khalid Bakdash

We demand peace, bread and freedom for the people.

Bakdash

Khalid Bakdash represents a radical school whose adherents tried to solve Arab problems by associating themselves with an international movement and consciously sought to change the very foundation of Arab society in accordance with the ideological goals and methods of that movement. It is true that almost all other leaders accepted in varying degree some foreign ideas and reform measures, especially the ones who sought to conform to one variant of socialism or another, but these leaders tried to adapt or modify the international concepts to meet essential local needs. Arab communists, however, stand unique among their contemporaries by their tacit agreement to subordinate national to international values. They were prepared to modify immediate goals and methods as circumstances dictated, but the underlying principles remained intact.

Khalid Bakdash, Secretary-General of the Syrian Communist Party for over forty years, is the communist leader *par excellence* for his personal qualities, dedication, and loyalty in carrying out ideological goals in accordance with Soviet strategy and guidance.

155

Collectivist ideas were not new to Arabs and were introduced, despite initial opposition, by methods not altogether incompatible with local traditions.[1] But communists, in contrast with other leaders, displayed a kinetic energy and discipline the like of which Arabs had not witnessed before. Bakdash has set a remarkable example of communist methods in an effort to achieve power, even though the road to this ultimate goal is still long and filled with almost insurmountable obstacles.

II

Khalid Bakdash was born in 1912 to a family which had not yet been fully assimilated by Arab society. His parents were of Kurdish descent and lived in the Kurdish—often called the Muhajirin (émigrés)—quarter of Damascus, where most Kurds had long resided. The Bakdash clan had not distinguished itself either in nationalist or social activities, despite the fact that Khalid's father had served first in the Ottoman Army and then in the Arab army under the short-lived Faysal regime in 1920. Thus Khalid grew up in a social environment of relative deprivation and insecurity and could rely on practically nothing of real significance in his family background, although he claimed later in life that his father had served with distinction in the Ottoman army.[2] From his youth, however, Bakdash possessed charm, native intelligence, and vigor—qualities that would enable any young man to make his way in society and overcome deprivation and a humble background.

Like most boys of his age, Bakdash entered government schools which had just been reorganized under the French Mandate after the fall of the Arab regime. During the next ten years, he completed his primary and high school education but could not pursue his studies at the Law College either because he failed to take the examination (according to one informant) or because he was expelled for political activities (according to another informant). While still in high school, he took an interest in politics and read the political literature that had bearing on questions of the day. From

[1] See my *Political Trends in the Arab World* (Baltimore, 1970), Chap. 5.

[2] Qadri Qal'achi, *Tajribat 'Arabi Fi al-Hizb al-Shuyu'i* [The Experience of an Arab in the Communist Party] (Bayrut, 1960), p. 154.

the collapse of the Arab regime in 1920 to 1935, nationalist leaders instigated anti-French agitation in which students were often enlisted to participate in protest demonstrations. An activist, and not inclined to be scholarly, Bakdash was drawn early in life into the Syrian politicized society of the interwar years. Since leaders of the National Bloc then dominated the scene, Bakdash was attracted to them, and with them he tried to make his way into politics. Although still young, he began to realize the inadequacy of traditional leadership for achieving national goals.

In 1930 Bakdash suddenly joined the Communist Party. It is not yet clear why he broke with nationalist leaders with whom he seemed to have maintained fairly good personal relations. It is possible that his Kurdish descent and social background, of which he was always conscious, made him realize that he could never be fully accepted into the company of professional politicians who represented wealth and aristocratic houses. Nor were those leaders working for a truly modern democratic society in which liberal-minded young men could participate; rather, they identified themselves as pan-Arab leaders, stressing Arab and not Syrian identity. Minority groups, both religious and ethnic, often resented this type of identity and preferred a territorial basis of nationalism which would put them on an equal footing with their compatriots rather than the historical or religious basis of nationalism. As a liberal-minded Kurd, Bakdash perhaps felt the lack of full identity with Arab nationalism and felt more at home in the company of politicians who would assert an international rather than a national or traditional mode of loyalty.

But there was another reason that tempted Bakdash to join the communist movement. From its very beginning, the Communist Party did not make much headway in Syria and Lebanon and was confined to religious minorities, especially Christians and Armenians; very few Muslims were willing to join even as sympathizers. For this reason, it was realized that unless leadership passed to Muslim hands, the activities of the Communist Party would remain confined to these minority groups.[3] It is said that this situation was keenly pointed out by a Soviet leader during a visit to

[3] The leadership of the Communist Party had passed from Yusuf Yazbuk to Fu'ad al-Shamali, both Christians from Lebanon, and it was deemed necessary to entrust leadership to a Muslim from Syria in order to spread the movement in Syria and break religious barriers.

Damascus in 1930. He found in Bakdash the potential leadership qualities and arranged for his visit and study in Moscow in preparation for future leadership of the Syrian Communist Party. After he joined the Communist Party in 1930, Bakdash was twice arrested for political agitations in 1931 and 1933; he served a term of four months in prison in 1931 and escaped after a second arrest in 1933. At this time he translated the *Communist Manifesto,* the first translation into the Arabic language, and published it in 1933. He left shortly afterward for study in Moscow.[4]

Bakdash seems to have studied communist theory and practice at more than one institution in the Soviet Union. It is exceedingly difficult to know the names of all the schools he attended and whether he joined them as a regular student or an auditor. It is reported that he attended first the Lenin Institute of Moscow and then the University of Tashkent. He learned the Russian language, which he now speaks with relative fluency, and is well read in Russian literature. We do not know much about Bakdash's activities in Moscow, but his name appeared on the list of heads of delegations to the Seventh Congress of the Comintern in 1935. He returned to Damascus either in 1935 or early in 1936.

III

Even before he went to Moscow, Bakdash became the secretary of the Syrian group within the Communist Party of Syria and Lebanon. After he returned from Moscow, he first began to consolidate his position and then to take over leadership of the party as Secretary-General. After he joined the party in 1930, Bakdash entered into a personal alignment with Rafiq Rida, a Muslim from Tripoli, and with Artin Madoyan, an Armenian activist leader, who agreed to entrust the position of Secretary-General of the party to Bakdash. When Faraj-Allah al-Hillu and Niqula (Nicola) Shawi, two Christians from Lebanon, joined the party and headed the Lebanese group, they also supported Bakdash's leadership. As a result, Bak-

---

[4] It is not certain when Bakdash actually left to study in Moscow; some writers say he left in 1930 and returned in 1932. See Qadri Qal'achi, *Tajribat,* p. 57; and S. Ayyub [Sami Ayyub al-Khuri], *al-Hizb al-Shuyu'i fi Suriya wa Lubnan* [The Communist Party in Syria and Lebanon] (Bayrut, 1959), pp. 70-71. Other reliable informants say that he went for study in Moscow in 1933 and returned two years later.

dash had no great difficulty in replacing Fu'ad al-Shamali, a trade-
union leader who had become Secretary-General in 1928, when
Ibrahim Yazbuk left the party.

In 1936, when the Popular Front, supported by French communists, formed a government in France under Leon Blum, Bakdash
became very active in Damascus. He supported the leaders of the
National Bloc, who came to an understanding with the Blum government to negotiate a treaty which would end the French Mandate
and recognize Syrian independence. He went to Paris to solicit the
support of the French Communist Party in the treaty negotiations
between the Syrian delegation and the French government. By his
good offices, the Syrian leaders met Maurice Thorez, Secretary-
General of the Communist Party, and some communist members of
Parliament who were prepared to impress upon the Blum government the need to sympathize with Syrian national aspirations. The
Franco-Syrian and Franco-Lebanese treaties, signed in September
1936 and providing for the independence of Syria and Lebanon,
were hailed as a great success, for which Bakdash claimed some
credit. After his return to Damascus, two members of the Communist Party—first Rafiq Rida and then Fu'ad Qazan—went to
Paris to insure that the French Communist Party would continue
to support the Syrian government.[5]

As a *quid pro quo* for communist participation in Syrian and
Lebanese negotiations for independence, Bakdash was allowed to
spread communist propaganda. He could not have found more
favorable circumstances to spread communist propaganda than in
the guise of national liberation. For the next three years, from
1936 to 1939, he sang the praise of democratic France and of national freedom; in reality, he and his followers fully exploited the
freedom given them by propagandizing their own slogans on a
larger scale than ever before. For the first time, an official organ of
the party, *Sawt al-Sha'b* (The Voice of the People), was issued in
1937, and Bakdash's speeches and other communist circulars were
published without censorship or restrictions. Bakdash's image suddenly changed from that of an underground rebel and a fellow trav-
eler to a patriot whose activities were not merely confined to liberat-

---

[5] See Khalid Bakdash, *Fi Sabil Hurriyyat al-Sha'b al-Wataniya wa al-Dimuqratiya* [Toward
the People's National and Democratic Freedoms] (Damascus, 1937), and *Fi Sabil Najah
al-Hukm al-Watani* [Toward the Success of the National Regime] (Damascus, 1937).

ing peasants and workers but encompassed national freedom, unity, and independence. His influence began to extend beyond the Levantine coast, and his leadership was acknowledged without dispute.

Syria and Lebanon ratified the treaties of independence a few months after they were signed in 1936, but the French Senate refused to ratify them after the fall of Leon Blum from power in 1937. Very soon Syrian nationalists began to realize that there was little or no hope for French ratification, despite their readiness to reconsider all matters relating to defense and minority rights to meet French demands. In protest against France's failure to ratify the treaty, the President of the Syrian Republic resigned in 1939. The French High Commissioner, seizing the opportunity, dissolved Parliament and appointed an administrative Cabinet responsible directly to him. This arrangement lasted until the Allied forces, in cooperation with General de Gaulle's Free French forces, entered Syria and Lebanon in 1941.

Despite these adversities, Bakdash continued to call for Syrian cooperation with France because he maintained that the Senate's failure to ratify the treaty after Blum's fall was caused by fascist machinations, and he hoped that once fascist forces were defeated Franco-Syrian relations could be normalized. In June 1941, when Hitler attacked the Soviet Union, Bakdash gave the signal to his followers that the time had come to support the Soviet Union and its Western allies. The British and the Free French forces, after entering Syria and Lebanon in August 1941, gave freedom to all elements who had opposed the former French authorities in the Levant— described as fascists by the communists—and both communists and nationalists called for Arab support of the democracies. *Sawt al-Sha'b,* which had been suspended in 1939, reappeared early in 1942, and communist propaganda began to spread far and wide not only in the Levant but in the Arab world as a whole. Meanwhile, Bakdash, whose activities had been temporarily suspended, began to coordinate the communist parties of the Arab countries.

In 1943, three events may be singled out as having had far-reaching effects on spreading communist propaganda in the Arab world. First, on June 9, 1943, it was announced that the Comintern was dissolved. This action, which relieved communists from nationalist accusations that their activities were inspired by a foreign power, gave Bakdash the opportunity to speak of the Syrian Communist

Party as a national party working for unity and independence and to claim that it had become independent from foreign (international) control. Second, Bakdash ran for election in the first stage of the electoral process as a secondary elector. Although he failed in the second stage, which returns members to Parliament, his victory as a secondary elector, the first in his party's history, was regarded as an encouraging sign for future possibilities of victory at the polls. In his own constituency—the Kurdish quarter—Bakdash received enthusiastic support which induced him to run again in later elections. Third, the Communist Party held a National Congress (December 31, 1943-January 2, 1944), often referred to as the Second National Congress, in which the party's aims and methods were reconsidered. A National Covenant laid down by the Executive Committee stressed national and democratic rather than communist principles. Moreover, the revolutionary process was renounced in favor of peaceful and constitutional methods of achieving power.[6] In 1944 the Syrian Communist Party, in a joint statement with the Lebanese Communist Party, declared that the two parties had become independent of each other in accordance with the principles of pursuing national lines of action, although they would continue to work closely together. These developments, though changing but little the basic communist doctrines, gave the communist parties the opportunity to create as patriotic an image as the other parties. Though it was clear that the aims embodied in the National Covenant were transitory and not ultimate goals, Bakdash began to express moderate views and to show readiness to cooperate with democratic elements. As a result, a host of intellectuals and sympathizers gave their ready support to him.

After the war, Bakdash began to bring his party into closer contact with other communist parties, especially in Europe, and to take part in international conferences. In 1946, he went with Faraj-Allah al-Hillu, leader of the Lebanese Communist Party, to London to confer with British communist leaders. On his way he attended secret communist meetings in northern Italy and became acquainted with Italian communist activities. He also kept in touch with communist activities in other Arab countries, especially in the Fertile Crescent, over which he exercised some influence. In 1947, he at-

[6] For the text of the National Covenant, see al-Khuri, *al-Hizb al-Shuyu'i*, pp. 118-26.

tended the Nineteenth Congress of the British Communist Party as
an official delegate. These and other activities abroad enhanced
Bakdash's prestige at home and made him a well-known leader in
international communist councils. Consequently, he was appointed
by the Cominform as Party Director of Arab countries in 1948.
The Syrian and Lebanese parties recombined into the Syro-Lebanese
Communist Party, though the two parties remained outwardly independent, and Bakdash was named Secretary-General. A Central
Committee, coordinating the activities of the two parties, was set
up under Bakdash's leadership. Between 1947 and 1949, when
Arab agitation against the partition of Palestine and the first Arab-
Israeli war marked a high watermark of sorts and communists were
accused of supporting Soviet policy in favor of partition, Bakdash
visited Haifa in secret to confer with Israeli communist leaders on
new plans for dealing with popular outbursts and perhaps to urge
them to dissociate their policy from the newly created state of
Israel. No incident had affected communist propaganda in the Arab
world more adversely than Soviet support for the partition of Palestine and Soviet recognition of Israel. But this situation, as subsequent events demonstrated, proved to be short-lived.

IV

What were Bakdash's methods and objectives?
As a confirmed believer in Stalinist doctrines, Bakdash showed
on the whole a remarkable consistency in trying to expound communist teachings as well as carry them out in Arab lands in accordance with Soviet strategy and methods. In theory, the ultimate
objective of communist strategy was first to seize power in one or
more Arab countries by means of a proletarian revolution and then
to link them with other countries or unite them with the Soviet
Commonwealth. But in reality these aims proved incompatible with
Arab national and religious traditions—indeed, with the national
traditions of many other countries—and Soviet leaders soon realized
that they had to change their methods in order to avoid resistance.
In 1928 the so-called colonial question was formally discussed at
the Sixth Congress of the Comintern and a new strategy, in which
communists in colonial countries would be urged to cooperate with

national organizations struggling against ruling classes and seeking national freedom, was laid down.[7] Bakdash, for purely local considerations, did not begin to apply the new strategy immediately after his return to Damascus.

What kept Bakdash from following the new strategy? There were personal as well as circumstantial reasons for so doing. In the first place, the Syrian and Lebanese Communist parties were supported by minorities, both religious and ethnic, and the principal reason these minorities became communists was their opposition to nationalist organizations which tended to discriminate either on ethnic or on religious grounds. Some minority leaders (especially Christians) preferred to identify themselves as nationalists rather than as communists in the guise of nationalists since Arab nationalists often called on Christians to join their ranks. Second, Khalid Bakdash, though a Muslim and thoroughly at home in Arabic culture, was a Kurd who spoke the Kurdish language and was dependent in part for his political activities on Kurdish support. It is true that while he was still in high school, he had identified himself as a nationalist and supported the National Bloc, but his Kurdish descent and the outdated methods of nationalist leaders had induced him to join the Communist Party. For these reasons Bakdash was not very enthusiastic about fraternizing with nationalist organizations.[8] We should also remember that the Syrian and Lebanese Communist parties had been given inspiration and support first by the Palestinian Communist Party and then by the French Communist Party before Bakdash began to receive direct guidance from Moscow. The former party, which exercised an increasing influence on the Levantine communist parties, did not adopt national symbols until the formation in 1936 of the Popular Front, to which the French Communist Party had given support in an effort to counteract the rising tide of fascism.

Recognizing the difficulty—indeed, almost the hopelessness—of an immediate seizure of power by his country's communists, Bak-

[7] For a discussion of this new strategy in Arab lands, see my *Political Trends*, pp. 116 ff.

[8] For Bakdash's views on communist doctrines and methods before he adopted national symbols, see Khalid Bakdash, *Tariq al-Istiqlal* [The Road Toward Independence]; Alias Marqus, *Ta'rikh al-Ahzab al-Shuyu'iya Fi al-Watan al-'Arabi* [History of Communist Parties in the Arab Fatherland] (Bayrut, n.d.), pp. 203-16.

dash called for a truly democratic and socialist order to be achieved by peaceful and constitutional methods. The dissolution of the Comintern and the circumstances of World War II gave further justification to the assertion of national symbols at the party convention of 1943. In the general elections of 1943 and 1947, Bakdash made speeches in which he clearly stated that he would not make extreme demands; he wanted only moderate social reforms and a truly democratic system, repudiating any claim for radical or revolutionary changes. Like members of other nationalist parties, he called for national freedom, unity, and democracy. From this moderate platform, Bakdash was able to win for the first time national support which almost carried him to Parliament.

After independence, Bakdash may have found it more difficult to maintain an alignment with nationalists since the national demands which formed the basis of cooperation between nationalists and communists had been achieved. But perhaps more important was Soviet support of the United Nations Partition Plan resulting in the establishment of Israel. The Soviet action was so disappointing to the Arabs that it led to an immediate conflict between nationalists and communists. Many an Arab who had joined the Communist Party reverted to nationalism and accused those who remained in the communist camp of treason. Arab communists who supported partition were told to do so on the grounds that it would be easier for communists to dominate two new states in Palestine than one Palestine state under traditional Arab leadership, and that the Arab-Jewish conflict would become meaningless when both the Israeli and the Arab Palestine states became communist states.[9] However, the Palestinian Arabs did not agree to form a separate state nor did Israel become a communist state, as communists had expected; on the contrary, Arab nationalists reacted violently against communists and refused to compromise with them. Old regimes—regimes dominated by bourgeois leaders in alliance with Western imperialists, as communists viewed them—were gradually replaced not by communists but by even stronger nationalist dictatorships opposed to communist doctrines. This occurred first in Syria (1949), then in Egypt (1952), and later in several other countries. This revolutionary process has not yet reached its full development.[10]

[9] See Mustafa al-Zayn, *Khams Sanawat Ma' al-Shuyu'iya* [Five Years with Communism] (Damascus, 1959), pp. 76-84.

[10] For a discussion of the nature and drives of this process, see my *Political Trends,* Chap. 6.

Bakdash was not unaware of the error of Soviet strategy on the Palestine question, but he could do nothing at first to change it. Very soon it became clear that if communism were ever to make progress in Arab lands, communist adoption of an Arab policy vis-à-vis Israel was deemed a necessity. Some communists argued for immediate Soviet support for the Arabs, but Soviet leaders moved gradually because most Arab leaders were still inclined to cooperate with Western nations.

The shift in Soviet strategy toward Arab-Israeli conflicts was prompted by Western defense plans in the Middle East. More directly exposed to the Soviet threat, Turkey and Greece accepted the Truman doctrine as a measure of self-defense; but the Arab countries, separated from the Soviet Union by non-Arab barriers, felt more directly threatened by Israel than by the Soviet Union. Consequently, 'Iraq rejected the Portsmouth mutual defense plan with Britain in 1948; Egypt rejected the Four Power Defense Plan (Britain, the United States, Turkey, and Egypt) in 1953; and though 'Iraq accepted the Baghdad Pact in 1955, she repudiated it later in 1958, and when Jordan was invited to join in 1956, she refused. Egypt came to an agreement with Britain on the Suez base in 1954 and repudiated it in 1956. These and other proposals demonstrated Western desires to re-entrench themselves in key military positions regarded as barriers to communist penetration in the Arab world. Israel tried at the outset not to take sides in the East-West conflict; but when she had to make a choice, her interests dictated that she should depend on American rather than on Soviet aid. These as well as other reasons prompted the Soviet Union to support Arab against Israeli claims, and Bakdash must have felt a great relief in reassociating his party's aims with Arab nationalist aims and calling for the rejection of Western defense plans in the Arab world.[11]

V

The Soviet desire to support the Arabs against Israel having become known, the door for communist-nationalist cooperation was

---

[11] For Bakdash's views on these questions, see Khalid Bakdash, *Fi Sabil Ihbat al-Hilf al-Turki = al-Iraqi wa Jami' al-Ahlaf al-Isti'mariya = al-Harbiya* [Toward the Demolition of the Turko-'Iraqi Pact and All the Imperialistic and Military Pacts] (Damascus, 1955).

thrown open. The Ba'th Party and other young nationalists entered
into an alignment with communists and formed a National Union, a
cherished communist demand, in an effort first to overthrow the
Shishakli military regime and then to oppose Western pressures, including Western support to Israel. After Shishakli's fall from power
in 1954, communist-nationalist cooperation continued since there
were other grounds for cooperation between communist and Ba'thists:
both regarded themselves as leftist in outlook and opposed to the
Syrian National (formally called the Social Nationalist) Party, which
Shishakli seems to have supported. Bakdash was quick enough to
take advantage of this new alignment and began to prepare himself
for the forthcoming elections of 1954. Meanwhile, when Syria refused American technical assistance, the Soviet Union, to Bakdash's
great delight, offered both military and economic aid with easy
terms. More specifically, Soviet participation in the Syrian International Trade Exposition, in which Soviet technical skills were ex-
hibited, so impressed the Syrians that the Communist Party felt
strong enough to participate in the elections of 1954.

In opening the campaign for the elections, Bakdash gave a
speech on September 10, 1954, in which he explained his platform.
The speech was given in the Kurdish quarter, Bakdash's stronghold,
to a crowd estimated to have numbered over 20,000. He began by
reminding his audience that he had been there some seven years
earlier—in 1947—when he was running in the elections. Those seven
years, he said—at least the last five of them—were, according to
some, lean years. But to him, he added, they were really rich years—
the years of trials and tribulations under military rule—from which
the Syrian people had gained invaluable experiences. Bakdash then
proceeded to outline his platform. What did Syria want, he asked?
Syria, he said, wanted a national democratic regime which would
insure freedom for all and provide bread for workers, soil and water
for peasants, and health and schooling for children. He also said that
Syria was in need of increased national production—both industrial
and agricultural—and of protection for small industrial enterprises.
He also stressed the need for the revival of Arab culture. Syria,
Bakdash told his listeners, expected the new members of Parliament
to achieve all these aims.

Bakdash then turned to foreign policy. He said that Syria,
which had just achieved independence and the evacuation of French

and British forces, did not want to pass under American domination or to become an American military base. Syria, he said emphatically, needed members of Parliament who could stand up and say no to anyone who desired to impose defense plans or extend colonial influence in the country. He then went on to admonish his countrymen that they should never be afraid of American imperialism, since imperialism was on the defensive. "There are now forces working against it," he said, "the forces of peace, democracy and socialism generated by over 800 million people inhabiting the vast region extending from Peking to Berlin, led by the Soviet Union—the country of workers and peasants, the bastion of socialism, and the great friend of the Arabs."

What did the Soviet Union stand for? Bakdash asked. The Soviet Union, he said, stood for socialism, but this socialism was not just any kind of socialism—"it is scientific socialism." "This kind of socialism," he explained, "is the socialism which undertakes to control the means of production and distributes goods among people on the basis of need, not personal profit. Each individual must work in accordance with his ability and receive his compensation accordingly, not on other grounds." There should never be exploitation of man by man, or oppression of one by another. All men should live in peace, prosperity, and equality. "But is Syria now ready for this kind of socialism?" Bakdash asked. "No," he said. "We have first to emancipate Syria and its resources from colonialism and feudalism before achieving socialism." Syria, he said, must pass through a transitional period of national liberation, democratic freedom, and peace before embarking on socialism. The first stage—the stage of national liberation—said Bakdash, was a national objective of all parties, and "we communists are prepared to cooperate with others to achieve these aims." We do not intend, he promised, to put forth now any other claim.[12]

On the strength of this moderate program—which he reiterated later in Parliament—he was elected as the first communist to occupy a parliamentary seat in an Arab country. This speech was a candid statement of policy: it reiterated the basic principles of the National Covenant (1943), the various statements and declarations made since the war, and Bakdash's own position on domestic and

[12]Khalid Bakdash, *Khitab Khalid Bakdash* (September 10, 1954) (Damascus, 1954).

foreign affairs. It delineated communist aims in the transition toward the ultimate goal—a socialist state.

Bakdash's victory at the polls was due not only to the fact that he was a communist. There were other contributing factors. Because of his heritage, he was supported by virtually all Kurdish voters. He was also supported by young nationalists who were then in alliance with leftist groups. And Bakdash's personal merits and growing prestige contributed in no small measure to his victory. In Parliament, Bakdash served with distinction. He became a member of several committees, including the Committee on Foreign Affairs, and attended their meetings regularly. He often spoke on domestic and foreign affairs and made extemporaneous remarks whenever the House debated an issue. I had the pleasure of attending a parliamentary meeting (July 9, 1955) in which Bakdash spoke eloquently in favor of draft municipal legislation; when during the debate he asked to speak again, Nazim al-Qudsi, Speaker of the House, remarked that Bakdash was the most frequent speaker in the House!

During the period in which Bakdash served in Parliament, from 1954 to 1958, communist influence reached perhaps a high watermark. Communists penetrated almost all departments of government and reached high military echelons. 'Afif al-Badhra (often called al-Bizri), their chief military spokesman, rose from the rank of colonel to brigadier in 1957 and became Chief of Staff; he did not officially join the Communist Party, but it became known, from actions if not from private utterances, that he was a communist at heart. As leader of the Communist Party, Bakdash became very active in official and nonofficial circles; he often visited President Quwatli and demanded official recognition of his party. He also paid several visits to Moscow and attended the parties of communist legations in Damascus. Twice, in 1956 and 1957, the communists tried to seize power but failed. These moves alarmed nationalist leaders, who saw power slipping gradually from their hands. Since both nationalists and communists were then talking about Arab unity, the Ba'th Party found itself losing ground and began to press for unity with Egypt to regain influence. The communists, though gaining, could not reject unity in principle and demanded that the form of unity should be federal rather than unitary. Nasir, the new spokesman for Arab unity, was no great friend of the communists, even though he was on friendly terms with the Soviet Union, and he accepted unity with Syria only after all political parties, except the Communist Party, agreed to dissolve themselves. For this reason, when the Syrian Parliament voted for unity (February 28, 1958), Khalid Bakdash was already on his way to Prague. His was the only vacant seat in Parliament when the resolution passed unanimously.

Since 1958, Bakdash has stayed in Prague whenever he has been unable to secure permission to return to Damascus. However, he has made several secret visits to Syria, and it was reported that twice, in 1961 and 1962, he was not allowed to leave the plane when he attempted to land at the Damascus airport. In 1964 he visited Damascus and met some of his party leaders. While living in Europe, he attended several international communist conferences and visited China, North Korea, and India. After eight years of exile, he returned quietly to Damascus in 1966, but made no serious attempt to resume an active role in politics. Bakdash has obviously not yet been able to recover from the setback he suffered in 1958. But his political career may well resume if circumstances once again become favorable. Needless to say, so long as internal tensions in Arab lands continue to exist and contending parties try to associate national claims with world ideological goals, it is always likely that Bakdash will find an opportunity to make a comeback.[13]

VI

"I do not know where the party's frontiers end," said 'Umar Fakhuri, a Lebanese Communist writer, "and where Bakdash's frontiers begin."[14] Fakhuri's cryptic remark is not meant to be a compliment but a reproach to Bakdash because he has put his own power and prestige above that of the party; but it may be taken as a compliment by a leader who wanted to identify fully his personal standing with his party's standing, since in the last analysis it is in

[13] During his eight years of absence, Bakdash has expressed his opinion on several domestic and foreign questions ranging from criticism of Nasir's attitude toward communists to the Sino-Soviet conflict. On domestic questions, see Bakdash's press interview published in al-Akhbar (Bayrut) and several other newspapers in December 1958. See also al-Watha'iq al-'Arabiya [Arab Documents], 1965, p. 32; and Qal'achi, Tajribat, pp. 117-18. For his views on international questions, see World Marxist Review, December 1965, pp. 16-19; June 1968, pp. 39-41; August 1964, pp. 16-18; April 1970, pp. 92-97.

[14] Qal'achi, Tajribat, p. 152.

the party's interest if the leader's stature and image rise high in the public eye. The party begins to suffer only when the leader subordinates public to private interests and makes arbitrary decisions contrary to strategy or basic principles.

Bakdash possesses certain qualities that qualified him for his party's leadership. In addition to being tall, well built, handsome, and distinguished-looking, he has moral courage, dash, vigilance, and perseverance. His personality also fits the role: he is sociable and amiable and has artistic tastes. Adept at public speaking, he could excite audiences even if they were not persuaded by his argument. He often recited poetry in his speeches and told entertaining anecdotes, making his extemporaneous speeches more effective than those he had prepared. His followers respected him, though they did not always love him, but all—friends and foes—acknowledged his efficiency and discipline.

Suave and dexterous in dealing with officials, he often misled the police and fled the country before he could be arrested. Consequently, he escaped prison more often than many other underground leaders, although he did serve some short prison terms.

As an administrator, Bakdash was both efficient and hardworking. It is true that he was jealous of his powers, often failing to delegate authority to subordinates, but he did not shrink from responsibility and worked hard to carry out the details of administrative functions. He has also been criticized for acting unilaterally, without the knowledge or consultation of the party's Executive Committee. Differences on procedural and personal grounds have taken their toll on all Arab parties and organizations, but Bakdash has often been reproached by comrades for differences resulting from whims and occasional mishandling of personal problems. Since communists have shown tenacity and suffered hardships in carrying out orders, they expect their leaders to have greater appreciation and understanding of personal problems and not to deal with them harshly and often unjustly. By blunt and often arrogant action, Bakdash unnecessarily alienated many devoted comrades who served the Communist Party loyally.

Bakdash has often spoken about freedom and democracy in such a way that many young men have been tempted to join the party in search for these principles, only to find to their surprise that freedom and democracy did not really exist under Bakdash's leadership.

On the contrary, he has often been curt and high-handed, which has prompted a number of members to leave the party. Moreover, Bakdash has offended some intellectuals who had long served the party with devotion. Since the Communist Party can not yet claim to be proletarian, the intellectuals and young men in high schools and colleges still form its backbone. Bakdash's alleged disrespect for intellectuals, probably initiated by personal differences, has resulted in the loss of several thinkers and writers who would have continued support to the party under a more careful and tolerant head.[15]

Above all, Bakdash's licentious propensities and relatively luxurious style of living did not escape critics, who remarked that they were unbecoming to a leader of toilers and peasants. Some have demanded to know how he could maintain a house and servants in Damascus, another in Bayrut, and still others elsewhere, along with two or more cars, on his modest salary as a member of Parliament or merely as leader of the Communist Party. Bakdash is known as a well-dressed man, almost a dandy, who frequented night clubs and was a heavy smoker and drinker—habits not very endearing to followers in the Arab world who expect men of responsibility to lead a dignified and austere life.[16] Most damaging of all were the rumors about his relations with women, a very sensitive matter in Arab countries, which aroused criticism and undermined the party's reputation in a conservative society. As early as 1949, Bakdash's social morality became a matter of concern to some members, especially after his return from Moscow in 1936. It was rumored that he had been married while he was studying in Moscow and that he had left behind a wife and daughter on his return to Damascus. His relations with a Kurdish girl, Wisal Farha, aroused concern, and only by marrying her in 1951 was he able to put an end to criticism. However, this marriage proved an asset to the party, since his wife became a vigilant propagandist of communism among women. Despite marriage, rumors about womanizing continued—a charge which was highly exaggerated in order to undermine his leadership.

---

[15] Qal'achi, *Tajribat*, pp. 156-59; al-Zayn, *Khams Sanawat Ma' al-Shuyu'iya*, pp. 30-33.

[16] Cf. Bakdash's habits with 'Aflaq's, who impressed followers by his frugal way of living (see p. 225, below).

Bakdash has shown remarkable flexibility and readiness to change his methods if they proved wrong or had an adverse effect on the party, but it has not always been easy to win back friends who have been deeply hurt. Personable and dexterous in manner, Bakdash may well be regarded as a successful leader. It is not an easy task to satisfy conflicting claims and sensitivities in an individualistic society, but on the whole he has been able to maintain fairly good relations with followers and sympathizers.

In his support of the international communist movement, Bakdash has shown remarkable consistency in endorsing Soviet aims and strategy, but he has not always been uncritical of the views of leading communists, Soviet or otherwise, in international communist conferences, where doctrines and methods were open for discussion.[17] Although he is aware of his dependence on Soviet support, he registered disapproval of Soviet support to Nasir's Egypt, which he regarded as basically opposed to communism, and only reluctantly did he pay tribute to Nasir before his untimely death.[18] As a professional politician, Bakdash served the Communist Party with ability; he also served the movement with his pen and tongue as an effective writer and speaker. Few indeed would doubt that he is a leader of the first order.

[17]See Khalid Bakdash, "The National Liberation Movement and the Communists," *World Marxist Review,* December 1965, pp. 16-19.
[18]See Khalid Bakdash, "Egypt and the Failure of the United Arab Republic," *al-Akhbar* (Bayrut), April 30, 1961.

PART THREE

THE MAN OF THE PEN
THE INTELLECTUAL
POLITICIAN

 Opinion before the courage
of courageous men;
It comes first and the other
runs behind.

Al-Mutannabbi (d. 965)

Ahmad Lutfi al-Sayyid

CHAPTER X

The Idealistic School
Ahmad Lutfi al-Sayyid

If we were to live with bread and water alone, the necessary food for
our life is quite adequate. . . . However, the real food with which we
live and love life is not merely to satisfy hunger: there is a kind of
food which is more important than bread and water and which has
become today our dearest and most highly prized demand—freedom.

Lutfi al-Sayyid

The task of the intellectual politician is more difficult and
complex than the task of the military or the professional
politician, for he tries to understand more profoundly the
nature of social change and to formulate his own goals, which he
then seeks to achieve by participation in politics regardless how long
the process may take. It requires a combination of qualities rarely
possessed by a single individual—qualities of the man of thought
who can formulate goals, and qualities of the man of action who
can carry them out. Rarely indeed in the experience of mankind
have men been found—Caesar, Jefferson, and Lenin, to mention but
three unique figures—who possessed the superior qualities of creative
thought and action and who left in varying degree indelible imprints
either on the course of events in their own countries or on the destiny of mankind as a whole.

Three types of intellectual politicians, each representing a different school of thought, may be distinguished for the purpose of
this study. First, there is the intellectual politician who displays an

interest in ideal goals and who refuses to compromise them by subordinating the ideal to the real. Aware that ideal goals cannot be achieved in the near future, he seeks to prepare a new elite who will be able by participation in politics to carry them out—*Serit arbores quae saeclo prosint alteri* (Caecilius Statius). Lutfi al-Sayyid, styled as the teacher of a generation, represents the idealist school of thought. Second, there is the intellectual politician who formulates goals that have closer relevance to reality and who seeks by direct participation in politics to carry them out. Muhammad Husayn Haykal, a writer, journalist, and leader of a political party, eminently represents the realistic school of thought. Third, there is the intellectual politician who seeks changes in accordance with ideological goals and tries to carry them out by revolutionary methods. Michel 'Aflaq, a writer and founder of an Arab socialist party, represents the ideological school of thought.

II

When Lutfi al-Sayyid entered public life toward the end of the nineteenth century, Egypt had achieved notable social and economic progress under British control, but she had not made corresponding political and cultural progress. Some critics maintained that it was the deliberate policy of Britain's proconsul—Lord Cromer—to pay particular attention to economic reform to enable Egypt to pay foreign debts but to neglect cultural and political progress in order to perpetuate the British occupation. By the turn of the twentieth century, after almost twenty years of British control, the country began to show signs of restlessness and the call for the termination of the occupation had become both persistent and vocal in press and political circles.

The most outspoken opponents of the occupation were two groups who styled themselves as Pan-Islamists and nationalists. Both called for the *status quo ante* the British occupation of 1882, when Egypt was an integral part of the Ottoman Empire and her ruler, the Khedive, governed as the Sultan's viceroy. Although the nationalists advocated an Egyptian national identity, they supported the Pan-Islamists in asserting the Sultan's sovereignty in order to bring Ottoman pressure on Britain to terminate the occupation.

The Khedive, reduced by Lord Cromer almost to the status of figurehead, secretly encouraged the nationalists under the leadership of Mustafa Kamil to launch a campaign against the occupation both inside and outside the country. Mustafa Kamil's nationalist call, expressed in highly eloquent and emotional terms, was particularly appealing to young men because it inspired them with a romantic love for their fatherland. His attack on Britain aroused the sympathy of liberal circles in Europe when he concentrated on particular grievances, but his agitation was on the whole confined to opposition to the British occupation and failed to give a positive content to the nationalism he preached. He invoked the supreme authority of the Sultan over Egypt, and thus his views differed but little from the Pan-Islamists who supported the Sultan's caliphial authority on religious grounds. Neither the Copts, Egypt's native Christians, nor thinkers who stressed Egypt's own identity apart from Ottoman connections were satisfied with Mustafa Kamil's vague concept of nationalism.

Mustafa Kamil's call attracted at first many young men, but very soon some began to fall under other influences when they discovered that Kamil was essentially supporting the Khedive's position against Cromer regardless of his authoritarian tendencies and that he said almost nothing about the people's right to participate in government. There was another group, small but increasingly influential, which derived its inspiration from Afghani and 'Abduh and had either sympathized with or participated in the 'Urabi movement. This group, often referred to as the 'Abduh group (Hizb al-Imam), consisting of such men as Sa'd and Fathi Zaghlul, Qasim Amin, and Lutfi al-Sayyid, was looked upon by the Khedive with suspicion and disfavor because of its sympathies with 'Urabi. Since the 'Urabi revolt had failed, 'Abduh and his disciples had abandoned revolutionary activities and concentrated on basic social reforms as the best way to prepare the country for public responsibility when the occupation had come to an end. Impressed by its moderation, shortly before he left Egypt Lord Cromer began to encourage the group to form the Umma Party in order to counter the influence of Kamil's nationalist followers.

It was in this social and political milieu that Ahmad Lutfi al-Sayyid began to play a role in the politics of his country. At first he was attracted by Mustafa Kamil, but very soon he was drawn into the circle of 'Abduh and showed grave concern about the Khedive's desire to exercise authoritarian powers. Like 'Abduh, he preferred to follow peaceful rather than violent methods; he even avoided mass agitation or any other form of demagogic performances. He envisaged his role primarily as preparing the people for eventual responsibility when the occupation came to an end and emancipating them from slavish submission and lethargy.

III

Ahmad Lutfi al-Sayyid was born in 1872 to a wealthy family. His father was an 'umda (village headman) and a notable in one of the villages of the Delta. Thus from early life Lutfi was relieved from worries about material security, which often forced other intellectuals to take positions contrary to their convictions. On more than one occasion, he could afford to resign posts which put him in disagreeable positions and return to his country house until called upon to resume work on his own terms.

The second important fact about Lutfi was his keen interest, from early life, in learning. He learned the Qur'an by heart at a *kuttab* school before he moved to a government school at the age of ten. In 1885, after three years in the district primary school, he went to the Khedival School in Cairo where he met his future law partner and intimate friend, 'Abd al-'Aziz Fahmi. Before he graduated in 1889, he had already read widely in Arabic literature. After high school he entered the School of Law, where he met some of Egypt's future political leaders; he also met Muhammad 'Abduh who seems to have given him encouragement in learning. He showed particular interest in journalism and edited with Tharwat and Isma'il Sidqi, two future Premiers, a magazine—*al-Tashri'* (Legislation)— which contained commentaries on legal decisions of the day. His interest in journalism led him to visit the editors of Cairo's influential papers and periodicals and to come into contact with leading intellectuals.

In 1893, a year before he graduated, Lutfi spent the summer vacation in Istanbul. This visit to the Ottoman capital must have made an adverse impression on him because he observed at first hand the Porte's censorship and police surveillance; he was later to warn against Egypt's dependence on the Sultan's mercy.[1] While there, he frequented the house of Jamal al-Din al-Afghani, who seems to have impressed him with his fluency of speech and power of argumentation, which he himself displayed later in conversations with disciples. In his spare time, he read literature and philosophy—the works of Comte, Mill, and Spencer in particular—the impact of which was revealed in his writings.

His studies completed, Lutfi first entered government service for two years and then practiced law for another year. From both he learned much about public life and bureaucratic abuses. Free from government service, he began to take an interest in politics. In 1896, he formed with 'Abd al-'Aziz Fahmi, a classmate, a secret society whose main purpose was to work against the British occupation. Mustafa Kamil, who knew about the society, approached him about joining another secret society, in which the Khedive himself was a member, working for the same goals. Lutfi was advised to spend a year in Switzerland in order to obtain Swiss nationality, which would give him protection under the capitulations, and to edit a newspaper for the dissemination of views opposed to the British occupation. This arrangement did not work and Lutfi returned to Cairo without Swiss citizenship; his relations with the Khedive and Mustafa Kamil began to cool, presumably because he had become a friend of Muhammad Abduh, whom the Khedive mistrusted. These experiences strengthened his conviction that the ruler's absolute powers should be restricted before independence was achieved and drove him to work in other political circles.

The next major event was Lutfi's decision to work in journalism. Favorable circumstances prompted him to found a newspaper and to use it as a means to expound his ideas about social reform. The conflict between the Khedive and Lord Cromer had become intense, and the nationalist press attacked British policy indiscriminately. When the Fashoda incident developed, the press naturally supported France. But when the Ottoman Porte claimed 'Aqaba, Lord Cromer was not a little surprised that the nationalists within Egypt then supported the Porte's claim for no other reason than to oppose Britain, even though she tried to protect Egyptian interests.

It was held by the British authorities that those who agitated

---

[1] Lutfi al-Sayyid, *Qissat Hayati* [Story of My Life] (Cairo [1963]), pp. 33-34.

against the occupation were either men of Ottoman origin (i.e., the Khedive and his palace entourage) or younger men who followed Mustafa Kamil and that the Egyptian landowner and wealthy class, who represented the "real interests" of the country, were silent about political issues. In order to bring the upper classes into active politics, Lutfi appealed to them to defend the country's real interests, which should be placed above personal interests, regardless of the policies of the contending parties. A meeting of Egyptian notables was held in which it was decided to organize the Umma (Nation's) Party and to issue a paper, *al-Jarida* (Journal).[2] The party, whose nominal leadership was entrusted to Mahmud Sulayman Pasha, was dominated by the rich and aristocratic families of Egypt. Lutfi, himself a representative of vested interests, became the editor of *al-Jarida* and secretary of the party. It was declared that the purpose of the party was to achieve Egyptian independence—Egypt was to belong neither to the Ottoman Porte nor to Britain—and to demand the promulgation of a constitution. These aims seem to have pleased Lord Cromer, as they were in accord with the ultimate purpose of the occupation in principle. They also counteracted the agitation in favor of the Khedive and the Ottoman Porte.

From 1907 to 1914, Lutfi devoted most of his time to reflecting on conditions of Egyptian society, demanding in particular freedom from absolute rule. His ideas, though intelligible to an educated class, failed to influence a public ready to be moved only by fiery slogans and emotional speeches. The leaders of the Umma Party complained about his editorship, because *al-Jarida* attracted only a small circle of intellectuals and failed to compete with other papers which enjoyed a greater popular appeal. But supported by a number of aristocratic houses, he remained in control of the party's organ.

In July 1914, when Britain declared war on Germany, Lutfi became more active in high government circles. He contended that this important event should be exploited to Egypt's advantage. He called on Husayn Rushdi, the Prime Minister, and urged him to propose to the British government that it recognize Egypt's independence if the Ottoman Porte should enter the war on Germany's side. He went on to suggest that Egypt might participate in the war

[2] *Al-Jarida* was issued on March 9, 1907; and the party was formally organized on December 21, 1907.

on Britain's side as the price for independence, if Britain so desired. He talked in the same vein to 'Adli Yakan, Egypt's Minister for Foreign Affairs, to Ronald Storrs, Oriental Secretary at the British Residency, and to Ronald Graham, British Adviser to the Egyptian Ministry of the Interior. Graham was not very encouraging and told Lutfi candidly that, if Egypt were to be declared independent, her government might be forced to support the Ottoman Empire against Britain, and not vice versa, because public opinion was manifestly sympathetic to the Sultan and hostile to Great Britain. Storrs, more optimistic, promised Lutfi to present the matter to higher authorities. Thereupon, Rushdi, Yakan, Lutfi, and Storrs met to prepare a set of proposals which would grant Britain the right to protect her interests in Egypt for the present in exchange for recognition of Egyptian independence after the war. When Rushdi submitted these proposals for consideration to Reginald Wingate, Acting British Resident in Egypt, Wingate was not very optimistic but promised to forward them to the British government. The British reply must have been negative, for it came to the knowledge of Rushdi and Yakan that Britain was not prepared to consider Egypt's demand for independence. On the contrary, when the Ottoman Sultan entered the war on Germany's side in October 1914, Britain declared Egypt to be under her protection to the great disappointment of Lutfi and his group.[3] A year later, in 1915, Lutfi resigned the editorship of *al-Jarida*—a task which had become difficult under wartime censorship—and retired to his country house. "I have decided to break my pen," he said in a moment of despair, "and to withdraw from politics."[4] He was persuaded to serve as Director of the Khedive's Library, which became the National Library after the war, and spent most of his time in reading and in translating Aristotle's *Ethics* into Arabic.

In November 1918, when the war came to an end, Lutfi returned to politics to make, with a few other politicians, another attempt to secure his country's independence. He and four others— Sa'd Zaghlul, 'Abd al-'Aziz Fahmi, 'Ali Sha'rawi, and Muhammad

[3] Lutfi al-Sayyid, *Qissat Hayati*, pp. 162-66. Ronald Storrs recorded in his memoirs that the British government was contemplating the "annexation" of Egypt to the British Empire and that the declaration of the "protectorate," made at the suggestion of the British Agency in Cairo, was a compromise between Egyptian and British interests (see Storrs, *Orientations* [London, 1949], pp. 136-40).

[4] Lutfi al-Sayyid, *Qissat Hayati*, p. 165.

Mahmud—formed a "delegation," the nucleus of the so-called Wafd
Party, and began, under Zaghlul's leadership, to demand negotiations
with Britain to achieve independence. Zaghlul and two other members of the delegation went first to see Wingate to demand independence. Rebuffed, they decided to proceed to Paris and present
their demand to the Peace Conference on the strength of the principle of self-determination. For the next two years, from 1919 to
1921, Lutfi took an active part in nationalist activities, but then he
decided to withdraw again from politics for two reasons.[5] First, he
had come to the conclusion that Britain was not really prepared to
end the occupation and recognize Egypt's independence and that
negotiations might continue indefinitely without real success. Second, from the time that nationalist activities began after the war,
he had been aware of a power struggle among the politicians,
particularly between Zaghlul and 'Adli Yakan. He saw in this
rivalry grave danger to the country because national interests were
being subordinated to personal interests, with Britain the only
beneficiary. He concluded that his goals could not possibly be
achieved by direct participation in politics and decided to devote
the rest of his life to the preparation of an elite that would guide
the nation toward the achievement of national goals. He maintained that reform of society depends on reform of the individuals who compose it. For this reason, he devoted most of his time
to cultural and educational rather than political activities, although
on more than one occasion he was drawn into politics by essentially personal considerations to serve in the Cabinet.[6]

IV

Lutfi al-Sayyid took the long view in trying to achieve social
goals. Like other nationalists, he wanted to reestablish his country's

[5] The events of these years are related vividly by Lutfi's friend and collaborator, 'Abd al-
'Aziz Fahmi, *Hadhihi Hayati* [This Is My Life] (Cairo, 1964), pp. 72-117. See also Lutfi
al-Sayyid, *Qissat Hayati*, pp. 178-81.

[6] In 1954 Colonel Nasir proposed to offer Lutfi the presidency of the Republic, but he
declined, pleading old age, although he was pleased by the offer and gave his blessings to
Egypt's new regime. Taking into consideration his dislike of violence, Lutfi could not
possibly have agreed to participate in politics with army officers who had achieved power
by force. For Lutfi's life and thought, see Afaf Lutfi al-Sayyid, *Egypt and Cromer* (London, 1968), Chap. 8; and "Lutfi al-Sayyid al-Insan," *Hiwar* (Bayrut), Vol. IV (1963), pp.
14-21.

independence, which had been lost long ago as the result of successive foreign dominations. But to Lutfi this was only one step in the national struggle, since the liberation of the individual from persecution and from submission to native and foreign rulers was the ultimate goal. Although he realized that individual freedom had rarely been enjoyed by his countrymen in the past, he saw it as a prerequisite for a responsible citizenry, which in turn was essential before authority could be transferred from foreign to native hands. He went so far as to argue that before national freedom could be achieved, the individual must be liberated from tyranny and oppression. His concern about individual freedom was perhaps the fundamental issue separating him from Mustafa Kamil, whose desire to bring the occupation to an end at the earliest possible moment included no concern about the relationship between the rulers and the ruled after the British had departed.

How can the individual be freed from absolute and oppressive rule? Lutfi held that the individual would be free if the ruler's powers were restricted by constitutional guarantees and if the people were to share authority with the ruler. He called for the promulgation of a written constitution that would specify the limitations of executive power and establish the people's right to participate in government by representation in a national assembly. In other words, he desired to establish a parliamentary form of government and to organize political parties whose representatives in Parliament would speak on behalf of the people. He maintained that democracy was the best form of government that man had yet developed to guarantee individual freedom.

It is important to remember, if we are not to misunderstand Lutfi, that his call for democracy and liberty was in his own mind essentially a call for checks against authoritarian rule and oppression; his political doctrine, if he may be said to have had one, was not popular democracy but parliamentary democracy, presided over by an enlightened elite imbued by patriotism and such ideas as progress and welfare and morality. His ideas of the functions of the state were based on individualism and free enterprise—the authority of the state in domestic affairs was not to extend beyond the functions of the courts, police, and army. The other areas of life in society were to be left to the individuals.

However, before democratic institutions can possibly work there must exist in the country an enlightened public and an elite that can guide the public and represent it in government. When Lutfi entered public life, representative institutions had not yet developed in his country nor was there an educated citizenry—the great majority of the people were totally ignorant and incapable of expressing an opinion on public affairs. He was quite aware that democracy could not be established overnight; he, therefore, called for the gradual adoption of constitutional-representative institutions and for the preparation of an elite to guide the public.[7]

Lutfi's preoccupation with freedom as a fundamental social goal stemmed from personal experience as well as from European liberal thought. When he entered public life first as a government official in the department of justice and then as a practicing lawyer, he found that freedom in judicial proceedings did not exist in Egypt, because of the absolute character of Egyptian governmental authority and its interference in judicial decisions, and because both judges and lawyers lacked dedication and often subordinated vocational to personal and political considerations.[8] Very soon he was to discover that these propensities also existed in other branches of the government. It is true that he found relative freedom of the press under the Cromer regime when he himself was an editor, but this freedom had not existed before nor did it continue after Cromer.[9] Finding freedom of the press replaced by censorship when World War I broke out, he retired from his editorship.

Lutfi's love for freedom was intensified by his reading of European thought, especially, as we have noted, nineteenth-century liberal thought—Mill, Spencer, August Comte, and others—and it was the nineteenth-century conception of freedom that was echoed in his writings. When he began to translate Aristotle's works, he realized the extent to which these European thinkers had drawn on Greek thought and the need for the study and translation of clas-

---

[7] For Lutfi's ideas about freedom, see Lutfi al-Sayyid, *Ta'amulat* [Meditations] (Cairo, 1946), pp. 55-60; *al-Muntakhabat* [Selections] (Cairo, n.d.), Vol. I, pp. 296-98, 299-302, and Vol. II, pp. 60-63; and *Mabadi' Fi al-Siyasa wa al-Adab wa al-Ijtima'* [Views about Politics, Literature and Society] (Cairo, 1963), pp. 38 ff. For an exposition of Lutfi's thought in general, see Albert Hourani, *Arabic Thought In the Liberal Age* (London, 1962), pp. 171-82; and J. M. Ahmad, *The Intellectual Origins of Egyptian Nationalism* (London, 1960), pp. 84 ff.

[8] Lutfi al-Sayyid, *al-Muntakhabat*, Vol. I, pp. 61-63, 117-20, 290-92. See also Lutfi al-Sayyid, *Qissat Hayati*, p. 39; and Fahmi, *Hadhihi Hayati*, pp. 51-54.

[9] Lutfi al-Sayyid, *Qissat Hayati*, pp. 58-87.

sical Greek works. From European thinkers, he learned the deeper meaning of freedom and other liberal concepts, but the relevance of these concepts to society as expounded in his writings was the product of his own reflections and personal experiences. His thoughts about Egyptian society were derived from an analysis of the weaknesses of the Egyptian individual—his tolerance, his submission to rulers, and his fear of authority. It is true, he said, that tolerance may be regarded as a virtue, if tolerance is combined with strength of character. But in Egypt, he noted, tolerance stemmed from resignation; it reflected, therefore, weakness and cowardice.[10] These weak elements, he went on to explain, were the product of a long history of absolute rule and oppression. The general level of morality in a society, he pointed out, tends to deteriorate under absolute rule. Continuous oppression, he said, forces the individual to be on the defensive, even though at heart he detests the rulers. This outward submission had become a traditional behavior pattern in Egypt handed down from generation to generation, and it had created an ungenuine type of loyalty to authority.[11]

While weaknesses were the causes of the individual's submissive attitude toward authority, they were also the product of authoritarian rule. This situation, needless to say, created a vicious circle, and, Lutfi said, it is not easy to break vicious circles. However, he observed, the nation which "twice gave birth to civilization" should be able to "break the fetters that [hold] it down." In their new awakening, the people would learn how to live in the modern world. He never doubted the ability of his countrymen to achieve progress: "All we need is to go on learning—the biggest enemies of progress are despair and lethargy."[12]

From this view of the individual, Lutfi turned to the nation. His concept of the nation, derived from European thought, was territorial and not Islamic or ecumenical. Egypt, he said, is composed of all the individuals who inhabit its territory—Muslims, as well as Copts, regardless of religious differences—and who share common interests and values. Pan-Islamists and Mustafa Kamil's nationalists, he noted, stressed either religious or Ottoman identity and thus

---

[10] Lutfi al-Sayyid, *al-Muntakhabat*, Vol. I, pp. 49-56, 107-9.

[11] *Ibid.*, pp. 104-6, 107-9.

[12] Lutfi al-Sayyid, *al-Muntakhabat*, Vol. II, pp. 104-7; *Ta'amulat*, pp. 65-67.

alienated the Copts, who were discriminated against on religious grounds. Lutfi rejected traditional views of loyalty and advocated an Egyptian national identity based on her continuous history, in which Islamic rule was but a chapter, as well as on the territorial, social, and economic conditions which shaped and continue to shape the life of the Egyptian people. Lutfi's call for national unity gained the support not only of Copts but also of the intelligentsia, who were attracted by the modern concept of nationalism.[13] The idea of Egyptian nationalism was not new, since 'Urabi had called for "Egypt for the Egyptians" in 1880, but Lutfi stressed secular rather than religious elements. He recognized that Islam was the religion of the majority of Egyptians but that other religions were just as important to other people who lived in Egypt; and he asserted that religion should be a matter of individual conscience.[14]

Lutfi's stress on secularism, especially the relegation of religion to the individual level, aroused critics, who denounced him as a mulhid (atheist).[15] But Lutfi's own views about religion, as it has been noticed, are absent in his published writings and can be known only from his private conversations with disciples and friends. I have already had occasion to notice that Lutfi took pains to impress on others his respect for their personal views on religion and would not say anything *contra bonos mores*. In the course of one conversation, however, he told me that the Shari'a (religious law), long in a state of stagnation, was no longer adequate to meet the new conditions of life and that it should be radically changed. Sanhuri, a close friend of Lutfi, told me that shortly before his death Lutfi seriously questioned traditional religious beliefs. "One who is very old," Sanhuri observed, "would rather tend to avoid raising doubt about religious convictions, but Lutfi expressed serious doubts about them." Lutfi remained a sceptic to the end of his life.

[13] Lutfi al-Sayyid, *Ta'amulat,* pp. 61-64, 65-67, 68-71. For the effect of Lutfi's teachings on Copts, see Salama Musa, *Tarbiyat Salama Musa* (Cairo, 1948), pp. 60-62, 68-75; translated by L. O. Schuman, *The Education of Salama Musa* (Leiden, 1961), pp. 42-44, 48-52.

[14] Lutfi al-Sayyid, *Safahat Mitwiya* (Cairo, 1946), pp. 96-101, 102-5; *Qissat Hayati,* pp. 73-77.

[15] "Lutfi al-Sayyid," 'Abd al-Rahman al-Rafi'i, the lawyer-historian, once told me, "was the shaykh of the mulhids." Sanhuri, who overheard this remark said, "the shaykh of the Mulhids was Shibli Shumayyil and not Lutfi," although Lutfi was one of the mulhids. Rafi'i added that Lutfi, as Rector of the Egyptian University, defended such mulhids as Taha Husayn, Mansur Fahmi, and Haykal.

From a secular conception of the nation, Lutfi proceeded to the second logical assumption that Egypt, like every other nation, must possess national freedom. He believed that this freedom is inherent in the nation, presumably arising from the natural rights of people to govern themselves.[16] But, he observed, the Egyptian people had so long been governed by foreign rulers that they could not achieve national freedom quickly. In modern times, toward the latter part of the nineteenth century, the Egyptian people had begun to awaken and demand self-government, but 'Urabi's military uprising precipitated foreign intervention and gave Britain the opportunity to occupy the country. Although reproached for criticizing 'Urabi, whom many Egyptians regarded as a national hero, Lutfi believed the 'Urabi uprising had impeded an already growing nationalist movement which would have matured into a constitutional-representative government. The 'Urabi revolt, he said, threatened foreign interests and gave the British an excuse to reestablish the Khedive's absolute rule, in which the British agency shared. He felt it was true that the British occupation brought about stability and material progress but that it had not helped to promote parliamentary government or to improve the moral character of the people. On the contrary, he noted, the occupation, like all foreign rule, accentuated the feelings of submission and lack of genuine loyalty to authority. The ultimate cure for this anomalous situation would be national freedom.[17]

But how could Egypt achieve national freedom? Britain was too strong for Egypt to persuade her or to force her to withdraw. Lutfi was aware of Egypt's weak position, and he reproached nationalists who were engaged in fruitless opposition to Britain; he was persuaded that there were perhaps some advantages in cooperation with Britain to improve Egypt's internal conditions. These conditions, he maintained, could be improved if the authority of native rulers was restricted and the people were given an active part in government. To achieve this end, he saw the need for the development of representative government and political parties, which he helped organize. He was hopeful that Egypt would eventually gain representative institutions, and that the time would come when

[16] Lutfi al-Sayyid, *Ta'amulat*, pp. 55-60; *al-Muntakhabat*, Vol. II, pp. 60-63, 67.

[17] Lutfi al-Sayyid, *al-Muntakhabat*, Vol. I, pp. 252-56, and *Safahat Mitwiya*, pp. 69 ff.

both Britain and Egypt would realize that their mutual interests could be best protected by the termination of the occupation.[18]

V

What were Lutfi's methods?

Neither government service nor law practice seems to have been very attractive to Lutfi when he entered public life. Nor did his entry into the Cabinet stir his interest, for he preferred to influence politics indirectly rather than by direct methods. Journalism was the means nearest to his heart for achieving his goals. Even before he graduated from school, he collaborated with two classmates in editing a magazine. In 1907 he founded *al-Jarida,* which was intended to influence public opinion, but to Lutfi, it had another and more remote purpose—to instill in the minds of readers his thoughts about fundamental issues and social goals. He wrote dispassionately, using a rational and detached method of argumentation, and expressed his ideas in logical and precise terms devoid of the verbose and elegant style of contemporary writers. For this reason, Lutfi's exhortations appealed only to a limited audience and his influence scarcely went beyond the intelligentsia. It was not surprising that the founders of the *Jarida,* who had expected a wider circulation, became disappointed with Lutfi's editorship, since they had expected the party's organ to influence the masses and gain their support against nationalists and Pan-Islamists. Lutfi was not unaware of his limited influence, but he looked to the distant future when the new elite that had come under his influence would be able to awaken the nation to play a more responsible role in public affairs.[19]

Lutfi was a good conversationalist; he enjoyed talking to young men and expounding his ideas about freedom and democracy and other liberal thoughts relevant to Egyptian society. These young men frequented his office or his house and sat with him in cafés

---

[18] Lutfi al-Sayyid, *Safahat Mitwiya,* pp. 7-24; *Ta'amulat,* pp. 46-50. Lutfi took no interest in the national freedom of other Arab countries; indeed, he advised against the association of Egypt's freedom with that of other Arab countries (see Fathi Ridwan, *'Asr wa Rijal* [Age and Men] (Cairo, 1967); pp. 402-3).

[19] Lutfi al-Sayyid, *Qissat Hayati,* pp. 46-47, 90-91.

during holidays and vacations. He always impressed his listeners with the breadth of his learning and with the persuasive and cogent manner in which he expounded his ideas and ideals. He likewise commanded their respect by his congeniality and polite manners: he looked dignified and reserved, although perhaps a little puritanical and austere. It was not mere flattery that he was often called with admiration the "teacher of a generation," for in his leisurely talks he always fascinated his listeners, including the present writer who had the pleasure of conversing with him in his later years.

Lutfi's interest in the preparation of an elite prompted him to serve in cultural and academic institutions after he had given up journalistic work. He served for a short time as Director of the National Library and participated in the founding of the Egyptian University, becoming its first rector when the university was reorganized and attached to the Ministry of Education in 1923. In these capacities, he participated in the spread of higher education and in throwing open the university's doors to men and women alike.

Apart from short incursions into politics, Lutfi spent most of his retirement years as head of the Academy of the Arabic Language, whose chief function was to coin Arabic words for new concepts. In this capacity, he tried to fulfill one of the fundamental purposes of his life—to render into the Arabic language the achievements of Western thought. From early life, he maintained that his age was one of translation and not of creation. Realizing the extent to which Europe had outdistanced his country in culture, he admonished his countrymen to first learn what Europe had achieved during the past few centuries before embarking on creative work. He urged them to translate the works of European thinkers. Believing that modern European knowledge in turn owed much to Greek thought, he devoted much of his time to the translation of Aristotle's works into Arabic. Aristotle, to be sure, was not unknown to Muslim philosophers in the past—indeed, he was held in high esteem and called the First Master—but ancient translations of and commentaries on Aristotle had been lost. Thus, Lutfi deemed it necessary to reintroduce Aristotle to his countrymen. He himself owed many of his ideas about authority and freedom to Aristotle, and he encouraged his disciples to study Greek thought. Within the span of twenty years, he published translations of the *Ethics* in 1924, *On the Universe* and *On Generation and Destruction* in 1932, *On Nature* in 1935, and the *Politics* in 1940.[20] Although these works were translated from the French, not from the original Greek, their clarity of style in Arabic was acknowledged by critics.[21] The study of Greek thought thus had an impact not only on his own secular thought but also on his disciples'.[22]

Taking the long view in achieving social goals, Lutfi did not expect to achieve immediate results from his participation in politics. From the time he entered public life, he did not play a very active part in the Umma Party. Nor did he show great interest in the activities of the political parties after independence. He seems to have taken it for granted that his social goals lay in the future, to be achieved by other hands than his. His hope that young men would achieve his ultimate goals reflected an optimism that he never lost and that was one of his salient characteristics which inspired all disciples.

In his participation in politics after World War I, Lutfi seemed to repudiate or, at any rate, to ignore in practice what he had preached in theory. He was in favor of constitutional guarantees and parliamentary democracy in principle, but he ignored these principles when he served in 1928 in a government headed by a Premier—Muhammad Mahmud—who suspended the constitution and governed by decree. He also served in 1930 in a government of Isma'il Sidqi which replaced the constitution of 1923 by another giving the crown and the executive such power as to encroach on Parliament and the electorate. These were not two isolated instances or acts done under exceptional circumstances, for Lutfi served again under the same Premier in 1937 and 1946, but demonstrate his preparedness to disregard the democratic principles which he had preached before.

Nor was this all. Lutfi had kept aloof from the public and rarely tried to fraternize with the common people even when he ran for

[20] Lutfi al-Sayyid, *Qissat Hayati,* pp. 168-69.

[21] See reviews of some of these translations by Husayn Haykal, *Fi Awqat al-Faragh* (2nd ed.; Cairo, 1968), pp. 152-58; and Taha Husayn, *Hadith al-Arbi'a* (Cairo, 1962), Vol. III, pp. 47-57.

[22] See Muhammad Kamil Husayn, *Mutanawwi'at* [Miscellaneous] (Cairo, n.d.), pp. 111-17. Emulating his master, Husayn translated directly from the Greek some literary masterpieces under the title *Min al-Adab al-Tamthili al-Yunani* (Cairo, 1923), as well as *Nizam al-Athiniyyin* [Constitution of Athens], by Aristotle. Husayn also lectured on Greek history and literature at the Egyptian University. For the reaction to Husayn's teachings of classics, see my *Political Trends,* pp. 221-22.

election to a District Council or the Legislative Assembly before
World War I. He failed in one election and won the other only when
his opponent gave up to challenge irregularities committed by those
who had campaigned on his behalf.[23] After World War I, he never
ran for an office or participated in general elections when parliamentary democracy was established. On the contrary, his contacts
with the people were limited to an even smaller circle of friends
and disciples who frequented his house or visited him in his office.

Some critics maintained that the aristocratic and wealthy class
to which Lutfi belonged was responsible for his personal behavior
and that his call for constitutional guarantees and parliamentary
democracy before World War I had been intended only to limit the
Khedive's power and enable his class to govern the country. At that
time the Umma Party, representing the wealthy class, whom Lutfi
called the "real interests" (i.e., vested interests), had demanded
representative government so as to govern the country on behalf of
the people. After World War I, when parliamentary democracy was
established and the Wafd Party championed the cause of the common people, the aristocratic and wealthy class organized a new party—
the Liberal Constitutional Party—which received the support of the
palace entourage and vested interests. Lutfi, though not formally
enrolled in this party, was fully identified with it and participated
in governments whose members were drawn from it.

This apparent discrepancy between Lutfi's theory and practice
may not be explained solely on the basis of class structure. By nature and upbringing Lutfi preferred to keep to himself and he shied
away from the public. His family's wealth, providing material security, may have accentuated these propensities; but it also protected
him from dependence on official resources which might have forced
him to compromise his views. Had he been an extrovert, he might
have been prepared to fight for his convictions and would probably
have attracted a larger following who might have helped him achieve
his goals more quickly and effectively. As an introvert, he preferred
to take a defensive attitude and consciously tried to avoid offend-
ing others or taking the initiative in fights for causes that might
bring injury to his pride.

---

[23] See ['Abd al-'Aziz al-Bishri], *Fi al-Mir'at* [In the Mirror] (Cairo, 1947), pp. 39-43;
Ridwan, *'Asr wa Rijal*, pp. 393 ff.

Believing in the intrinsic value of freedom and democracy as well as other liberal principles, Lutfi hoped that his countrymen might enjoy the benefit of these principles when they were ready for them. As one who had studied Aristotle's *Politics,* he must have pondered on Aristotle's exhortation that the citizen must be educated in the spirit of the constitution under which they live. For this reason he called first for the gradual adoption of representative institutions in order to give the people time to accommodate to them. After parliamentary democracy began to operate under the Constitution of 1923, Lutfi realized that the public was not yet ready to exercise the full freedom provided under that constitution, and he supported the Sidqi and Muhammad Mahmud governments in their endeavors first to carry out internal reforms before granting the country democratic freedoms. Lutfi's political activities should not, therefore, be considered as attempts to achieve ultimate goals but as preliminary steps to prepare the people for the exercise of their rights. As he grew older, he became convinced of the need for fulfilling this task, and he began to lay more stress on moral and cultural development and on the preparation of an elite who would guide the nation along the road to progress. What held him in high respect was the consistency throughout his life of his moral and intellectual attitudes—he was a remarkable example of the intellectual politician who insisted on applying reason and intellect to private and public affairs.

CHAPTER XI

The Realistic School
Muhammad Husayn Haykal

> Political issues, including major constitutional questions, should be
> ultimately decided by public opinion. . . . Public opinion will decide
> in accordance with the national interest only if it were guided by
> political leaders who are in accord on fundamental issues; however,
> if the leaders were divided, and the division among them was
> sharpened by particular interests, public opinion would be unable
> to make decisions in the national interest, but is often misled to
> subordinate national to particular interest.
>
> *Haykal*

Haykal was a disciple and a great admirer of Lutfi al-Sayyid.
He kept in close touch with Lutfi, but after he entered public life, he began to pursue his own goals. Some of his ideas
and goals were later to undergo changes which suggest that Haykal
had begun to weigh them on a scale of practical considerations
which Lutfi would have been unable to appreciate. In his mature
years, he tried to strike a balance between ends and means—he chose
to pursue goals which appeared to him to be within the realm of
possibility. Like the professional politician, he became increasingly
preoccupied with methods; but, as an intellectual, he never lost sight
of goals. Haykal's struggle to relate goals to conditions must be assessed in the light of his experiences and frustrations.

Muhammad Husayn Haykal

II

Muhammad Husayn Haykal was born in 1888 to a relatively well-to-do family. His father, an 'umda in one of the villages of the Nile Delta, became too preoccupied with the affairs of a big family to pay particular attention to each child. He married a second wife eight or nine years after young Haykal was born and had a number of children with both his first and second wives. After his father's second marriage, young Haykal no longer attracted his father's attention, and Haykal seems to have resented his strict and authoritarian attitude.[1] Unlike Lufti al-Sayyid, who seems to have enjoyed his father's affection, Haykal grew up with a certain feeling of insecurity from childhood, which was often reflected in his suspicion of other people. This sense of insecurity may have been responsible for his readiness to compromise with reality. On the other hand, his father's neglect may have prompted him to depend on himself, thus strengthening his spirit of independence and self-reliance.

Haykal went to study first in a kuttab school in the district, and then in Cairo, where he completed his primary and high school education in 1905. He entered the School of Law at the suggestion of Lutfi al-Sayyid, who seems to have been on friendly terms with Haykal's father. Family ties, especially in rural districts, created a deep sense of personal loyalty and solidarity among children of the same locality, which was often manifested in their desire to cooperate and help one another after they had moved into big towns or cities. While studying in Cairo, Haykal often paid visits to Lutfi al-Sayyid and sought his inspiration and guidance. Lutfi became his mentor and the man who had the greatest single influence on him. As a young man, Haykal was attracted to liberal thought and read Mill and Spencer, who made a great impression on him. He supported, in the first article he contributed to the *Jarida*, Qasim Amin's call for the emancipation of women. After he graduated from the Cairo Law School in 1909, he decided to pursue further legal study in Paris, at Lutfi's suggestion.

In France, Haykal's ideas received further impetus. He arrived

---

[1] Preferring not to record these early unhappy experiences, Haykal begins his memoirs with his life in school (see his *Mudhakkirat fi al-Siyasa al-Misriya* [Cairo, 1951], Vol. I, pp. 24 ff; hereafter referred to as *Mudhakkirat*).

in Paris on the eve of July 14, the national day, when Frenchmen display emotional and social gaiety without restraints. "The expression of individual and national freedom appeared vividly before my eyes," writes Haykal in his memoirs, "experiences the like of which I had never had in my country."[2] Parisian life demonstrated for Haykal ideas which Lutfi had spoken about in the abstract in Cairo and which he now was able to observe with his own eyes. He found the exercise of liberty present in almost all walks of life. He read French philosophy and literature which taught him the methods of literary criticism, objective analysis of problems, and methods to search for the truth. He began to question his own religious beliefs, which he had always taken for granted, as he recorded in unpublished entries in his memoirs, and his intellectual outlook ever afterward became more secular, although belief in God seems to have persisted despite momentary scepticism. He found great inspiration in Jean Jacques Rousseau, who combined spiritual values (regarded by Haykal as containing an Oriental prophetic element) with love for freedom, and he later wrote a book about him.

Despite the excitement of learning and the attraction to some Parisian cultural and social activities, Haykal often experienced profound homesickness, especially for the countryside of his birthplace. He found relief in his participation in the Egyptian Society, organized by young Egyptians studying abroad, and in his attendance at a conference in Brussels, sponsored by the Egyptian National Party, at which the Egyptian question was discussed. He also wrote a novel, entitled *Zaynab,* describing life in the countryside of his childhood. He was inspired to write this novel by his visits to the French countryside as well as by his reading of French novels, whose influence is revealed in the plot of *Zaynab.*

In 1911 Haykal returned to Egypt to gather material for his doctoral dissertation. While in Cairo, he was invited to edit the *Jarida* temporarily because Lutfi al-Sayyid had come into conflict with leaders of the Umma Party over three articles he had written which advocated Egyptian neutrality in the Italo-Turkish War of 1911-12. Haykal agreed with Lutfi's views in principle and defended his right to express his opinions, but his own articles in the *Jarida* were quite sympathetic toward the Porte in deference to public

[2] Haykal, *Mudhakkirat,* Vol. I, p. 40.

opinion, an early example of his readiness to compromise with reality. After he returned to Paris, Haykal received his degree in 1912. His research for the dissertation, which was entitled *La dette publique Egytpienne,* strengthened his conviction in Egypt's right to national freedom and deepened his nationalist feelings.

His studies completed, Haykal returned to practice law in al-Mansura, one of the Delta's principal towns, and often visited Cairo and contributed to the *Jarida.* He was in close touch with Lutfi al-Sayyid, and both watched with keen interest the lively discussion in the Legislative Assembly of questions commented upon in the *Jarida,* since both Lutfi and Haykal were in favor of representative institutions. In his spare time, Haykal continued to lecture and write on liberal subjects. He seemed to have settled into a pattern of life as a successful lawyer and distinguished critic, and there was still no sign that he was destined for political leadership.

In 1914, when World War I broke out, Haykal began to make known his views about Egypt's position in the war. He maintained that Egypt, though under British control, should remain neutral, since public opinion was in favor of the Ottoman Porte and hostile to Britain. But Lutfi, who was urging Premier Rushdi and Foreign Minister 'Adli Yakan to demand independence as a *quid pro quo* for Egypt's support of Britain against the Ottoman Empire, advised Haykal against neutrality, at least until the outcome of the negotiations between Egypt and Britain were known. When Britain rejected the proposal for independence and declared a protectorate over Egypt on December 18, 1914, Haykal began to publish articles in the *Jarida* that could be construed as unfavorable to Britain, even though Lutfi continued to warn that it was not in Egypt's interests to criticize Britain.[3] Despite disagreement, master and disciple remained on good terms to the end of the war. After the suspension of the *Jarida,* they also suspended their political activities. Lutfi retired to his country house and Haykal turned to law practice. Meanwhile, Haykal began to write the life of Jean Jacques Rousseau; the first volume was published in 1921 and the second in 1923 (these with a third were republished in a one-volume edition in 1965).

After the war Haykal resumed his incursions into politics in close collaboration with Lutfi. At first he and Lutfi held essentially

[3] *Ibid.,* p. 67.

the same views about liberty and freedom of the press, but very soon Haykal's views about parliamentary democracy and public opinion began to differ from Lutfi's. Haykal asserted that ultimate decisions should be made by the public through representation in Parliament, while Lutfi regarded parliamentary procedures merely as a check against authoritarian rule.[4] Under the influence of Rousseau, Haykal's views about private ownership and free enterprise also differed from Lutfi's; he held that private ownership should be qualified by proper attention to public welfare, and he endorsed this principle when he joined the Democratic Party.[5] With regard to national freedom and sovereignty, he held more extreme views than Lutfi. Haykal acquired these views partly from his participation in the activities of and discussions with young men of his generation and partly from his own studies of modern Egyptian history.[6]

Haykal differed in another matter with his master: Lutfi maintained that his age was one of translation from Western thought rather than of creation, while Haykal, who proved to be a writer in his own right, combined the competences of transmission and creation. Haykal did not translate literally from works of Western writers, except for a few articles, but he transmitted the product of Western thought in his own books and articles, explaining that he was either summarizing certain Western thinkers or adopting their views with changes and therefore was entitled to claim authorship.[7] He was a prolific writer, and some of his works on Egyptian culture reveal insight and creativity.

After World War I, Haykal continued his law practice in al-Mansura for another two or three years before he became fully involved in politics, and he regularly visited Cairo for a weekly lecture at the Egyptian University. He was constantly in touch with Lutfi and with young men of his generation who had organized the Democratic Party. Lutfi introduced him to 'Adli Yakan, Tharwat, and

---

[4] See p. 183, above; and Haykal's *Mudhakkirat,* Vol. I, pp. 39-41.

[5] See Haykal, *Mudhakkirat,* Vol. I, pp. 80-81; and Haykal's own introduction to *Jean Jacques Rousseau,* pp. 20-21.

[6] Haykal, *Mudhakkirat,* Vol. I, pp. 42-43, 52-54.

[7] See Haykal's translation of Levy Bruhl's introduction to a book on Auguste Comte in *al-Siyasa al-Usbu'iya* (Cairo), September 2 and 9, 1927; reprinted in Haykal, *al-Iman wa al-Ma'rifa wa al-Falsafa* [Belief, Knowledge and Philosophy] (Cairo, 1964), Chap. 2.

Muhammad Mahmud, future leaders of the Liberal Constitutionalist Party, and other politicians who encouraged him to participate in his country's domestic politics. The entrée to—and good reception in—high political circles as well as his name as a critic and frequent contributor to the press on questions of the day made him appear indeed a very promising figure in politics.

On February 28, 1922, the protectorate over Egypt was terminated and independence was declared. Tharwat, who became Prime Minister, appointed a Constitutional Committee, of which Haykal became a member, to prepare a draft constitution. Work in this committee gave Haykal an opportunity to express some of his views on parliamentary democracy and exchange ideas with a number of the country's eminent leaders.[8] Meanwhile, he had also become editor of al-Siyasa (Politics), organ of the newly organized Liberal Constitutionalist Party, at Lutfi's recommendation. This party, headed by 'Adli Yakan, included Tharwat, then Premier, Muhammad Mahmud, Isma'il Sidqi, and others who stood for parliamentary democracy and free elections. As editor, Haykal revealed his talents as an effective writer and forceful spokesman for his party. He was to continue as editor for fifteen years, until 1937, when he became a member of the government of Muhammad Mahmud, new leader of the Liberal Constitutionalist Party.

Before he became a minister, Haykal's role in politics was manifested in two different but closely related fields of activities. First, in addition to the party's organ, al-Siyasa, he edited the weekly al-Siyasu al-Usbu'iya, devoted essentially to literary and cultural subjects. This periodical provided a forum for liberal intellectuals, and Haykal, with Taha Husayn, initiated a new school of thought advocating modernism and secularism. The group of writers who contributed to al-Siyasa al-Usbu'iya, calling themselves "moderns" (al-Majaddidun) and advocating a new critical approach to problems, stood in opposition to the "ancients" (al-qudama'), representing a traditional mode of thought.[9] Under Haykal's guidance, the "moderns" were expected to influence public opinion in favor of the

---

[8] For Haykal's work in the Constitutional Committee, see his *Mudhakkirat,* Vol. I, Chap. 3.

[9] For the role and ideas of these groups, see my *Political Trends in the Arab World* (Baltimore, 1970), pp. 219 ff. For Haykal's literary views, see exchange of letters with Taha Husayn in *al-Siyasa al-Usbu'iya* (Cairo), June 25, 1927, pp. 10-11; July 2, 1927, pp. 10-11; August 13, 1927, pp. 10-11.

Liberal Constitutionalist Party. As author and editor, Haykal published a number of books and articles on various subjects and, in contrast to other liberal writers, developed eventually his own school of thought.[10]

Haykal also took part in politics through the activities of the Liberal Constitutionalist Party, both as member and as writer. He defended the party when the party's activities became subject to official investigations, and he became its spokesman in meetings with leaders of other parties. Moreover, his own writings on behalf of the party came under censorship. In all these activities, Haykal served the party to the best of his abilities with loyalty and intellectual integrity. He was almost always consistent in thought and action; he often had to threaten resignation rather than jeopardize his principles. During the first decade of his political career he was able to maintain a fairly good balance between personal convictions and convenience, perhaps with a margin in favor of personal convictions.

III

Almost a decade after he became active in politics, Haykal began to modify some of his ideas and goals. Changes in one's own views are not unnatural; they often reflect maturity and deeper understanding—*Nemo doctus umquam . . . mutationem consilii inconstantiam dixit esse* (Cicero). In the short span of a decade, he became involved in a number of political activities—he worked in the Constitutional Committee which prepared the Constitution of 1923, he was active in the Liberal Constitutionalist Party and edited its paper, and he participated in other capacities. He campaigned for some of his party's candidates (as well as for himself) in general elections, and he wrote speeches and articles to insure his party's success and to further its program, for which he stood. But the fruits of his endeavors and the causes for which he fought did not always stand the test

[10] Before he became a Cabinet Minister, Haykal published the following books: *Zaynab* (Cairo, 1914); *Jean Jacques Rousseau* (Cairo, 1921-23); *Fi Awaqat al-Faragh* [During Leisure Time] (Cairo, 1923); *'Ashrat Ayyam Fi al-Sudan* [Ten Days in the Sudan] (Cairo, 1927); *Tarajum* [Biographies] (Cairo, 1929); *Waladi* [My Son] (Cairo, 1931); *Thawrat al-Adab* [Literature's Revolt] (Cairo, 1933); *Hayat Muhammad* [Life of Muhammad] (Cairo, 1935); and *Fi Manzil al-Wahi* [In the Birthplace of Revelation] (Cairo, 1937).

of experience. Were his ideas and goals wrong in principle, or were they incompatible with reality? Were they ahead of his time? These questions necessarily came to Haykal's mind, and he began to redefine and improvise some of his methods and goals.

Three major events may have greatly influenced Haykal's life, and they seem to have gradually, almost imperceptibly, led him to modify his fundamental ideals and methods. First, after the Constitution of 1923 had been promulgated and the first parliamentary elections had been scheduled, both the Liberal Constitutionalist and the Wafd parties began to make preparations for the forthcoming elections. The Liberals, who had contributed in no small measure to the establishment of parliamentary democracy, naturally expected to win the elections and to form the first Cabinet under the new constitutional regime. Instead, the Wafd Party, which had denounced the Constitution of 1923 as incompatible with national demands, won an overwhelming majority, thanks to the very liberal principles enshrined in the Constitution. The Wafd leaders launched a fierce campaign in which they attacked the Liberals—'Adli Yakan, Tharwat, and Muhammad Mahmud—with scathing words denying their integrity and loyalty to the country. "We would rather have [foreign] protection under Sa'd Zaghlul [leader of the Wafd] than independence under 'Adli [leader of the Liberals]," according to one of the slogans. The Wafd, winning a majority of 195 seats against 19, proved to be the beneficiary of the very principles which Haykal and the Liberals had worked so assiduously to embody in the Constitution of 1923. Haykal's experiences in this as well as several other elections in which he participated and failed demonstrated to him that the country was not yet ready for the principles and goals for which he and the Liberals stood.

Second, the rivalry among the parties had become so intense after the establishment of parliamentary democracy that the principal objectives of political leaders were not to achieve power in Parliament but to denounce their opponents and cause their fall from power by demagoguery and agitation even if the consequences of their actions were contrary to public interests. Political leaders often indulged in recriminations—accusing one another of treason and disloyalty—with the result that confidence in all leaders suffered considerably in the public eye. Haykal gradually began to realize that the party system, at least insofar as it worked in his lifetime, was inadequate to serve the best interests of the country, and he often called for cooperation and alignment among the parties, especially among dissident groups. Although he remained loyal to his party to the very end of the old regime, he lost confidence in the party system and tried to pursue his goals by other methods.

Third, when Muhammad Mahmud, new leader of the Liberals, formed a government in 1928, he ignored the Constitution of 1923, although his party had always defended that Constitution, and he suspended Parliament for three years and governed by decree. In 1930, when Isma'il Sidqi, a former member of the Liberal Constituionalist Party, formed a government, he replaced the Constitution of 1923 by another constitution that gave extensive prerogatives to the crown. Although the Liberals, supported by the Wafdists, criticized Sidqi's actions and called for the restoration of the Constitution of 1923—and it was indeed restored in 1936—the whole constitutional regime had become meaningless.

Consequently, there was ample justification for Haykal to review his goals and political objectives and to modify them in accordance with his country's immediate needs. The process of modification was very slow and the changes were more apparent in some goals than in others. The most radical change was, of course, in his attitude toward religion; but he also modified some of his political ideas, especially those concerning free elections and the parliamentary system. He began to realize that some of his ideals were simply impossible to achieve; others would have to be modified if they were ever to be realized.

In December 1925, Haykal lost his son. This tragic event seems to have profoundly grieved him and affected his family life. It took his wife several years to overcome the shock, and he tried by three successive trips to Europe to erase the memory of the lost child. He began to find consolation in reflective thoughts on religion, to which he had given little or no attention before.[11] In 1926 Haykal published three articles in the weekly al-Siyasa al-Usbu'iya (June 12-July 24, 1926) entitled "Religion and Science," in which he argued that there was no essential conflict between science and religion, if religion was understood to define ideals and science to describe

[11] The account of the trips to Europe and their impact on Madame Haykal are recorded in Waladi, dedicated to the lost son. For the significance of the event, see Fathi Ridwan, 'Asr wa Rijal [Age and Men] (Cairo, 1967), pp. 465-66, 520-22.

realities. He went on to argue that the conflict was not between
science and religion but between men of science and men of religion,
and he pointed out that this conflict had existed from ancient
times.[12] The notion that the conflict between religion and science
is essentially a conflict between theology and science is not new,
but Haykal brought it home by applying it to the Islamic religion
in persuasive arguments reminiscent of the Afghani-'Abduh modernist
interpretation of Islam. In 1927 Haykal published another set of
articles on religious belief in which he reiterated the idea that there
was no conflict between science and religion; but, perhaps more significant, he now began to argue that moral and spiritual values were
always more important in the life of nations than material objects.
He stated that the full realization of this truth had come to him
during one of his trips to Luxor where he saw the temples of the
ancient Egyptian pharaohs and became convinced that no civilization could possibly survive unless it was based on some type of
belief system. He saw the future faith of the emerging civilization
as a combination of the findings of science and religion.[13]

But it was not only Haykal who changed his views about parliamentary democracy. The leaders of the Liberal Constitutionalist
Party had already come to the conclusion that before calling for
freedom and parliamentary democracy they should raise the standard of living and improve social and economic conditions. Thus,
when Muhammad Mahmud, leader of the Liberals, formed a government in 1928, he began to carry out a program to improve living conditions, including the construction of roads and bridges and
the draining of marshes, rather than concentrating on freedom of
the press and free elections. Haykal, for his part, became more
critical of opponents in order to defend his party's actions. In 1930,
Haykal with other writers launched a campaign against the Sidqi
government. Meanwhile, the press had reported that some Christian
missionaries were trying to persuade Muslims to become Christians
and the name of the American University of Cairo was involved.
The opposition press seized the opportunity to attack Prime Minister Sidqi, who himself had received his early education in a Jesuit
school, for his reluctance to suppress these missionary activities and

---

[12] Haykal's articles are reproduced in *al-Iman*, pp. 9-40.
[13] *Ibid.*, pp. 86-114.

put an end to alleged incidents of apostasy. As a member of a committee in the Muslim Brotherhood to counteract missionary activities, Haykal supported the suggestion that pressure should be brought on the government to stop missionary proselytizing; but as a writer he tried to use his pen in a positive manner to save the public from succumbing to missionary propaganda. He began by publishing an article in *al-Siyasa al-Isbu'iya* on the life of the Prophet Muhammad, the substance of which was taken from a book by Emile Dermenghem—a French Orientalist who wrote a sympathetic study of Muhammad's life.[14] The article was well received in religious circles and there was a demand for further writings on the subject. Haykal accordingly began a study of the original sources on the Prophet's life which occupied the next four years, and in 1935 he published his bestseller *Life of Muhammad*.[15] Unexpectedly, this work brought Haykal higher esteem and far greater pecuniary remuneration than all his other works. In the following year, Haykal performed the pilgrimage and in 1937 published a readable account of the visitation as well as of his spiritual experiences in the cradle of Islam.[16] Although Haykal's private life remained unaffected by these religious rituals, his public image began to change considerably— from the spokesman for free thought to the defender of the faith. It has been maintained, not without exaggeration, that *Life of Muhammad* elevated its author to a Cabinet post; but Haykal had already been on his way up in the hierarchy of the Liberal Constitutionalist Party and the time had come for him to be rewarded by a seat in the Cabinet. His *Life of Muhammad,* which enhanced the prestige of his party in religious quarters, entitled him to his reward. Haykal's brilliant success in his writings on Islam prompted other younger writers to emulate him, which contributed in no small measure to the widespread religious revival during the 1930s. Viewed in retrospect, Haykal's works on Islamic studies were not mere apologies for traditionalism, since they were composed by a modernist-oriented writer who tried to reconcile reason and revelation with considerable success. Had Haykal begun his early career with an interest in religious subjects, he would have been hailed by modernists as

[14] See *al-Siyasa* (Cairo) (supplement), September 1933.

[15] Haykal, *Hayat Muhammad* (Cairo, 1935).

[16] Haykal, *Fi Manzil al-Wahi.*

having pushed 'Abduh's thought a step forward; but since he began his career as a liberal thinker, his new interest in spiritual and religious subjects was construed not as a bona fide change of heart but as an expedient political move.[17]

Haykal's defection from liberal thought created a crisis of conscience among liberal thinkers and caused widespread disenchantment with secularism and liberalism. It is true that several other liberal thinkers, Taha Husayn, in particular, began to publish works on Islam which were widely read; but these works were not taken very seriously in religious circles, as it was not believed that their authors had written them with full conviction.[18] Haykal's writings, however, were received with esteem and great enthusiasm, and Haykal himself gave the impression of deriving personal satisfaction from his defense of religious beliefs and values.

But did Haykal really derive inner satisfaction and did he honor religious beliefs in his own private life? It was no secret that Haykal did not perform the daily prayers, nor did he fast or observe other religious duties; he only prayed on ceremonial occasions when he was in the Cabinet, and his visitations to Makka and Madina were ritual performances from which he knew he would derive prestige and high esteem. In private, he continued the secular practices to which he was accustomed to the end of his life—he frequented the theater, went to cocktail parties, and never stopped drinking even when he was engaged in the composition of his *Life of Muhammad* and other works on Islam.

Inwardly, Haykal must have passed through a crisis of conscience before he began to give the outward impression that he was satisfied to pay lip service to religion in public while following an entirely different way of life in private. This dissimulation did not mean the absence in Haykal's life of moral principles; for, in comparison with some professional politicians, Haykal maintained a high level of personal integrity and was immune to political influence for pecuniary remuneration or other corrupt practices. His dissimulation was entirely political to improve his own image in an essentially

---

[17] For evaluations of the *Life of Muhammad* by contemporary writers, see *al-Siyasa*, May 15, 1935, contributed by friends and admirers of Haykal; cf. N. Safran, *Egypt in Search of Political Community* (Cambridge, Mass., 1961), pp. 169-75. For an appreciation of Haykal's works on Islam by a traditional writer, see Ridwan, *'Asr wa Rijal*, pp. 592-97.

[18] See my *Political Trends*, pp. 182-83, 226-27.

religious society and to rally religious leaders to his party's support. His own personal conduct was never questioned on moral grounds— his sense of justice, loyalty to party and friends, and respect for the opinions of others were indeed personal qualities for which he was held in high esteem.[19]

Haykal used his pen as the natural instrument of the intellectual politician who lacked certain qualities which professional politicians ordinarily possess. Had he been a popular leader in the Wafd Party, which had great influence on the masses, he might not have felt the need to arouse religious sentiment to achieve goals and ambitions; but the Liberal Constitutionalist Party, to which he was committed, was a minority party which needed his active support through his pen as much as he needed it to achieve his objectives. Why did Haykal join the Liberal Constitutionalist Party rather than the Wafd Party?

It was perhaps the accident of Haykal's early association with Lutfi al-Sayyid, who recommended Haykal as editor of the Liberal's paper, that dictated his choice. The reason for his continued attachment to this party was, however, Haykal's initial commitment to the liberal principles for which the Liberal Constitutionalist Party stood. As a successor to the Umma Party, to which Lutfi al-Sayyid had attracted young intellectuals before World War I, the Liberal Constitutionalist Party became the party of the intelligentsia after that war. In reality it was founded by wealthy politicians who represented aristocratic houses; some of them were highly cultured personages who received their education in European institutions. Lutfi al-Sayyid, a pivot of the intellectuals, himself belonged to the aristocracy and not unnaturally was a great supporter of the Liberal Constitutionalist Party as the instrument of both the intelligentsia and the aristocracy. As a disciple of Lutfi and an intellectual committed to liberal thought, it was therefore natural that Haykal should join not the Wafd but the Liberal Constitutionalist Party. This was the party that sponsored the preparation and promulgation of a liberal consti-

---

[19] Even to his opponents in political battles, Haykal was considerate and fair when the battle was over. It is to his credit that when he was called to testify against a political opponent—Siraj al-Din, Secretary of the Wafd—at the Military Tribunal in 1954, he gave accurate, fair, but never vindictive testimony, although the opponent was responsible with others for the loss of the presidency of the Senate when the Wafd formed a government in 1950.

tution and the party that advocated freedom of speech, free elections, and other liberal principles.

When the Constitution of 1923 began to operate, it was the Wafd Party, more closely representing the common man, that proved to be the beneficiary of the Constitution and defended it, while the Liberal leaders ignored its principles in practice and came to power not as the result of victory at the polls but by an alignment with the court entourage and a coalition with other small political parties. Thus, when Muhammad Mahmud, leader of the Liberals, formed governments in 1928 and in 1937, he suspended the Constitution of 1923 and governed with repressive measures in order to prevent the Wafd Party from achieving power in free elections or by popular pressures. Haykal had to make up his mind whether he belonged to the Liberals or whether he would join the Wafd. His decision was in favor of the former because he disliked electioneering and popular fraternization—at least in the way they were practiced by Wafd leaders—and preferred the aristocratic methods of the Liberals with whom he shared many values by upbringing and education. He felt bound accordingly to subordinate goals to conveniences and modify ideals by realities so long as he wished to continue his role in politics.

By the mid-1930s Haykal had become a well-known national figure, highly respected as writer and journalist, and his position in the Liberal Constitutionalist Party had become very influential. His elevation to Cabinet rank was, therefore, expected whenever his party's leader formed a government again. The opportune moment came when Muhammad Mahmud, after the Wafd had fallen from power, formed a new government in 1937. From this time to the seizure of power by the military in 1952, Haykal served as Minister of Education in five Cabinets—three under Muhammad Mahmud, leader of the Liberals, and two in coalition Cabinets in which Liberals and Sa'dists, a dissident Wafdist group, cooperated. He became leader of the Liberal Constitutionalist Party after Mahmud's death in 1942, and President of the Senate from 1945 to 1950. He came very near to forming a government himself when Ahmad Mahir, head of a coalition Cabinet in which Liberals and Sa'dists cooperated, was assassinated in 1945. The King, upon Haykal's advice, invited Nuqrashi, a Sa'dist, to form the new government, which Haykal supported, hoping that he might succeed Nuqrashi as Prime Minister.

As Minister of Education Haykal was able to provide direction, distribute and coordinate work, and formulate general policy for the department over which he presided with efficiency. He also supervised the administrative staff of the editorial and publication boards of the *Siyasa* and gained the respect of all those who worked under him. Professional politicians in the Arab world, indeed in many other countries, are liable to fall victim to corruption and nepotism; but Haykal proved immune to these practices, although he may occasionally have yielded to pressures for the transfer of functionaries on political grounds. In general, he displayed a high degree of integrity and maintained correct relations with subordinates, for which he was given credit even by critics.

Haykal was not a popular leader nor could he mix easily with the common man; but he was able to win many friends who gave him full support. As a speaker he was calm, direct, and even persuasive, but he was not a fiery or effective orator who could sway an audience. He was highly esteemed for devotion, moral courage, and hard work—qualities which endeared him to followers but did not make him a popular leader who could obtain votes for his party in general elections. In his political career, he reached the highest position in the hierarchy of his party but failed to become Prime Minister, which seems to have been one of his cherished aspirations, although he told King Faruq once that he would prefer to devote his time to reading and writing rather than becoming Prime Minister.[20] When the opportunity to devote his time fully to his pen came after the Revolution, he felt that he had been compelled prematurely to withdraw from political activities and resorted to reading and writing only as a consolation.[21]

After the Revolution, the military asked party leaders who wished to take part in politics to purge their parties of corrupt elements, and Haykal made a final attempt to participate in politics under the new regime. It soon became clear, however, that the military had no intention of transferring power to civilian hands. Haykal began to realize that parliamentary rule in the form that had existed under the old regime was over, and that the eventual development of a truly parliamentary democracy as he had en-

[20] See Haykal, *Mudhakkirat*, Vol. II, pp. 329-30.
[21] See Ridwan, *'Asr wa Rijal*, pp. 472-73.

visioned it was an illusion. Owing to his clean record, he was able
to withdraw from politics unscathed, but some of his fellow professional politicians were either detained or thrown into prison for
corruption and other charges. Haykal's involuntary withdrawal
from politics must have been a great disappointment since none of
his goals were acceptable to the military and his wishful thinking
that he might still participate in politics came to naught when
political parties were abolished. Only as a writer did his pen continue to participate to the very end of his life at the age of sixty-
eight.

In a conversation with Haykal in 1955, a year before his death,
I asked him what in his opinion were the causes of the failure of
parliamentary democracy under the old regime? He replied that
Egypt, despite independence, was never really free to develop a
truly democratic regime; foreign pressures and intervention in domestic affairs prevented the parliamentary system from taking
roots in the country. The parliamentary system, he said, had
emerged in highly advanced countries, but it was adopted by countries entirely unprepared for it. Though Egypt had freely adopted
this system, she should have modified it long before 1952 to conform to her traditions and internal social conditions. Moreover,
Egypt should have modified her parliamentary system by peaceful
rather than by violent methods until that system became suitable
to her needs and expectations. The replacement of the parliamentary system by military rule was not a guarantee that a better system would be established. He maintained that democracy was the
best system of government that man has so far developed, and he
hoped that Egypt would eventually adopt a democratic system, because it was the only safe way toward progress and stability. He
saw no sign, however, that the military leaders were preparing the
country for democracy and realized that if the military could not
be persuaded or forced to transfer power to civilian hands, it would
take Egypt a very long time before she would again be on the path
of normal growth of political institutions.

From the time of his withdrawal from politics until his death
in 1956, Haykal devoted most of his time to writing and to lecturing inside and outside the country. He published the second volume
of his political memoirs, but he died before completing the third.
He also wrote a second novel, entitled *Hakadha Khuliqat* (Thus She

Was Born), published in 1955, in which he described the religious
experiences of an old woman, reminiscent of his own experiences;
he also wrote a few minor studies, some of which are still incomplete,
on the history and culture of Islam.[22] Shortly before his death,
Haykal began to realize that his claim to immortality might well
rest essentially on these works, some of which undoubtedly consti-
tute an important contribution to the modern culture of Egypt. It
is not as a politician but as a man of letters that Haykal's name will
be remembered by his countrymen.[23]

[22] Haykal's son, Ahmad, is now engaged in the process of collecting these studies, some
of which have already appeared in print.

[23] In homage to Haykal, fellow members of the Arab Academy contributed papers and
speeches to a volume entitled, *al-Ductur Muhammad Husayn Haykal,* edited under the
supervision of Ahmad Lutfi al-Sayyid (Cairo, 1958). For a more critical study, see Baber
Johansen, *Muhammad Husain Haikal* (Bayrut, 1967).

CHAPTER XII

The Ideological School
Michel 'Aflaq

One Arab Nation having an eternal message.

'*Aflaq*

Lutfi al-Sayyid and Haykal, though differing in methods, both advocated constitutional and parliamentary democracy and sought by peaceful and evolutionary processes to achieve their goals. Both were opposed to the use of force because violence was contrary to the spirit of their social and political doctrines. In contrast with Lutfi and Haykal, Michel 'Aflaq consciously advocated violent methods because he felt that his social goals would scarcely have any chance of success unless old regimes were overthrown by coups d'état (inqilab) and new elites were entrusted with power in order to shape the new regimes in accordance with new ideas and ideals. Although not gifted in oratory, 'Aflaq identified himself with the new generation and often went to harangue crowds of young men and to participate in street demonstrations.

What influenced 'Aflaq to pursue goals and methods radically different from Lutfi al-Sayyid and Haykal, who were also not, strictly speaking, traditional intellectual politicians?

II

'Aflaq was born in 1910 to a relatively well-to-do family, although not really rich even by local standards. His father was a

211

Michel 'Aflaq

grain merchant, whose income was occasionally very handsome but could provide no real security for the family. His religious affiliation was to the Greek Orthodox Church, and he lived in the Maydan quarter, a center of nationalist agitation, of Damascus. These two facts provided young 'Aflaq with a favorable background for participation in politics early in life. The Greek Orthodox Church was regarded by Arabs as a national, not an ecumenical, church, and its members tended to identify themselves with nationalist activities. 'Aflaq's parents took a keen interest in politics, and his father was known to have taken part in nationalist activities and to have been arrested for his opposition to the French Mandate over Syria. Thus 'Aflaq grew up in a family where both parents often discussed political questions, and his mind must have been further inflamed by the political strikes and demonstrations he witnessed at first hand in the quarter where his house was located.

In school, where nationalism is ordinarily mixed with education, 'Aflaq received further political indoctrination before he went abroad to pursue his studies. An introvert and shy by nature, he seldom participated in social activities, but his talent and industry won him a government scholarship in 1928 which enabled him to spend the next four years in Paris. At the Sorbonne he read history, but his own personal interests covered a wide range of subjects, especially literature and philosophy. He seems to have had a strong interest in Anatole France and André Gide, but he was especially influenced by Marx and Nietzsche; he also read Dostoevsky, Tolstoy, and Bergson. He was attracted not only to the ideas of these writers, but also to their literary styles and techniques. From their varied styles, he developed his own vivid, though often abstract, romantic style. Underneath this interest in literature and philosophy lay a fervent spirit which found expression first in short stories and then in speeches and political writings.

While still in Paris, 'Aflaq began to take part in student political activities. He met Arab students from other countries, whose nationalist aspirations and grievances against foreign rule he shared, and founded an Arab Students' Union calling for the independence and unity of Arab lands. His experiences with Arab students taught him that the political problems of his country were essentially the same as the problems of other Arab countries. These experiences inspired in him the idea that the aims and political activities of each

Arab country should be coordinated with the aims and political activities of the others. His love for freedom, partly the product of
French thought and partly from personal experience, was confirmed by lengthy conversations with other students and evolved
into two of the fundamental principles of the future Ba'th ideology—
freedom and Arab unity.

But Paris had another significant impact on 'Aflaq's mind.
While still a student, he was lured by communists to attend some of
their meetings and became acquainted with their literature. Although he did not become a member of the Communist Party, he
seems to have been fascinated by Marx and may have become in
theory, if not in practice, a Marxist. Above all, he was most impressed by communist discipline and tenacity, which taught him at
first hand the practical methods of a highly organized political party.
These experiences proved invaluable when he himself began to organize a political party. He accepted Marx's criticism of the social and
economic orders, but he seems to have had certain mental reservations about the international character of Marxist thought. He remained an ardent nationalist at heart, and even when he supported
the Communist Party after his return to Syria, he did not identify
himself as a communist sympathizer.[1] Some of the conflicting views
between Marxism and nationalism must have troubled him before
he made up his mind about a possible combination of the two doctrines into one—Arab socialism.

His studies completed, 'Aflaq began to teach in one of his country's high schools—the Tajhiz of Damascus—in 1932. From his
school days, he had developed an intimate personal connection
with Salah al-Din al-Baytar, a member of a Muslim family reputed
for its learning and strong nationalist leanings, with whom he often
discussed political questions of the day. For the next four years, he
and Baytar cultivated the company of students and discussed politics
with them. These students became potential supporters of the future
Ba'th Party. Meanwhile, 'Aflaq and Baytar began to fraternize with
political leaders known for their outspoken nationalist views. These
extracurricular nationalist activities were preparatory to their entry

---

[1] According to some of my informants, 'Aflaq's support of the Communist Party in the
1930s gave the impression that he was a communist sympathizer, but at heart he never
really was.

into politics in 1942 when they resigned from their academic posts presumably in protest against encroachments on academic freedom. Even before they resigned, they had been in touch first with nationalists and then with leftist groups, but in all these endeavors they spoke essentially on behalf of and sought support from young men. The entry of 'Aflaq and Baytar into politics intensified the involvement of youth in political activities, although many young men had already been politicized by nationalist indoctrination.

The political activities of 'Aflaq and Baytar were not confined only to young men. Although they did not formally join any nationalist party, they participated in some of their activities and supported in particular the Nationalist Bloc—a group of politicians who distinguished themselves in the independence movement which bore fruition during the war. They campaigned for nationalists in the general elections of 1943, and 'Aflaq offered himself as a candidate. He failed to be elected to Parliament, probably because of lack of support from nationalist leaders. Very soon he became disenchanted with the nationalists and began to criticize their outmoded methods. In 1947 he sought support of leftist groups in the general elections. He failed again to be elected. He tried for a third time to run as a candidate of his newly organized Ba'th Party in 1949, but he failed once more, this time presumably because the government was opposed to Ba'th representation in Parliament, notwithstanding the fact that he was a member of the Cabinet—Minister of Education—which supervised the elections. The three defeats in parliamentary elections demonstrated to 'Aflaq the inadequacy of democratic processes to achieve his goals, even though his defeat in one or two may have been caused by his tampering with the elections. He never ran again for an elected post, and he began to speak openly in favor of the use of violence for social and political change.

For his surreptitious activities 'Aflaq had to endure some physical inconveniences. It was not uncommon practice in Arab lands for outspoken critics of the government to suffer exile or imprisonment, and 'Aflaq was arrested several times. But his delicate physique could not always endure the hardships—indeed, he was almost always suffering from one kind of illness or another—which prompted him on one occasion to write a letter to Husni al-Za'im, author of the first military coup d'état in 1949, in which he requested pardon and promised to withdraw from politics, contrary to the pride and dignity of nationalist heroes.[2] 'Aflaq had been imprisoned twice before, in 1939 and 1948, but on this occasion, it is reported that he was either threatened or exposed to torture. He served short prison terms again in 1952 and 1954 under the dictatorial regime of Adib al-Shishakli; after Shishakli's fall in 1954, he was released from prison and became a hero. These trials and tribulations enhanced 'Aflaq's prestige, since exile and imprisonment were considered a form of heroic struggle against unpopular regimes and contributed indirectly to their eventual overthrow.

After a short experience in the Cabinet—he served only three months in 1949—'Aflaq began to realize that he was not really fit for executive positions, and he never again served in an official post. He seems to have come to the conclusion that his role in politics should be confined to formulating goals and counseling and guiding party leaders rather than taking direct responsibility. Consequently, he preferred to be called the founder and philosopher of the Ba'th Party rather than its leader, although it became clear that he played a more important role than court philosopher; in the absence of an effective leader, he often served as chairman of the National Command and arbiter and coordinator among rival leaders, leaving the implementations of party programs to followers.[3]

III

Before 'Aflaq began to formulate his party's goals during and after World War II, he had spent several years in contemplation and study and had written a number of articles and essays in which he expounded some of his ideas and reflections on social and political

[2] For the text of 'Aflaq's letter to Colonel Za'im, see Mahmud 'Abd al-Rahim, *Qiyadat Hizb al-Ba'th al-Murtadda* (Cairo, n.d.), pp. 6-7. For the possibility of a forgery or of the letter's having been signed under threat, see Sami al-Jundi, *al-Ba'th* (Bayrut, 1969), pp. 54-55.

[3] 'Aflaq preferred to be called officially Secretary-General of the Ba'th Party and unofficially the philosopher of the Party. Although he deserved the latter title, he tried to play both leader and philosopher and failed in the former. For a brief account of 'Aflaq's life, see Muta' al-Safadi, *Hizb al-Ba'th* [The Ba'th Party] (Bayrut, 1964); and K. S. Abu Jaber, *The Arab Ba'th Socialist Party* (Syracuse, 1966). A critical study of 'Aflaq's life has yet to be written.

questions of the day. As a writer, he developed his own literary
form and wrote short stories in which he criticized the social order
and outmoded values and traditions. The theme in most of these
stories centered on the lives of young men who had experienced
certain tensions culminating in a sudden revolt either against bureaucratic practices, family repressions, or inertia and their own
barren way of life. Having rid themselves of traditional restraints,
the young men could then begin to lead a new way of life—a life
which would realize their cherished aspirations. In all these stories,
'Aflaq described the absurdity of stereotyped and corrupt practices,
which, he maintained, always created tensions and disaffection in
Arab society, and the necessity of achieving a complete change in
one's own life by revolutionary rather than by evolutionary processes.[4]

Meanwhile, 'Aflaq published articles and essays in which he
criticized deprivation, poverty, and misery in particular and called
for the adoption of socialism as the panacea for these social ills.
But socialism was not intended to meet only material needs—these
needs, 'Aflaq contended, were taken for granted; he called for a
type of socialism which would stress above all spiritual values.
Socialism of this description, he said, calls

> . . . not only to speed production, but to increase the richness
> of life. . . .
> It has been too long to regard life as a bestial oven in which
> millions of men were consumed to produce a grain of gold. . . .
> I can still remember those who perished in their graves while
> struggling to achieve their cherished aspirations; life was de-
> prived of the sterling qualities of love and goodness of these
> men who could not spread them. . . .
> I have never regarded socialism merely as a means to satisfy
> hunger. . . . I am not concerned about hungry men merely be-
> cause they are hungry, but because of the potentialities hidden
> in them which hunger has prevented from displaying. . . . If I
> were asked to define Socialism, I would not seek a definition

---

[4] Most of 'Aflaq's short stories were published in a newspaper called *al-Ayyam* (Days) and
a periodical called *al-Tali‘a* (The Vanguard) of Damascus. For a summary of these stories,
see Shakir Mustafa, *Muhadarat ‘An al-Qissa fi Suriyya* [Lectures on the Syrian Story]
(Cairo, 1958), pp. 305 ff.

in the writings of Marx and Lenin, but I would rather say that
it is the religion of life, and life's ability to overcome death.[5]

'Aflaq's early writings, whether in the form of essays or short
stories, combined a description of the misery and inner contradiction of social life with a critical analysis of the forces that produced
them. "Only those who have had similar experiences," he once said,
"will understand the meaning of our complaints." No less than a
complete change from the traditional way of life could relieve the
individual from tensions and deprivations. The road to this complete change, he said, is a revolution which would achieve a new
mode of living—Arab socialism.

A critical exposition of 'Aflaq's ideas about Arab socialism—a
blend of nationalism, socialism, and democracy—has already been
presented to the reader in a companion volume,[6] but a word about
the relative significance of the three ingredients of Arab socialism
in 'Aflaq's eyes might be in order. I asked 'Aflaq: What, in his view,
is the relationship between nationalism and socialism? Socialism,
in attempting to liberate the individual from deprivation, is only
the means, he replied; but nationalism, in supplying spiritual values,
is the end. Democracy as a form of government, he added, would
be established only after society had become socialistic. Nationalism,
by necessity, is third in the order of things, since social change
must be accomplished first by revolution before peaceful changes
can take place by democratic processes.

Nationalism is the overriding principle in 'Aflaq's scheme; it is
the "destiny" of Arab life today, aiming at rehabilitating the Arabs
morally and materially to take their deserved place among the nations of the world. The Arab nation—divided and decadent—must
first be revitalized and reunited to form, or re-form, a nation in the
modern sense. Thus socialism and Arab unity—the movement to
unite all Arabs into one nation—are the direct means by which the
Arabs may play their role as a great nation in the national hierarchy.

'Aflaq's views—indeed, the Ba'th ideology as a whole—are stated
in vague and abstract terms, acceptable in principle to young men
imbued with idealism but never really spelled out as a party pro-

[5]Michel 'Aflaq, "Tharwat al-Hayat" [Richness of Life], al-Tali'a (Damascus), Vol. II
(June 1936); for a summary, see Mustafa, Muhadarat, p. 303.
[6]See my Political Trends in the Arab World (Baltimore, 1970), pp. 153-59, 194-98.

gram. 'Aflaq may have been right in stating that he, as the party's philosopher, provided only general principles—a conceptual framework for the party's program—and that it would be the duty of the party's leaders to work out a detailed program. The National Command, composed of representatives of the various regional units, was originally designed to formulate goals and provide strategy and general guidelines. But since 'Aflaq was head of the National Command and so intimately involved in the party's leadership, there may be justification in making him responsible for the failure to formulate a detailed program. As a result, dissension split the party and each faction tried to provide its own interpretation of general principles. Thus the Ba'th today no longer remains one party.

IV

What was 'Aflaq's role as an intellectual politician?

'Aflaq began his political activities by lecturing his students on social and political doctrines; he talked with them in school when he was still in the teaching profession and in his house and other meeting places after he resigned. Arab students in Syria as well as in other countries have become highly politicized, especially since World War II, and have shown readiness to listen to ideological groups who approached them to enlist their support in organizing strikes and street demonstrations. As an intellectual, 'Aflaq found the company of students quite congenial, for they were ready to sit at his feet and listen with fascination to his articulate exposition of ideas and personal opinions relevant to their country's conditions. He is not very fluent in speech—he often pauses before he completes a sentence—but he expresses himself in well-chosen words and can get his ideas across in terse and synoptic sentences which carry conviction. He often speaks like a school teacher, and his audience listens to him like students in a classroom. The disciples spread the master's words to larger audiences and eventually to the masses. Students and other young men, who form the core of 'Aflaq's supporters, have played the role of vanguard for his political movement; in the last analysis his political strength has depended on them as the vehicles of his political ideas.

As a Christian intellectual, 'Aflaq was able to influence only

young Muslims to whom religious loyalty had become subordinate
to national loyalty; but older men, to whom religious affiliation
was still a primary consideration, were not easily won over by
the same arguments, even though 'Aflaq often paid high tribute to
Islam as a necessary spiritual ingredient of Arab nationalism. Nor
did he possess the qualities of a fiery speaker who could with a
fluent tongue influence and excite a crowd, as could Faris al-Khuri,
a Christian political leader who became Prime Minister after World
War II. 'Aflaq was essentially a withdrawn person who preferred to
converse with small groups and to exercise influence from behind
the scenes, although against his personal inclinations he did on more
than one occasion participate in street demonstrations. After the
Ba'th Party was established, he depended on certain party members,
especially Baytar, who often acted as the leader of the party, to
perform executive and other functions. But neither Baytar nor
other members possessed the requisite leadership qualities, least of
all the charisma necessary for popular appeal. As a result, 'Aflaq
continued to play the role of the "spiritual leader," while a few
other members, often guided by him, operated as bosses in various
capacities.

   After the Ba'th Party was officially organized in 1947, 'Aflaq
tried to control the party through the principle of collective leadership. This principle was embodied in a National Command composed of representatives from various Arab countries, each controlled by a regional command.[7] 'Aflaq acted nominally as the
Secretary-General of the National Command, but in fact he failed
to provide effective control over the party when differences among
leaders arose. Elaborate in structure, the central command lacked
coherence and effective coordination.

   Early in 1954 the Ba'th merged with the Socialist Party, led by
Akram al-Hawrani, a young professional politician; but Hawrani,
though active and a good speaker, could not command the respect
of Ba'th leaders, and the lack of effective leadership continued.
The type of charismatic leadership that the Ba'th needed to excite
young Arabs was to be found elsewhere—in the Nile Valley where
Jamal 'Abd al-Nasir had just emerged as a popular hero following
his successful arms deal with the Soviet Union in 1955. Nasir's

[7]See *ibid.*, pp. 158-59.

prestige was enhanced when he nationalized the Suez Canal Company and opposed the tripartite attack on Egypt in 1958. 'Aflaq saw in Nasir the kind of leader his party needed—a man possessing leadership qualities with a charisma appealing to the masses. A marriage between Nasir and the Ba'th, 'Aflaq held, would provide the Arab nation with her immediate need—an ideological party with effective leadership. 'Aflaq himself hoped to play the role of court philosopher.

This marriage took place in 1958. The Ba'th leaders contributed in no small measure to the achievement of the Syro-Egyptian union;[8] but contrary to expectations, the experiment proved utterly disastrous to their party. Nasir, who cooperated at the outset with Ba'th leaders, paid little or no attention to their ideology; he was apparently interested in the Ba'th only as a means to dominate Syria. Consequently, some Ba'th leaders, especially Baytar and Hawrani, turned against Nasir and supported Syria's secession in 1961. This move, which seems to have been opposed by the majority, caused a serious split among party leaders which 'Aflaq could neither prevent nor repair. Consequently, he suffered a loss of control over the bosses, and the split in leadership has continued to exist.[9] Each faction, including 'Aflaq's own, is now claiming to represent the true principles of the Ba'th ideology; some members defected on the ground that Nasir no longer had faith in the Ba'th Party. 'Aflaq's failure to exercise effective leadership proved to be not only the principal weakness of the party but also the rock on which its entire structure has been wrecked. Today, the Ba'th is not one party but several rival groups.

V

In 1964 'Aflaq, no longer in control over the party, left first for Europe and then, after a short visit to Syria in 1966 (relinquishing

---

[8] A study of the establishment and dissolution of the United Arab Republic is the subject of a doctoral dissertation done at the Johns Hopkins School of Advanced International Studies by Robert Mertz.

[9] The major splits took place in 1959 and 1961. First, 'Abd-Allah al-Rimawi and then Fuad al-Rikabi resigned to organize separate nationalist-socialist groups under Nasir's leadership; in 1962, Akram al-Hawrani resigned to reorganize his own Socialist Party; and in 1964, 'Ali Salih al-Sa'di resigned to organize his radical revolutionary group. See my *Political Trends,* pp. 171-75.

his position of Secretary-General in favor of Munif al-Razzaz), for Brazil to live with relatives for some two years. He was still in Brazil when the Arab-Israeli war of June 1967 broke out. Despite defeat in the war, military officers continued to dominate the Ba'th Party, although leadership changed hands from one officer to another. Disenchanted with military control, the civilian leaders have either withdrawn from the party or ceased to support it.

In Syria, the humiliation suffered during the Six-Day War was attributed to the military's failure to stand up to the challenge and to decisions made in the name of the Ba'th without consultation with civilian leaders. Consequently, the regional commands of the other Arab countries felt compelled to act independently, and there was a growing feeling that the time had come to reinstall 'Aflaq in his former position of leadership. 'Aflaq made no move to return from Brazil until after the 'Iraqi Ba'th leaders seized power in 1968 and began to urge Ba'thists in other countries to acknowledge his control over the National Command.

While still in Brazil, 'Aflaq began to prepare the way for his return to party leadership. Arab defeat in the war of 1967, for which Ba'thists leaders were partly responsible, shocked 'Aflaq. He felt it to be his duty to inspire Ba'th followers with confidence and to urge them to resume the struggle and wipe out the consequences of defeat. In June 1967, immediately after the Six-Day War, he sent a letter to one of his followers in which he said:

> The beginning point to eliminate the consequences of the present situation, as I see it, is the same as that where we started a quarter of a century ago: to go back to the real source of our strength—the people. We should talk candidly and tell them the truth; we should arouse their feeling of responsibility so as to restore confidence and cooperation with them, even if these candid talks should lead to an embarrassing criticism of the [Ba'th] Party.
>
> Face-to-face talks with the people . . . is the normal exercise of the principle of popular democracy in which our Party believes; it is the only way to abandon the habits of individual decisions, isolationism and rivalry among leaders—qualities which had characterized the period before the tragedy [of the Six-Day War] . . . .[10]

[10]Michel 'Aflaq, *Niqtat al-Bidaya: Ahadith Ba'd al-Khamis Min Huzayran* [The Beginning Point: Talks (on the Period) after the Fifth of June] (Bayrut, 1971), pp. 41-42.

In this as well as in other dispatches, 'Aflaq tried to appeal directly to Ba'th members over the heads of party leaders, especially those in power in Syria, in order to revive Ba'th activities on the popular level. After the 'Iraqi Ba'th leaders seized power in July 1968, 'Aflaq returned to the Arab world, presumably at the invitation of Ahmad Hasan al-Bakr, Ba'thist President of the 'Iraq Republic, to reassume his position as Secretary-General of the party.[11] Since his return, 'Aflaq has again become active in politics and has tried to rally popular forces behind the 'Iraqi leaders; this put him in disfavor in the eyes of Syrian Ba'th leaders—indeed, these leaders were so enraged that they condemned him to death *in absentia* in 1971.

In the formative years of the Party, 'Aflaq appealed to young men as the "vanguard" (al-tali'a) of the Ba'th movement; he now also appeals to workers, as the toiling class of society, and reminds them that the crisis through which the Arab world is passing today is most crucial—it is the struggle for life or death.[12] Ba'thists, he has said, should prove that they are equal to the challenge and can, with popular support, transform defeat into victory.[13] He has called for cooperation with Marxists and other leftist groups and warned against assuming a hostile attitude toward the Soviet Union, since today it is the chief protagonist of progressive socialist programs and the greatest supporter of the Arabs since the Six-Day War.[14] In all these exhortations, 'Aflaq has repeated with great firmness the overriding principles of nationalism, socialism, and democracy; he has said that Arab need for these principles in their peremptory aspects is more pressing than ever before, especially Arab national unity, which should be realized by revolutionary methods. Only by pursuing these goals, he has often repeated, can the Ba'th correct past errors and resume the Arab procession toward progress.[15]

---

[11] In June 1968, while visiting Baghdad, I had the pleasure of meeting some Ba'th leaders, including Ahmad Hasan al-Bakr, who were then active in the preparation of the military coup that brought them to power in the following month. In a conversation with Bakr I mentioned 'Aflaq's name, and Bakr volunteered the information that he was hoping soon to invite him to visit 'Iraq!

[12] 'Aflaq, *Niqtat al-Bidaya*, pp. 42, 48, 77-81.

[13] *Ibid.*, p. 43.

[14] *Ibid.*, pp. 51, 52-53.

[15] 'Aflaq has said that the Arabs should regard themselves as in a state of continuous war in order to achieve national goals (*ibid.*, p. 60).

The initial favorable response to 'Aflaq's appeal demonstrated that the Ba'th movement has not yet spent itself and that the principles for which it stands, especially in the wake of the Arab-Israeli war, are still popular among young men who consider Arab weakness toward Israel the direct result of the division and rivalry among leaders vying for power. However, it is doubtful that 'Aflaq will be able to provide today more effective leadership than before and to reconcile rival factions within the party. He seems still to enjoy the respect and loyalty of some rival factions, but most have preferred to remain apart and have refused to unite into one party, each claiming to represent fundamental Ba'thist principles more faithfully than the other. In short, the lack of effective leadership continues to exist despite 'Aflaq's renewed efforts at coordination.[16]

VI

'Aflaq, in contrast with Lutfi al-Sayyid and Haykal, is the intellectual politician *par excellence;* he possesses an ability to formulate goals and has the intent to carry them out. Like Lutfi, he is a dedicated man and loyal to his party; indeed, he has gone beyond Lutfi by advocating revolutionary methods in trying to create the conditions necessary to achieve his party's goals. Haykal stands between Lutfi and 'Aflaq because he tried to relate goals to realities and to modify basic principles; neither Lutfi nor 'Aflaq would approve of altering principles in order to achieve goals. 'Aflaq, unlike Lutfi and Haykal, is committed to revolutionary principles and is ready to destroy by force barriers which might stand between him and his goals. Lutfi in particular would prefer to withdraw from politics rather than use violence in the pursuit of goals, even if conditions were favorable for achieving them. True, 'Aflaq failed in his efforts to achieve his goals, but he tried earnestly. Lutfi possessed the talent to formulate goals but lacked the ability for implementing them. Haykal possessed the intent but failed to achieve most of his goals,

---

[16]'Aflaq reluctantly agreed to become the Secretary-General of the 'Iraqi Ba'th, but he seems to have some reservations about the conduct of 'Iraqi leaders. The fact that he prefers to live in Bayrut rather than in Baghdad—although he pays occasional visits to the 'Iraqi capital—gives the impression that he is not fully in favor of Ba'th activities in 'Iraq.

even though he gave full support to some—free enterprise, freedom of the press, the multiple-party system, and others. Needless to say, these principles are no longer relevant to his country's existing regime, but they are still held in esteem and may well be reasserted in practice if civilian rule should ever be reestablished.

Since 'Aflaq is still active and the Ba'th Party (or parties) is still operating in some Arab countries, it is exceedingly difficult to evaluate his role and to pass final judgment on his achievements. It is perhaps less difficult to assess the roles of Lutfi and Haykal, since both have passed away, even though the span after their disappearance is too short for a proper perspective. I have known 'Aflaq more intimately than Lutfi and Haykal; yet his character and personality seem more enigmatic than theirs. He lives a modest life, almost frugal (especially before his marriage), and gives the impression that he has no desire for power—judging by the obvious fact that he has often refused to hold political posts. But one suspects that beneath his shyness and pious desire to avoid official functions there is a persistent desire to exercise political influence. He never desired to become Prime Minister—he always urged Baytar to hold this post—but he did influence, if he did not directly control, Baytar whenever he was in the saddle. Like a king's mother, he does not pretend to rule, but he exercises power from behind the throne. Although essentially an intellectual, he is not devoid of political ambition and his conduct, despite loyalty and dedication to the party, has been open to charges of charlatanism. However, he has never used his personal influence, nor that of his party, for pecuniary reward. Had he possessed the qualities of a charismatic leader, he might have been able to play a more constructive role in Arab politics. He has already passed his sixtieth birthday and he lives almost in retirement, but his political career is not yet over, for he continues to issue directives to disciples and is ready to give counsel to any politician likely to carry out his party's goals by peaceful or revolutionary methods. There seems to be an element of adventurism in 'Aflaq, but this is not necessarily the product of political opportunism or lack of honesty; it is perhaps a function of the revolutionary principle which he deems necessary to achieve goals. In the last analysis he is a visionary and a romantic type of intellectual politician, which is not out of place in Arab society.

CHAPTER XIII

Conclusion

> The realm is guarded by the sword and administered with the pen.
> People disagree about the sword and the pen, as to which of the two
> is superior, and takes precedence. Some think that the pen has it
> over the sword, and urge, in support of their view, that the sword
> guards the pen, and so stands to it as a guardian and servant. Others
> think the sword superior, and urge that the pen serves the sword
> because it provides the soldiers with their pay, and so is a servant to
> it. Others say they are equal and that neither of them can function
> without the other.
>
> Ibn al-Tiqtaqa, *al-Fakhri* (A.D. 1302)

We have seen that the dozen personalities who form the
subject matter of this study were drawn into politics either
because they consciously sought to pursue a political career
or because events coincidentally thrust them onto the scene to play
a political role. Whether political involvement comes by accident
or by choice, to survive as a political leader one must possess certain qualities and qualifications for the game of politics. Are the
qualifications or the circumstances responsible for drawing a man
into politics to play a constructive role?

Like their Western counterparts, Arab writers have disagreed on
this question as well as on the relative importance and precedence
of the factors involved. Traditional biographers of great men assert
that the leader's qualifications are overriding. For example, the
Prophet Muhammad, Mu'awiya, Salah al-Din(Saladin), and in modern times 'Abd al-'Aziz Ibn Sa'ud and Nasir are but a few who were

involved with great events in the Arab world and who, by the strength of their characters, left an impact which transcended circumstantial forces. On the other hand, modern social analysts consider great men as the product of social forces long in progress. According to this view, when such forces matured to produce a movement, the man who proved capable of riding the crest of a wave became the great leader of the time. As representative leaders, the experiences of the men scrutinized in this study may throw light on this question.

In the Arab world, as in several other regions, a plethora of political leaders appeared in periods of stirring events—national revival, two world wars, and social and political upheavals. These events created opportunities for many men to be drawn into politics, but only a few rose to the occasion to play constructive roles. Most of them failed either because their ideas were not relevant to conditions or because they lacked the requisite leadership qualities. For example, the idealists who refused to subordinate ideals to realities either preferred to withdraw from politics—'Aziz 'Ali and Lutfi al-Sayyid—or continued to play the political game without success—the Mufti and Chadirchi. The ideological leaders, on the other hand, tried to change conditions by violent means in order to carry out their ideals—indeed, they often succeeded in changing conditions but failed to achieve their goals. Only a few leaders who possessed the requisite qualities succeeded in playing constructive roles, because the circumstances in which they entered politics proved favorable. For example, Nuri al-Sa'id, Muhammad Husayn Haykal, Faysal, and Bourguiba are four distinguished leaders who played constructive roles because of the favorable circumstances following two world wars—the first two after the first war and the other two after the second war.

It follows that both qualifications and circumstances are necessary for a leader to succeed, but the point of interest is to inquire as to which of the two variables—men or circumstances—is in the last analysis overriding? The cases of the four men just cited may suggest a clue to correlate the operating factors of men and circumstances. Nuri and Haykal, two highly qualified leaders, succeeded in the favorable circumstances of the years between the wars but failed in the shifting circumstances of the years following the second war. Conversely, Faysal and Bourguiba, no less highly qualified, made no progress in the unfavorable years between the wars but succeeded perhaps beyond their expectations after the second war because the new circumstances of the postwar years turned in their favor. It follows that neither the man nor the circumstances alone can produce the constructive leadership role; it is the confluence of the man's requisite qualifications with the right circumstances. In other words, it is neither the man nor the circumstances, but the man-in-the-circumstances. The stronger the man's qualities and the more favorable the circumstances—in short the higher the point of confluence on the scale of men and circumstances—the greater and more transcending the leader's achievements.

II

Of the dozen political leaders, three—'Aziz 'Ali al-Misri, the Mufti, and Lutfi al-Sayyid—belong to an idealist school. They failed to carry out the goals with which they were identified primarily because those goals were either too advanced for or incompatible with existing conditions and traditions. Two—'Aziz 'Ali and Lutfi—decided to withdraw from the scene, revealing unwillingness or inability to subordinate ideals to reality. In other words, they were bona fide or confirmed idealists. The other—the Mufti—continued to play the political game despite failure because he possessed the skills of a professional politician. Thus, the Mufti was not a bona fide idealist, since he traded on his ideals for political survival.

The so-called idealists appeared on the political scene at the turn of the twentieth century, each representing in his own country a certain school. As such, they were pioneers in the *terra incognita* of their political endeavors. No leader had preceded them to experiment with ideas relevant to conditions and to provide guidance for successors.

The generation that succeeded the pioneer idealists had learned that success depended on adjusting goals to conditions. This set of leaders belonged to the realistic school. It is true that Nuri, Bourguiba, and Haykal were by nature practical men; they were also quick enough to see the futility of their mentors' struggles to achieve impossible goals. Thus the realistic school followed logically a pioneering idealistic school. This is not to suggest that all the leaders who succeeded idealists belonged to a realistic school. There were indeed some who paid no heed to the lessons of predecessors and developed their realism as a result of their own experiences. Even as a realist, the leader's goals must be constantly tested by experience if he is to survive.

A third generation of young leaders, dissatisfied with half-measures and the outmoded methods of the realists, turned to radical goals. This new school, growing out of postwar Arab politics, sought to disestablish old regimes by violence and to replace them. These leaders, belonging to an ideological school, sought to achieve a new society by revolutionary methods. Although a number of ideological leaders have entered the political scene, none has yet been able to achieve power save by an alliance with army officers. However, such a collaboration has been disastrous for the ideological leaders: if they remained loyal to their ideology, they had to abandon politics; if they wanted to continue political participation, they had to compromise with the military, hence becoming realists. We have had an occasion to examine three ideological leaders—Nasir, the officer who adopted an ideology to legitimize military rule; Bakdash, a civilian leader who refused to subordinate ideology to military rule; and 'Aflaq, an ideological leader who achieved power—more specifically, his party achieved power—because he came to terms with the military. None was able to subordinate the military to ideology.

III

It will be noted that the categorization of political leaders in accordance with goals—idealist, realist, and ideological—and the pathways (political ladders) by which they entered politics cut across one another. This demonstrates that political pathways do not necessarily become obstacles that restrain or prohibit leaders from the pursuit of goals to which they are committed, although it is commonly held that professional politicians tend to exhibit greater flexibility in bypassing obstacles than military and intellectual politicians. Of the six professional politicians scrutinized in this study, two were committed to extreme or radical outlooks—the Mufti (extreme traditional) and Bakdash (communist)—which inhibited them from accepting compromises; three were committed to moderate goals—Faysal (moderate traditional) and Chadirchi and Junblat (social democrats)—which in varying degrees affected their behavior patterns; only one—Bourguiba—displayed a readiness to accept compromises and pursued flexible methods to achieve goals that had relevance to reality.

It is a commonplace that men who have been trained in military or intellectual disciplines are likely to be inhibited in their actions as political leaders. Refusing to subordinate principles to convenience, 'Aziz 'Ali al-Misri and Lutfi al-Sayyid were restrained from direct participation in politics; the former insisted on purist military standards in other walks of life and the latter disliked trading ideals for half-measures. But Nuri al-Sa'id, who received his training in military sciences, and Haykal, who was trained in intellectual disciplines, were quite prepared to modify their ideas and goals in accordance with existing conditions. Both realized that politics requires an approach different from professions in which purist standards are highly valued. Consequently, they were prepared to subordinate their standards to political convenience in order to survive as political leaders. Nonetheless, both were able to maintain a high level of integrity and immunity from corrupt practices widespread among professional political leaders.

Politics is essentially an art; to practice it successfully men learn to operate realistically, unfettered by the processes through which they achieve their goals. It is true that essential commitments to the needs and aspirations of one's country must be made as a matter of principle and for political survival, but these commitments must then be adjusted to political realities. The experiences of Arab leaders have shown that, regardless of the way they entered politics, they had to subordinate discipline and goals to the realities of life. These experiences—shared in varying degrees by leaders in almost all other countries—have been the subject of reproach by writers old and new; Shakespeare, in one of his plays, has put it in the mouth of Brutus, as follows:

'Tis a common proof,
that lowliness is young ambition's ladder,
Whereto the climber-upward turns his face;
But when he once attains the upmost round,

He then unto the ladder turns his back,
Looks in the clouds, scorning the base degrees
By which he did ascend.[1]

IV

Arabs yearn for strong political leaders to preside over their destiny; if these leaders prove their integrity, straightforwardness, and strength of character, they often receive unlimited support and confidence and are likely to enjoy a long period of political survival. Competent men who possess the intent and qualifications for leadership have not always been able to obtain their countrymen's confidence either because they tried to enter the political scene by pathways deemed contrary to traditions or because their outlook conflicted with the country's needs and aspirations.

According to Islamic traditions, political leaders were either chosen by God through the angels or inspired by some superior power, and men were exhorted by divine orders to "obey those in authority among you."[2] In accordance with these teachings the Prophet Muhammad, after presenting himself as God's chosen Apostle, was acknowledged by his people as their leader. However, before his death, the Prophet provided no rules for succession save the vague guiding principle that matters of public affairs were open to consultation, and the angels seem to have been relieved of their burden to appoint leaders by divine orders. Consequently, the duty of choosing successors to the Prophet's mantle of leadership devolved upon his people, and the methods of choice have proved to be a perennial cause of dissension and conflict.

Prior to the era of nationalism, Arab leadership was in the hands of dynasts, who had come to power by political manipulation, or rival legionnaires, who seized power by violence. Ibn al-Tiqtaqa, a fourteenth-century writer, referred to these two pathways as the political methods of the sword and the pen.[3] In accordance with the political method of the sword, the legionnaire, following a successful coup de grace, would establish a new line of sultans or shahs,

[1] *Julius Caesar,* Act II, Scene 1, lines 21-28.

[2] For relevant texts on the subject, see Qur'an, II, 29; III, 31; VIII, 45; XXXVIII, 25.

[3] See the quotation at the head of this chapter.

which in turn would be replaced by other legionnaires. In almost every case, the religious leaders tended to support those in power on the strength of the principle that public quietude was in the best interests of the community; however, in reality, the beneficiaries of this rationale were the vested interests.

Foreign ideas and pressures caused a change in traditional patterns of leadership. Arab leaders often accommodated, rather than opposed, foreign intruders, which resulted in a conflict between the leaders and their countrymen. The traditional religious and tribal forces offered no viable alternative leadership, and, eventually, they were crushed by overwhelming foreign interventions.

With the rise of nationalism, a new type of leadership began to emerge, which has not yet superseded traditional behavior patterns. Combining qualities from traditional and European experiences, as is true of the dozen personalities chosen for our study, the contemporary leaders sought by various means to achieve goals derived from the needs and aspirations of their countrymen. Today, Arab leaders have been experimenting with political processes, ranging from extreme traditional to radical modern methods, but no single pathway acceptable to all has yet emerged. Once a stable regime (or regimes) has been firmly established in Arab society, Arab leaders may eventually develop their own political pathways, derived partly from their traditions and partly from Western experience. If social democracy, as I suggested in a companion volume,[4] eventually emerges out of Arab experimentation with diverse political systems, a corollary type of leadership will also have to emerge to operate in accordance with new political processes.

We have seen how the traditional leaders who resisted the influx of foreign ideas and pressures tended to pursue inflexible methods. The so-called revolutionary leaders, on the other hand, tried by authoritarian and violent methods to carry out the needed social change. Neither method seems to inspire confidence or insure progress and development. If a form of social democracy eventually emerges and if it is to survive, a new pattern of leadership is bound to evolve. More specifically, the new leaders will have to have qualities that will insure the stability and survival of the evolving system—

---

[4] See "A New Social Democracy?" in my *Political Trends in the Arab World* (Baltimore, 1970), Chap. 10.

the qualities of flexibility, temperance, and a sense of practicability. The stability of the system presupposes political pathways that conform to the political process. If the leaders ever resort to violence and military coups, they should be discredited by an enlightened public—a necessary instrument against authoritarian propensities in the evolving political system.

V

If we review the history of mankind, it is said, we will find an abundance of great scientists, great soldiers, and great men in every field of human endeavors—but how many great political figures? The truth of this synoptic view of the relative scarcity of great statesmen may well be attested by Arab experience, if first we try to clarify the meaning of the word "great" and then indicate the requisite conditions under which men become great.

Following World War I, when a new phase of Arab national existence began to take shape, a plethora of political figures was drawn into the political scene, as we noted earlier; but how many of these—at any rate how many of the dozen personalities scrutinized in this study—may be singled out as really great, if we mean by great only those men who possessed the animus and intent to exercise leadership and the ability to achieve goals relevant to their country's conditions? (This is not necessarily to suggest that great men have appeared in fields other than Arab politics, especially if they are compared with other great men in the world at large.) And even if they could claim some qualities of greatness, were they known to the outside world?

Apart from world recognition, let us examine the claim of our twelve personalities to greatness in the context of their national milieu. Of these twelve men, half were professional politicians in their own right and the other half had chosen military or intellectual endeavors before they entered politics. How many of the six professional politicians could distinguish themselves as great statesmen and how many of the other six as great in politics and/or other activities? If we take leadership qualities and the capacity to achieve national goals as the minimum standard of greatness, perhaps none would qualify for greatness. However, one or two among

the six professional politicians—Faysal and Bourguiba—might qualify for a modest claim to greatness according to this scale. Of the
three soldiers, two—'Aziz 'Ali al-Misri and Nasir—were highly rated
in military discipline and might have distinguished themselves as
great—indeed, 'Aziz 'Ali's contemporaries considered him as the
ideal officer—had they not attempted to achieve national goals
through the weapons of their profession. As for the three intellectuals—Lutfi al-Sayyid, Haykal, and 'Aflaq—they were all recognized as relatively great writers and their works were highly prized.
One of them—Lutfi al-Sayyid—had a more lasting imprint on his
country, because he prepared a new generation of elites and earned
the name of "the teacher of a generation" as a token of his intellectual influence. However, none of the three could qualify as a
great statesman—indeed, all had a deficiency in one, and perhaps
more than one, requisite quality of leadership in addition to their
failure to achieve cherished goals. Of the six men of the sword and
the pen, only Nuri al-Sa'id, judged at least by his record of achievements, might qualify as a great statesman, because he possessed the
qualities of a professional politician, although he was not a popular
leader and his life ended in the collapse of a regime he himself had
helped build.[5] Nasir, who became more widely known than Nuri
in the outside world, may well go down in his country's history as
a greater leader of men than Nuri, although a different final judgment of his achievements may be made by future scholars.[6]

   If Arab experiences tend to confirm the view about the scarcity
of great statesmen, will they also reveal to us the clue as to why
men who choose politics as a career find it more difficult than men
in other walks of life to achieve greatness? In our scrutiny of the
twelve personalities, we have already had occasion to notice that in
order to play a constructive political role the politician must await
certain favorable circumstances, regardless of his leadership qualities. Neither qualifications nor circumstances alone determine the
success of a political leader—his destiny necessarily lies in the happy
confluence of circumstances and qualifications. In such human
endeavors as science and art, where achievements are essentially

[5] Nuri's claim to greatness lay not so much in his support of the monarchy (which was
overthrown by the Revolution of July 1958) as in the achievement of his country's independence and in the postwar reconstruction schemes which survived the July Revolution.

[6] See p. 43, above.

brought about by talent and industry, circumstances are not as important; favorable circumstances for scientists and artists may make them celebrities, but they are not necessary to their mastery of their respective fields. We have already seen how 'Aziz 'Ali al-Misri and Lutfi al-Sayyid, to mention but only two examples, had become recognized figures in their respective fields primarily because of personal qualifications. But when they entered the political scene, they failed to succeed because of unfavorable circumstances, and they consciously refused to accommodate goals to conditions. Needless to say, men of science and art need not heed unfavorable conditions, for their achievements are essentially the product of natural faculties; but genius alone is not enough for a politician to succeed. Circumstances, which may seem to smile upon a prospective political leader, often shift beyond even the wit or will of a Napoleon, regardless of the reputation or the charisma he has developed. Rare indeed are the men who can become great statesmen; in Seneca's words: *Non est ad astra mollis e terris via!*—for them the way to the stars is not easy!

APPENDIX

A Case Study of the Conflicting Policies of Two Arab Leaders toward the Axis Powers [1]

Perhaps no other Arab statesman in modern times has followed a foreign policy so consistently friendly toward Great Britain as General Nuri al-Sa'id of 'Iraq. From the time when he joined the forces of the Arab revolt against the Turks in 1916 as the ally of Britain to the moment of his assassination in 1958, he had taken no important decision which ran contrary to British interests. He firmly believed that Arab nationalism was in need of British sympathy and support, which Britain indeed had readily given since World War I.

II

Nevertheless, *The Documents on German Foreign Policy,* captured by the Western powers during the last war and now made available to scholars,[2] supply evidence to the effect that General Nuri, at a time when his political opponents were busy negotiating with the Axis powers, himself made secret overtures to Axis representatives in 'Iraq conflicting with the policy he had advocated toward Great Britain. The story of Nuri's contact with the Axis, as given in the German documents, may be summarized as follows:

[1] This paper, appearing under the title "General Nuri's Flirtations with the Axis Powers," is reproduced with minor changes from *The Middle East Journal,* Vol. XVI (Summer 1962), pp. 328-36.

[2] The basic documents have been published in U.S. Department of State, *Documents on German Foreign Policy, 1918-45;* but the material relating to Nuri's offers of collaboration with the Axis remains unpublished.

During the autumn of 1940, when Nuri was Foreign Minister in the government of Rashid 'Ali al-Gaylani, there was a great concern in nationalist circles about the future of 'Iraq resulting from sweeping German victories. A few leaders began to call for an Arab-Axis alliance, irrespective of the Anglo-'Iraqi treaty. The Mufti of Jerusalem, al-Hajj Amin al-Husayni, who had arrived in Baghdad in October 1939, organized an Arab committee in whose name he initiated secret correspondence with Nazi representatives. Nuri himself was worried about the future of 'Iraq and began in early September 1940, to offer his collaboration with pro-Axis elements. He approached Jamal al-Husayni and Musa al-'Alami, two Palestinian leaders friendly to Nuri, and offered to work with the Mufti, if the 'Iraqi government could obtain an assurance of independence from the Axis powers. This offer, warmly recommended to the Mufti, was rejected on the ground that Nuri had been too long involved with the British. Nuri's offer, the Mufti contended, was merely designed to find out what the Mufti's secret arrangements with the Axis were in order to pass them on to the British authorities.

Despite this discouragement Nuri turned to Gabrielli, the Italian Minister in Baghdad, to whom he offered his collaboration. The Italian Foreign Minister, Count Ciano, apparently took the matter seriously at first and thought that Nuri's collaboration might be used to Italy's advantage. Nuri's flirtation with Italy, however, was short-lived; for, when the news of his secret contact with Gabrielli reached von Papen,[3] Germany's Ambassador in Ankara, with whom the Mufti was conducting secret negotiations in the name of the Arabs, he warned his government at once against Italy's treating with Nuri. On September 14, 1940, von Papen wrote the German Foreign Office stating that he was in contact with the Mufti through Naji Shawkat, the 'Iraqi Minister of Justice, and that Shawkat had told him that Nuri was regarded as a "traitor." On October 2, 1940, von Papen again warned the Foreign Office explaining that Italian collaboration with Nuri would be very disappointing to the Arab nationalists and pointed out that such dealings could not be kept secret very long. Von Ribbentrop passed on this warning to Count Ciano who in turn wrote to Gabrielli to stop his dealing with Nuri.

Nor was this all. Nuri seems to have intimated to several Arab leaders in the circle of the Mufti that he was ready to collaborate

[3] Von Papen heard the news from the Italian Colonial Secretary who met Dr. Schmid in Munich and told him about Nuri's contact with Gabrielli. Schmid passed this information to von Papen.

with the Axis powers. In December, 1940, he declared to the Mufti, in the presence of Jamil Mardam, a former Syrian Prime Minister who was then in Baghdad, that 'Iraq should seek an alliance with the Axis powers and that he was prepared to work with the Mufti to carry out such a policy. The Mufti, however, made no move to give Nuri any encouragement.

In an interview with the Mufti in Cairo (May 8, 1958), I asked him to comment on the information provided in the German documents concerning Nuri's offer to collaborate with the Axis. The Mufti confirmed the information concerning Nuri's offers of collaboration and stated that he was first approached through General Taha al-Hashimi.[4] Taha said, the Mufti went on to explain, that Nuri was willing to collaborate if he were allowed to participate in the Mufti's negotiations with the Axis. In his reply to Taha, the Mufti denied that secret negotiations with the Axis powers had been going on. He apologetically explained to me that it was not wise to disclose secret negotiations to General Taha who would pass them on to General Nuri. Moreover, the Mufti said that Nuri once complained to him, after a visit to Egypt (in the summer of 1940), that the British government would not give any pledge to the Arabs which might win them to its side, even though the military position in the Western desert was precarious. Thus Nuri hinted that he was willing to change his attitude toward Britain if the Mufti desired collaboration with him.

When I saw General Nuri in Baghdad on June 7, 1958, shortly before his assassination, I tried to verify some aspects of the information relating to his dealings with the Mufti. Avoiding asking him the embarrassing question concerning his offers of collaboration with the Axis, I put the question in the following form: "I heard that some of the Mufti's friends tried during the last war to repair your relations with the Mufti so that you and the Mufti would follow the same foreign policy." Nuri did not deny his approaches to the Mufti and replied in his characteristic vagueness that his contacts with the Mufti were never interrupted. He added that he had often discussed Arab affairs with him, but that he (the Mufti), who was then carrying on secret negotiations with the Axis, refused to disclose them to him. Nuri went on to explain that he tried to repair the relations between Great Britain and the Mufti

---

[4] General Taha, one of Nuri's supporters, was *persona grata* to the nationalists, owing to his active participation in the Palestine Defense Committee. See my *Independent 'Iraq* (2nd ed.; London, 1960), pp. 206 ff.

when Colonel S. F. Newcombe, who went to Baghdad in July 1940, opened semi-official negotiations with Palestinian leaders. The Mufti showed willingness to accept a settlement of the Palestine question on the basis of the White Paper[5]—a settlement which virtually would have put an end to Zionist aspirations to unlimited immigration by declaring that the Jewish National Home had been achieved.[6] Colonel Newcombe tried to find out the minimum demands of the Palestine leaders which the British government might consider as a basis for the Palestine settlement. Several meetings were held in the 'Iraqi Foreign Office at which, among others, Jamal al-Husayni and Musa al-'Alami, were present.[7] A scheme for the settlement of the Palestine problem was proposed, which Newcombe agreed to transmit to the British government. The White Paper was to be accepted as the basis of the Palestine settlement and the transition period was to be fixed at ten years. Both General Nuri and Prime Minister Rashid 'Ali, who attended the meetings, submitted the scheme to the 'Iraqi Council of Ministers and a decision was taken (August 1940) to the effect that in return of such a settlement the 'Iraqi government would make a formal declaration of war on the Axis powers and place one half of its forces (two divisions) at the disposal of the Middle East Command for service outside 'Iraq.[8] General Nuri went on to explain that he left for Cairo to communicate the decision of the 'Iraqi government to General Wavell, and the whole arrangement was referred to London, but there was no reply from the British government.[9] From that time on, said General

[5] The Mufti pointed out to the present writer that he made it clear to Nuri that the Newcombe conversations should not be based on the White Paper, but Nuri did not listen to him.

[6] *Palestine: Statement of Policy* (London, 1939), Cmd. 6019.

[7] Musa al-'Alami told the present writer (June 18, 1962) that he attended the meetings at the request of Colonel Newcombe, not as a representative of the Mufti. The news of Musa's mother's death on July 24, 1940, caused his absence from subsequent meetings, but when he saw Colonel Newcombe before his departure from Baghdad, the Colonel told him that he would receive a favorable message. Such a message never arrived.

[8] In an interview with the present writer in Cairo (April 5, 1958), Rashid 'Ali confirmed his agreement with the Mufti's representatives of the scheme proposed in the British Government through Colonel Newcombe and added that the 'Iraqi government decided to place its entire forces at the disposal of the British government. But, he said, the British government turned down the 'Iraqi offer.

[9] On August 26, 1940, a declaration was made to the effect that the British government could not depart from their declared policy in regard to Palestine. Winston Churchill, who disagreed with his Colonial Secretary, Lord Lloyd, rejected the Newcombe proposals and welcomed Zionist requests that they should be equipped for the defense of Palestine. See Winston S. Churchill, *The Second World War* (London, 1950), Vol. II, pp. 153, 559, 564; and George Kirk, *The Middle East in the War, 1939-45* (London, 1952), pp. 64, 237-38.

Nuri, the attitude of the pan-Arab leaders became increasingly hostile toward Great Britain.[10]

General Nuri's reference to the Mufti's representatives, Jamal al-Husayni and Musa al-'Alami, who attended the Newcombe conversations, prompted the present writer to seek the evidence of these two Palestinian leaders. Jamal al-Husayni, with whom I had the opportunity of discussing the Newcombe mission during my visit to Riyad (April 1955),[11] added no further details; but Musa al-'Alami, with whom I raised the whole question of Nuri's contact with the Axis powers, drew my attention to the relation between the failure of the Newcombe mission and Nuri's decision to contact the Axis powers.[12] Musa stated that the agreement reached between the Mufti's representatives and Colonel Newcombe on Palestine raised Nuri's hopes that at last he could rally the support of Arab leaders to his pro-British policy. After Newcombe's departure, however, while Nuri and the Mufti's representatives were expecting an invitation from the British government to establish a provisional Arab government in Palestine, no reply ever arrived, which demonstrated that no just settlement was contemplated in London. Nuri went to Cairo in August 1940, to discuss the matter with Richard G. Casey,[13] British Minister of State in the Middle East, but he returned empty-handed. Thereupon Nuri suggested to Musa al-'Alami to open negotiations with the Axis powers with a view to obtaining more favorable terms re the Palestine question. Musa, however, declined, pleading that he could not undertake such a heavy responsibility, and suggested for such a mission Amir 'Adil Arslan who, in turn, also declined. Nuri's failure to find a suitable messenger for direct contact with the Axis powers prompted him to suggest to Jamal al-Husayni that he (Jamal) should approach the Mufti with his offer of collaboration with the Axis, and was instructed to explain the reasons for such collaboration. The Mufti, however, rejected Nuri's offer. Nuri's offer of collaboration with the Mufti was probably sincere, since he was then disappointed with the British government's utter disregard for Arab interests, and its rejection of the 'Iraqi government's offer to participate in the war in lieu of a settlement favorable to the Pales-

---

[10] For an account of the Newcombe mission, see my *Independent 'Iraq*, pp. 171-72; and M. F. Abcarius, *Palestine Through the Fog of Propaganda* (London [1946]), pp. 212-13.

[11] After the war Jamal al-Husayni went to Saudi Arabia. He became a personal adviser on political affairs to the King of that country.

[12] The writer's interviews (June 12, 1961 and June 18, 1962) with Musa al-'Alami in Washington, D.C.

[13] Cf. Nuri's statement that he went to see General Wavell to p. 240, above.

tinian leaders disheartened him. He realized that Britain's unwillingness to settle the Palestine question during the war undermined his
position in 'Iraq and among pan-Arab leaders, who had already been
dissatisfied with Britain. Nuri now began to share the feeling of these
leaders.[14]

III

In analyzing the foregoing statements, both written and oral,
the evidence seems to prove beyond any doubt that General Nuri
did attempt to contact the Axis powers either directly or through
pan-Arab leaders. It also proves that he was anxious to know what
terms he or the Mufti could obtain from the Axis powers in favor
of the Arabs. Evidently Nuri utterly failed to establish a working
basis of collaboration and his initial success with the Italians was
short-lived,[15] for neither the Axis leaders nor the Mufti would trust
him.

What prompted Nuri to seek Axis collaboration is not clear
from available evidence. Did he merely want to obtain intelligence
concerning the Mufti's relations with the Axis in order to pass it
on to the British authorities, as the Mufti contended? Or was he
really disappointed with the British government, following its rejection of the Arab proposals transmitted by Colonel Newcombe, as
Musa al-'Alami stated? Or, again, did he, in a moment of despair,
seek to change his loyalty to Britain in order to save his own skin
and protect his country's interests from an association with a losing
party?

Before we attempt to find a clue, much less an answer, to these
questions we should recall the atmosphere of bewilderment and
clash of loyalties that followed the fall of France, which threw the
country's leaders into utter confusion. Syrian and Palestinian
emigrés, whose countries lay under the control of France and England, rejoiced at France's misfortune, while moderate 'Iraqi ele-

[14] Musa al-'Alami made the following comment: "Nuri's purpose for contacting the Axis
was his desire to settle the Palestine question. He had persuaded the Palestinian leaders to
rely on Britain for a just settlement, but when the Newcombe mission failed, he told those
leaders that since he had failed to obtain a settlement, they should feel free to contact the
Axis powers for a favorable solution of their country's problems."

[15] It is not yet known what went on between General Nuri and the Italians, since the
Italian war documents have not yet been published. The German documents merely men-
tion the fact, not the substance, of Nuri's conversations with Gabrielli. Unfortunately,
Gabrielli died before the present writer could make an arrangement to see him in Rome.

ments were alarmed to conclude that the loss of the war to England might lead to the loss of 'Iraqi independence. The prevailing opinion, however, was that England had no chance of survival, while Axis propaganda gave lavish assurances of a brighter and more prosperous life if Germany won the war. The pan-Arab leaders, especially the leading army officers, who always had a say in the politics of the country, were seemingly no wiser than those French generals who advised their head of government after their collapse that "in three weeks England will have her neck wrung like a chicken!" To these leaders the Anglo-'Iraqi alliance had become a liability, which put the very existence of their country in jeopardy, rather than an asset. British prestige reached its lowest ebb and 'Iraqi leaders were advised to reconsider their relations with the British government.

In June 1940, in the same month that France collapsed, the Mufti of Jerusalem dispatched a letter, the first in a series of correspondence with the Axis powers to von Papen. In July, when pan-Arab leaders became restless, Colonel Newcombe arrived in Baghdad and showed readiness to transmit specific proposals concerning the Palestine settlement to the British government. The failure of the Newcombe mission, as Nuri himself suggested, proved to be the turning point from which the elements still hesitating to break with Britain threw their lot with the pro-Axis party. At this critical point Nuri might have had a moment of second thoughts concerning 'Iraq's relations with Britain. He intimated, it is now known, to a few close friends in the Mufti's circle that he was in favor of collaboration with the Axis powers.[16] Sir Basir Newton, the British Ambassador in Baghdad, is reported to have informed his home government that even Nuri seems to have thought during 1940 that 'Iraq should take steps to safeguard her future irrespective of Great Britain.

Under the circumstances Nuri might have wanted to know what promises the Mufti had obtained from the Axis powers, not necessarily to pass the information on to the British authorities. In the meantime, Nuri was disappointed with the British government's attitude toward the Arab proposals for the settlement of the Palestine question, the rejection of which contributed to undermining his position vis-à-vis the pan-Arab leaders at the time he had come very near to securing their agreement to side with Britain. Hence, his conversations with Musa al-'Alami, prompted by his failure to ob-

[16] See the memoirs of the Mufti's secretary, 'Uthman Kamal Haddad, entitled *Harakat Rashid 'Ali al-Gaylani* (Sidon, 1950), pp. 16-17.

tain British support for his understanding with the pan-Arab leaders no less than his concern about 'Iraq's future, was designed to inform himself about the nature of Axis promises, in order to assess the value of Axis collaboration before he should change his loyalty to Great Britain.

Nuri's short-lived flirtations with Axis agents induced him to reconsider Britain's chances of survival and there was no doubt as to what his decision would be. Britain's ability to carry on the struggle alone before the entry of Russia and the United States inspired him to uphold his country's traditional policy toward Britain which he had so assiduously worked to establish. He seems to have reverted to an argument which he had often advanced during the first year of the war, and which had an initial favorable impression on the 'Iraqi Army officers before the fall of France, that the Soviet Union's nonaggression pact with Germany was "unnatural" and that eventually she would enter the war on the side of Britain.[17]

On second thought, Nuri might have also concluded that in more auspicious circumstances after the war, he would be able to influence his British friends to settle the Palestine question in favor of the Arabs if he submitted new proposals acceptable to the British government. The opportunity for taking the initiative for submitting such proposals came sooner than Nuri had expected; for no sooner had Anthony Eden made a statement on May 30, 1941, in favor of Arab unity, than Nuri submitted a set of proposals to Richard G. Casey, British Minister in the Middle East, setting forth his ideas about the form of Arab unity, including a settlement of the Palestine question.[18] Nuri's proposals to Richard Casey became the basis for inter-Arab conversations during the war which culminated in the establishment of the Arab League, designed to tackle the Palestine question after the war. Nuri's frustration in 1940, resulting from the failure of the Newcombe mission, was vindicated, though the Arab League utterly failed to rise to its task after the war.

IV

Even if Nuri's approaches to the Axis powers were encouraged by the Mufti, it is doubtful that Axis circles would have been con-

[17]See Sabbagh, *Fursan al-'Uruba fi al 'Iraq* (Damascus, 1956), p. 114.

[18]General Nuri al-Sa'id, *Arab Independence and Unity* (Baghdad, 1943). For a summary of Nuri's proposals see Colonel S. F. Newcombe, "A Forecast of Arab Unity," *Journal of the Royal Central Asian Society*, Vol. XXXI (1944), p. 158.

genial to Nuri. For long accustomed to be the leader of pro-British elements, he would not have agreed to be the junior partner with the Mufti. Nor would the Mufti have been willing, as his subsequent quarrel with Rashid 'Ali demonstrated, to surrender the leadership of the pro-Axis group to Nuri. Rivalry between these two formidable men would have driven Nuri back to where he always stood—the favored son of the British. Nor was the Mufti expected to trust Nuri, who had often ignored the Mufti's entreaties on behalf of pan-Arabs at the time when Nuri was Prime Minister.[19] By far more experienced in diplomacy than the Mufti, Nuri would probably have discovered the Mufti's weakness in his Axis negotiations and criticized him for obtaining neither a clear assurance of independence for 'Iraq nor specific advantages for the other Arab countries; while the Mufti, realizing these shortcomings, might have tried to conceal them from Nuri. In all probability Nuri would have soon discovered that the Arabs could gain no more from the Axis than what they had already obtained—or might obtain later—from Great Britain. Unless the Axis prospects were indeed promising, Nuri would not have remained long in Axis circles.

Nuri's confusion as to what course of action he should take to save his country out of a difficult position during 1940 was not unprecedented in the life of men who found themselves in similar circumstances. The Prophet Muhammad, in a moment of weakness during his struggle to uphold belief in God, made a concession to Makkan idols in order to end the estrangement between himself and his people. Very soon he discovered that he was listening to the suggestion of Satan, not to divine communication through Angel Gabriel, and he repudiated Satan's delusion in favor of the "truth."[20] Before him, other prophets, like Nathan and David, passed through similar experiences when they accepted Satan's suggestions but later had to reject them in favor of divine guidance.[21] The confusion between Satan's delusion and divine guidance reflects the difficulties in which those old sages found themselves during momentous crises. But prophets seem to have had the advantage of having always at their elbows the angels ready to correct their errors. In modern times we seem to have relieved the angels of their burdens and required men of responsibility to possess what the gods possess—the wisdom of making good judgment.

[19]Haddad, *Harakat Rashid 'Ali al Gaylani*, pp. 19-20.

[20]See Tabari, *Ta'rikh* (Leiden, 1879), Vol. I, pp. 1192 ff; and Ibn Hisham, *Sira*, ed. Wustenfeld (Göttingen, 1858), Vol. I, p. 214, Guillaume's translation, p. 165. See also A. Guillaume, *New Light on the Life of Muhammad* (Manchester, n.d.), pp. 38-39.

[21] 2 Sam. 7: 1-5, 12, 13; Kings 5: 3-5; 1 Chron. 21: 1-30, 22: 1-19.

At critical times it is not unnatural that men of public responsibility should pause either to iron out certain doubt about past actions or to gather momentum for a new departure. The nature of the decision taken reveals the quality of the man and the set of principles governing his judgment. He may prove to be an idealist or a Machiavellian and his decision may yield to his country a long- or a short-term advantage. It is indeed a heavy responsibility, for the slightest error in judgment might lead to a disastrous end. Lucky indeed would be the man who can correct an error before he faces a fatal disaster.

Index